"The Scientific-
Technological
Revolution" and
Soviet Foreign Policy

Pergamon Titles of Related Interest

Kahan/Ruble Industrial Labor in the U.S.S.R.
Kanet Soviet Foreign Policy and East-West Relations
Nogee/Donaldson Soviet Foreign Policy Since World War II
Schultz/Adams Political Participation in Communist Systems
Smith/Maggs/Ginsburgs Soviet and East European Law and the
   Scientific-Technical Revolution
Welsh Survey Research and Public Attitudes in Eastern Europe
   and the Soviet Union

Related Journals*

BULLETIN OF SCIENCE, TECHNOLOGY AND SOCIETY
ECONOMIC BULLETIN FOR EUROPE
SOCIO-ECONOMIC PLANNING SCIENCES
TECHNOLOGY IN SOCIETY
WORLD DEVELOPMENT

*Free specimen copies available upon request.

PERGAMON
POLICY
STUDIES   ON INTERNATIONAL POLITICS

"The Scientific-Technological Revolution" and Soviet Foreign Policy

Erik P. Hoffmann
Robbin F. Laird

Pergamon Press
NEW YORK • OXFORD • TORONTO • SYDNEY • PARIS • FRANKFURT

Pergamon Press Offices:

U.S.A.
Pergamon Press Inc., Maxwell House, Fairview Park, Elmsford, New York 10523, U.S.A.

U.K.
Pergamon Press Ltd., Headington Hill Hall, Oxford OX3 0BW, England

CANADA
Pergamon Press Canada Ltd., Suite 104, 150 Consumers Road, Willowdale, Ontario M2J 1P9, Canada

AUSTRALIA
Pergamon Press (Aust.) Pty. Ltd., P.O. Box 544, Potts Point, NSW 2011, Australia

FRANCE
Pergamon Press SARL, 24 rue des Ecoles, 75240 Paris, Cedex 05, France

FEDERAL REPUBLIC
OF GERMANY
Pergamon Press GmbH, Hammerweg 6 6242 Kronberg/Taunus, Federal Republic of Germany

Library of Congress Cataloging in Publication Data

Hoffmann, Erik P., 1939-
   "The scientific-technological revolution" and Soviet foreign policy.

   (Pergamon policy studies on international politics)
   Bibliography: p.
   Includes index.
   1. Soviet Union--Foreign relations--1945-   . 2. Science--Social aspects--Soviet Union. I. Laird, Robbin F. (Robbin Frederick), 1946-   . II. Title.
III. Series
DK274.H59 1982   327.47   81-19924
ISBN 0-08-028065-X   AACR2

Printed in the United States of America

To NANCY CROFT LAIRD and

HELENE and WILLIAM HOFFMANN

Contents

Acknowledgments

Our interest in the central themes of this book dates from the mid-1970s, and our collaborative work began in the late 1970s at Columbia University. We very much appreciate the intellectual stimulation and various forms of support provided by our colleagues at the Research Institute on International Change, initially directed by Zbigniew Brzezinski and currently by Seweryn Bialer, and at the Russian Institute, once again directed by Marshall Shulman. We are most grateful to the National Science Foundation for the research and travel funds essential to the production of this and a companion volume, The Politics of Economic Modernization in the Soviet Union, and we especially thank Gerald Wright and William R. Thompson of NSF's political science division for their assistance. Also, we express our appreciation to the Kennan Institute for Advanced Russian Studies of the Woodrow Wilson International Center for Scholars, particularly to Abbott Gleason and James Billington and their staffs, for numerous kindnesses during our stays there as visiting fellows. And Hoffmann appreciatively acknowledges support from the American Council of Learned Societies and the Social Sciences Research Council at the early stages of his work on Soviet technology and politics.

We have benefited from the informative observations of numerous Soviet, West European, and American scholars and officials. We particularly thank Raymond Garthoff for his thoughtful comments on our fourth chapter and several members of the U.S. Department of Commerce and the other participants in the 1980 and 1981 conferences on socialist law and scientific and technical change, sponsored by the National Council for Soviet and East European Research, for their helpful critiques of a shorter earlier version of our third chapter. Also, we express our gratitude to Caitlin McCormick

and Thomas Lancia, who ably and enthusiastically assisted us
in our research; to Kira Caiafa and the staff of Victor Kamkin,
Inc., who provided us with valuable Russian-language source
materials; to Addie Napolitano, who skillfully and speedily
typed the several drafts of this manuscript, and Maxine Mor-
man and Edith Connelly - all of the Graduate School of Public
Affairs of the State University of New York at Albany; and to
Angela Clark and Lynn Lauber of Pergamon Press, who effectively and patiently helped bring this book to completion.

   In addition, we thank the following publishers for permis-
sion to incorporate into this volume revised versions of some of
our earlier work: the two essays by Robbin F. Laird and Erik
P. Hoffmann and several pages of the editors' introduction to
Part V in The Conduct of Soviet Foreign Policy, edited by
Erik P. Hoffmann and Frederic J. Fleron, Jr. (Hawthorne,
N.Y.: Aldine Publishing Co., 1980); the chapter by Erik P.
Hoffmann and Robbin F. Laird in Law and Soviet Economic
Development, edited by Peter Maggs, Gordon Smith, and
George Ginsburgs (Boulder, Colo.: Westview Press, 1982); and
several pages from Erik P. Hoffmann, "Contemporary Soviet
Theories of Scientific, Technological, and Social Change,"
Social Studies of Science 9, 1 (February 1979), Sage Publica-
tions.

   Finally, we affectionately note the remarkable energizing
and enervating powers of our effervescent children, Anders
Hoffmann and Vivian and Caroline Laird. And in deep appreciation for their nurturing, encouragement, and counsel of
many kinds, we dedicate this book with love to Nancy Croft
Laird and Helene and William Hoffmann.

Introduction

Soviet political leaders and social theorists clearly recognize
that portentous scientific and technical changes have taken
place since World War II and are continuing rapidly worldwide.
Foremost among these developments are remarkable scientific
discoveries of new sources of energy and materials, and technological innovations in transportation, telecommunications,
information processing, manufacturing, agriculture, weaponry,
consumer goods, and many other fields. Also, Soviet analysts
contend that the social structure of an industrializing nation
undergoes transformations. For example, urbanization and the
growth of a highly educated technical and managerial strata
are thought to be having multifaceted consequences in all
types of societies. Furthermore, Soviet commentators maintain
that the relations among socialist, capitalist, and Third World
countries are changing continuously. For example, the specialization and concentration of industrial production are
perceived to be creating an international division of labor that
is restructuring the world economy and is hence reshaping
world politics.

Soviet officials and theorists affirm that such changes are
being decisively influenced by the contemporary "scientific-
technological revolution" (STR) and by the political and social
contexts in which it unfolds.(1) Soviet spokesmen argue that
the STR is a global phenomenon that shapes and is shaped by
the distinctive values and behavior of various peoples. That
is, scientific-technical and industrial development are thought
to be profoundly affecting - and to be profoundly affected by
- the political elites and citizens of different nations, the
socioeconomic relationships within nations, and the balance of
power among nations.

The primary purpose of this book is to help explain the
effects of the worldwide STR on Soviet foreign policy under

"the collective leadership" of Leonid Brezhnev. To do so, we describe and analyze how Soviet leaders and international affairs specialists perceive the STR to be influencing East-West relations and, to a lesser extent, North-South relations from the mid-1960s to the early 1980s. We carefully examine Soviet views about the interconnections between the STR, on the one hand, and the political, economic, and military dimensions of "peaceful coexistence" and "detente," on the other. In addition, we evaluate the impact of scientific discoveries, technological innovations, foreign economic relations, strategic arms development, and instability in Third World countries upon the orientations and perceptions that are central to our study. Finally, we analyze some of the functions performed by present-day Soviet perspectives on scientific-technical change and international politics. That is, we seek to understand better the effects of Soviet ideas and images upon Soviet policy.

Of particular significance is Soviet thinking about the influence of the STR on power, conflict, competition, interdependence, and cooperation in the rapidly changing international system of the 1970s and 1980s. Top Communist Party (CPSU) and state officials maintain that the STR is creating the preconditions for much greater interaction and interpenetration among the industrialized nations of the East and West. Nonetheless, Soviet leaders and theorists insist that the STR is having very different political consequences in different socioeconomic systems. Soviet analysts view the STR as a dynamic force that is strengthening socialist societies and weakening capitalist societies. At the same time, Soviet policymakers and foreign affairs specialists argue that the STR is generating pressures for new kinds of adversarial and collaborative relationships between socialist and capitalist states. Specifically, Soviet commentators affirm that compelling scientific-technical and sociopolitical developments ensure the eventual establishment of "peaceful coexistence" or "detente" throughout the world, thereby advancing Soviet interests while averting the possibility of a thermonuclear conflagration or a return to the confrontationist policies and attitudes of the Cold War.

One of the central questions facing Soviet leaders is whether the USSR and its allies should strive for greater economic self-sufficiency, or whether they should broaden and deepen ties with all or most of the highly industrialized capitalist countries. The STR underscores the possibility of becoming a more developed society either in terms of "a modernized fortress USSR" or "a technocratic interdependent USSR." Both strategies of development are clearly expressed in contemporary Soviet pronouncements, and the tension or conflict between them is often explicitly stated or thinly veiled. These competing conservative and reformist orientations are discussed in greater detail in successive chapters of this book, and they are the main theme of our companion study, The Politics of Economic Modernization in the Soviet Union.(2)

In the present volume we focus upon the basic parameters of consensus among leading Soviet officials and analysts. We attempt to distill for Western readers the essence of the Brezhnev approach to technological change and international relations. This centrist or "mainstream" Soviet interpretation has been consistently influential but has not remained static in the period under investigation. Hence, by reconstructing and assessing evolving Soviet perspectives, we describe and analyze the views that have had the greatest impact on the foreign policy of the USSR in the 1970s and 1980s.

Soviet leaders and specialists are closely examining many of the dynamic relationships between technology and foreign policy and their theoretical and practical implications for various kinds of societies. Soviet analysts focus on the reciprocal influences of the STR and the changing international system; of the STR and the changing polities and economies of the West; and of the STR and the changing political, economic, and military relations between the developed socialist and advanced capitalist states. These fundamental issues are the main themes of our book.

Chronologically, our study begins where William Zimmerman's Soviet Perspectives on International Relations, 1956-1967 leaves off.(3) By focusing on East-West relations our research is narrower than his, but by exploring the interconnections between perceptions and behavior our research is broader. Our book also can be compared to Morton Schwartz's Soviet Perceptions of the United States.(4) His volume offers more detail on certain themes, but our conceptual orientation, subject matter, and data base are more comprehensive. In addition, our book complements major works on individual topics, such as Philip Hanson's Trade and Technology in Soviet-Western Relations.(5) Because we analyze Soviet perspectives on a wide range of issues, and because Hanson concentrates on Soviet behavior in a single important sphere, our book is in some ways more ambitious and in other ways less ambitious than his.

Parts of our study elucidate "tendencies of articulation" in the USSR. Like Franklyn Griffiths, we emphasize issues rather than groups, and we recognize that a pattern of articulations may constitute an "aggregate [pressing common claims], a loose coalition of like-minded actors, or the parallel unilateral articulations of virtually atomized individuals."(6) Like Gordon Skilling and Timothy Colton, however, we think that tendencies of development are often closely linked to the interests of institutions or of segments of institutions.(7) Hence, we use the term "policy group" to suggest the bridging of shared expressed attitudes with diverse organizational, professional, and personal goals and loyalties. And we view "tendency conflict" as competition among organized and unorganized groupings, especially bureaucratic coalitions, over policy and power.

Furthermore, we have benefited from the burgeoning Western literature on the political economy of industrialized countries and on the impact of scientific-technical and industrial advances on international relations.(8) For example, we believe that the Soviet economy is becoming much more permeable to external economic forces, such as global prices, inflation, and recessions, and that the Soviet leaders are deliberately increasing certain interdependencies through long-term production and market ties with Western and Third World nations. But we do not view such developments as signs of Soviet vulnerability or weakness; nor do we think that Brezhnev and most other leading party officials assess their nation's present-day and future capabilities and policy alternatives in this light. Indeed, the USSR's greater sensitivity or openness to world economic trends and events may be enhancing its leadership's assertiveness, self-confidence, and capacity to manage problems in various geographical and issue areas, rather than increasing its restraint, indecisiveness, and inability to cope with dilemmas and uncertainties.

Soviet analysts consistently argue that East-West relations in the current era are part of an historical process whereby conflict and cooperation develop simultaneously.(9) We hope to shed light on important political, economic, and military dimensions of the conflict and cooperation that are being generated by a compelling "objective" pressure for change, the STR. At the same time, "subjective" assessments of the external and internal environments are playing a more and more significant role in international politics. In the increasingly complex, interconnected, and multipolar world, the components, distribution, uses, and effectiveness of political resources are not all self-evident. Governmental leaders' and technical specialists' perceptions of capabilities, opportunities, vulnerabilities, and problems - their own nations' and other's - are of ever greater importance in shaping the goals and conduct of foreign policy.

For example, Soviet "conservatives" maintain that the West's inability to link technical and social progress is rooted in capitalist forms of producing, as well as utilizing, advanced technologies. Soviet "modernizers," in contrast, stress that technologies generated by the profit motive are capable of furthering "progressive" ends. Modernizers insist that the key variable is the politics of technology - that is, the purposes to which native and imported techniques and approaches are put and the different interests they serve in different socioeconomic systems. Modernizers reject the conservative idea that many technologies and modes of technological development have distinctly "socialist" and "capitalist" characteristics. Most Western know-how, equipment, and management methods can and must be made to serve the political, economic, and social goals of the Soviet bloc countries, modernizers contend. Conservatives are much more wary about the capitalist values that may be embedded in certain systems of technology developed in the West (such as assembly lines), their harmful social effects (such as alienation), and the transferability of these problems from West to East. Nonetheless, conservatives and modernizers advocate the selective importation of Western industrial and agricultural technologies, and both groupings view the choices about when and how advanced technologies should be obtained, adapted, or installed as major political, as well as economic, decisions.

Influential Soviet orientations of this kind, especially conservative and modernizing attitudes, beliefs, and images regarding the STR and East-West relations in the rapidly changing international environment of the 1970s and 1980s, are of considerable relevance to Western policymakers. Soviet perspectives on scientific and technological advances and world politics, which are the primary concern of our book, must be closely and continuously examined for eminently practical reasons. For, in both the East and the West, "situations defined as real are real in their consequences."(10)

1 "The Scientific-Technological Revolution," "Developed Socialism," and "Detente"

"PEACEFUL COEXISTENCE" AND "DETENTE" IN SOVIET THEORY AND PRACTICE

The Soviet Constitution of 1977 declares that "The USSR's foreign policy is aimed at ensuring favorable international conditions for building communism in the USSR, protecting the Soviet Union's state interests, strengthening the positions of world socialism, supporting the peoples' struggle for national liberation and social progress, preventing wars of aggression, achieving general and complete disarmament, and consistently implementing the principle of the peaceful coexistence of states with different social systems."(1)

This is the most authoritative summary of the basic objectives of Soviet foreign policy, past and present. Nonetheless, Soviet leaders and theorists since Lenin have emphasized that the USSR's goals and policies must be adapted to the distinctive conditions of the current era. Each era has particular characteristics that are decisively shaped by the values and purposes of competing socioeconomic systems and by the balance of power among nations.

Soviet analysts identify two major periods in the history of the USSR's foreign policy. In the first period, from 1917 to 1945, the USSR struggled alone to build a socialist society. Capitalist systems were dominant, and Soviet Russia was weak and vulnerable. In the second period, beginning with the defeat of German and Japanese fascism in World War II and the establishment of "people's democracies" in Eastern Europe, socialism became a major regional and then a global power. "The cardinal feature of the second stage is that the world socialist community has firmly grasped the historical initiative."(2)

1

The essence of the second period, according to Soviet theorists, is "the shift of the correlation of forces in favor of socialism." A chief factor producing this shift is the disintegration of the capitalist colonial system. The weakening of direct Western political control over Asian and African countries means that the Third World no longer plays the role of a reserve and supply base for imperialism. An authoritative Soviet text concludes: "The formation of the socialist community and the appearance of new countries on the international political scene have fundamentally changed the balance of strength in the world. The possibilities of imperialists for pursuing an aggressive policy have narrowed substantially."(3)

Soviet authors attribute the ascendancy of socialism in part to what they term "the third phase of the general crisis of capitalism." The "first phase" was the decline of capitalist economies and societies after World War I. The successful Bolshevik revolution of 1917, the repulsion of Western and Japanese military intervention in the Russian civil war of 1917 to 1920, and the creation of the first socialist state "objectively" demonstrated the possibility of a noncapitalist path to development.

Moreover, "anti-Sovietism" and "appeasement" in the capitalist world spurred the rise of German, Japanese, and Italian fascism. Before and after the Nazi-Soviet nonaggression pact of 1939 to 1941, the fascist coalition threatened - and vigorously engaged the Red Army in - two-front wars in European Russia and in the Soviet Far East. Hence, a "second phase" was ushered in by the Allied defeat of fascism in World War II and by the emergence of new socialist regimes in Eastern Europe and revolutionary movements in the Third World. The formation and consolidation of an international socialist system was the major force shaping this second stage.

According to Soviet analysts, the current "third phase" of capitalism's decline, which began in the mid-1950s, is characterized by the mounting "antagonistic" and "interimperialist contradictions" within and among the major Western nations. The problems of the capitalist states are becoming more acute, it is argued, because of the increased influence of socialism upon world historical development. Soviet writers contend: "In the economic sphere capitalism's crisis is manifested by the fact that the leading imperialist powers are losing their supremacy."(4) Furthermore, "the sharply accentuated uneven development of the capitalist countries is leading to a further aggravation of imperialist contradictions and to an intensification of the competitive struggle, in which the USA's chief rivals are the Common Market and Japan."(5)

"Peaceful coexistence" with the West is perceived to have been pursued in two phases that parallel the rise of the power of socialism. The first phase (1917-1953), initiated by Lenin, was a defensive form of coexistence. Socialism had to be built and consolidated in the face of extreme hostility from the capitalist world. Soviet Russia, the first socialist state, was militarily and economically vulnerable and had to make the most of its very limited political and diplomatic resources. By contrast, the second phase is an <u>active</u> form of peaceful coexistence in which socialism is allegedly becoming the ascendent historical force. Under Stalin's successor, Nikita Khrushchev, peaceful coexistence became the cornerstone or "general line" of Soviet foreign policy. In the first half-decade or so of the Brezhnev period, peaceful coexistence was temporarily reduced to equal status with other goals and principles, as it had been under Stalin and Lenin.

Throughout the 1970s, however, peaceful coexistence – now more often referred to as "detente" – was returned to a central place in the theory and practice of Soviet foreign policy. With the winding down of the Vietnam War, Soviet leaders again viewed the expansion of East-West cooperation as possible and desirable, because the USSR's military power had protected – and would continue to protect – the socialist world from capitalist aggression. "Soviet foreign policy paralyzes the aggressive actions of the imperialists. The Soviet Union's immense military and economic potential serves the cause of peace."(6) In short, the new active phase of peaceful coexistence is characterized by a growing Soviet capability (real and perceived) to influence the course of historical development in favor of socialism. However, Soviet domestic and foreign policy initiatives, which are taking place in an increasingly complex international system, are becoming, by choice or circumstance, increasingly sensitive and responsive to external trends and conditions.

International relations generally and Soviet foreign policy in particular are more and more shaped by the worldwide STR, according to Soviet leaders and theorists. P. N. Fedoseev, member of the CPSU Central Committee and Vice President of the USSR Academy of Sciences, offers a comprehensive interpretation of scientific-technical and sociopolitical change since the mid-twentieth century:

> The dialectic of the present era is manifested in the fact that in a number of countries the socialist revolution has come before the STR, thereby providing the necessary social conditions for its completion. In these countries the STR serves to develop and multiply the achievements of social revolution. In other countries the STR has preceded social revolution, thereby preparing its material prerequisites and deepening the fundamental contradictions of capitalism. The sequence of the scientific-technological and social revolutions is a concrete expression of the basic contradiction of our era

(i.e., between capitalism and socialism), and is a manifestation of the many forms of historical development in the contemporary era.(7)

Momentous scientific, technical, and socioeconomic changes have indeed transformed capitalist and socialist societies and the relations between them since World War II. These changes have had both positive and negative consequences. On the one hand, the STR creates pressures for a more efficient division of labor in the global economy and for international cooperation in a broad range of scientific and technological fields. On the other hand, the STR has produced the danger of thermonuclear warfare, not only among the superpowers but among lesser powers as well. For the first time in world history, nations have the capability to annihilate one another and permanently to damage the earth and its environment. The very destructiveness of modern weapons technology, however, reduces the possible benefits of initiating an all-out war and thereby restrains potential aggressors.

It is to Khrushchev's credit that he not only recognized this fact, but adjusted the Soviet concept and policy of peaceful coexistence accordingly. The downing of an American U-2 spy plane in the Soviet Union in 1960 dramatically discredited Khrushchev's initiatives to improve political and economic relations with the United States, and it also exacerbated the Sino-Soviet split. Khrushchev and Mao Tse-tung already had sharp disagreements about the military assertiveness of the United States and about the appropriate uses of the Soviet Union's newly developed strategic weapons arsenal. The U-2 incident belied Khrushchev's contention that the United States now sought to extend its power only by peaceful means. Criticism from the Chinese and from conservative Soviet leaders no doubt contributed to Khrushchev's rash and extremely dangerous attempt to redress the East-West strategic balance by implanting nuclear weapons in Cuba in 1962. However, the signing of the U.S.-Soviet nuclear test-ban treaty less than a year later exemplified Khrushchev's efforts to reduce the international tensions and dangers produced by the awesome new weapons technologies. As a Soviet spokesman declared a decade afterward: "In the nuclear age, peaceful coexistence of the socialist and capitalist countries is dictated by the objective necessity of social development. Wars of plunder and conquest cannot be a method of settling international disputes. History poses the problem thusly: either peaceful coexistence or a catastrophic thermonuclear world war."(8)

Soviet analysts do not maintain that the avoidance of nuclear war through a policy of peaceful coexistence signifies the reconciliation of capitalism and socialism. Peaceful coexistence and detente, in Soviet theory and practice, consist of both conflict and cooperation in competing with major Western nations. "The contradiction between socialism and capitalism has been and remains the principal contradiction of our epoch. A political, economic, and ideological struggle has been and will continue to be waged between them."(9)

What do change, however, are the forms of competition between the two systems. "The main thing is to divert the historically inevitable class struggle between socialism and capitalism into a channel that is not fraught with wars, dangerous conflicts, or an arms race."(10)

This last goal has proved to be particularly elusive. Throughout the 1970s, while the United States was trimming its existing conventional military capabilities, the USSR launched a major buildup of strategic and conventional weapons and significantly expanded and upgraded its navy. Moreover, Soviet leaders, unlike their American counterparts, have repeatedly insisted that detente does not preclude intense competition between the USSR and the West in the developing world, including the use of Cuban proxy forces to promote selected "wars of national liberation," as in Angola, Ethiopia, and South Yemen. Furthermore, the harassment and incarceration of Soviet dissidents intensified during the 1970s, symbolized by the forced internal exile of Nobel Peace Prize laureate Andrei Sakharov. This third trend clashed sharply with President Jimmy Carter's particular concern about the suppression of "human rights" in the USSR.

Yet, in the early 1970s, the Brezhnev administration initiated a serious attempt to increase political, economic, and military cooperation with the United States and Western Europe. Brezhnev's stated purpose was to reduce East-West conflict for the long rather than the short term and to promote the interests of both the developed socialist and the advanced capitalist countries. The SALT negotiations, the settling of the postwar boundary disputes between Western and Eastern Europe, and the Soviet efforts to enhance East-West trade - especially the flow of advanced technology to the Soviet Union to develop the natural resources of Siberia and to help meet the energy and mineral needs of the West - were major elements of this initiative.

Differing views of detente in the East and West, and differing views of detente within and among the major Western powers, have substantially undermined the prospects for closer Soviet-American ties. Relations between the United States and USSR have deteriorated to the point where three American presidents have rejected the very term "detente," while Soviet leaders concluded that they had little to lose by U.S. displeasure over the forceful occupation of Afghanistan in 1979, the first combat use of Red Army divisions outside the Soviet bloc since World War II. One important consequence of this Soviet action was the immediate acceleration of the Soviet-American arms race. Both sides have now placed renewed emphasis on developing new military technologies that would offset the other's offensive and defensive capabilities. And both sides are more vigorously pursuing geopolitical advantage (e.g., in the Persian Gulf and the Horn of Africa) to preserve or enhance their perceived security and economic interests.

But the Brezhnev collective leadership has not abandoned peaceful coexistence. In the Soviet view, active coexistence may consist of various combinations of conflict and collaboration. Depending on the circumstances, Soviet policymakers place greater or lesser emphasis on expanding the areas of East-West cooperation and on the extent of cooperation with various Western partners, especially the United States, Western Europe, and Japan. As a Soviet analyst, buttressing his authoritative interpretation with quotes from Brezhnev, asserted shortly after the Soviet occupation of Afghanistan:

> Detente . . . has demonstrated its viability and stability. It advances thanks to its profoundly objective, historical basis, thanks to the political forces of our time, including the policies of certain Western countries, which realistically see the mainstream of history and work for the triumph of detente, for peace and security. . . . There is no reasonable alternative to detente in present-day international relations. It is noteworthy that in the complex situation at the beginning of 1980 the Soviet Union found it necessary to reaffirm its confidence in the vitality of detente. . . . Detente is an absolutely necessary and indispensable prerequisite for any constructive approach to the solution of crucial world issues."(11)

Soviet leaders and theorists emphasize the following three basic principles of peaceful coexistence and detente: (1) the repudiation of nuclear war as a means of resolving political disputes between industrialized capitalist and socialist countries; (2) the expansion of mutually advantageous cooperation between capitalism and socialism; and (3) the recognition of national sovereignty and noninterference in the internal affairs of other nations.(12) Unlike most Westerners, Soviet analysts do not find this third principle incompatible with the USSR's military and economic support for promising "national liberation movements" in Third World countries.

N.N. Inozemtsev, Central Committee member and head of the Institute of World Economics and International Relations, offers an especially clear interpretation of recent changes in world politics and of the interconnections among the STR, social revolutions, and detente.

The combination of deep-going revolutionary changes in social relations and the revolution in science and technology is a distinguishing feature of out time. . . .

If one were to ask: What is the fundamental difference between the world situation today and that of some 30 to 35 years ago, between capitalism of the 1970s and that of the early postwar years - the answer would probably be as follows:

- first, capitalism - if we take the industrialized countries - now accounts for only 18 percent of the world population and for about 50 percent of its industrial output. Though capitalism is engaged in combat with the other, opposite world system, socialism, it finds itself compelled to coexist with it, cooperate with it in different fields, in the conditions of the balance of forces steadily changing in favor of socialism;

- second, with the collapse of its colonial empires, capitalism has lost its hinterland, its colonial periphery; it is still keeping most of the developing countries within its economic orbit, but it has increasingly to reckon with their demands. While influencing these countries, it finds itself increasingly dependent on their energy and raw material resources, as was strikingly demonstrated in the mid-1970s.

The STR plays an especially important role in the current social changes, primarily in the altered balance of strength between the two systems. . . .

And so, the STR makes for far-reaching qualitative changes in the whole complex of human life and in the line-up of class and social forces throughout the world.(13)

Let us now examine Soviet conceptions of the STR more closely.

THE STR AND THE PRODUCTIVE FORCES OF ADVANCED
SOCIETY

There is not yet a single officially sanctioned Soviet definition or theory of the STR. Soviet scholars and bureaucrats offer a wide range of views about the nature or essence of the STR and its sociopolitical origins and consequences. Virtually all Soviet writers agree that the STR is a worldwide phenomenon, that it began in the USSR in the mid-1950s (and somewhat earlier in the West), and that it has portentous but predominantly favorable implications for the future of mankind, allegedly hastening the development of socialism and the fall of capitalism. Some Soviet authors emphasize that the essence of the STR lies in specific scientific or technical breakthroughs, such as logical and control operations, and in the automation of the processes of production and management. Other theorists stress the changing nature of work, the greatly enhanced problem-solving capacities of socialist leaders, and the growing capability of socialist societies to shape their physical and economic environments (for instance, to improve the productivity of labor). Still other theorists direct attention to the broader social implications of advances in scientific and technical knowledge - their impact on human needs and aspirations, job satisfaction, leisure, interpersonal relations, education, the professions, demographic patterns, and evolving attitudes toward nature and ecological questions. And still others insist that the STR consists of three interrelated elements: the natural-scientific and technical, the socioeconomic, and the philosophical-ideological.

An authoritative Soviet definition of the STR - and one that carefully distinguishes between its content and consequences - is offered by Fedoseev:

> The scientific and technological revolution is basically the radical qualitative reorganization of the productive forces as a result of the transformation of science into a key factor in the development of social production. Increasingly eliminating manual labor by utilizing the forces of nature in technology, and replacing man's direct participation in the production process by the functioning of his materialized knowledge, the scientific and technological revolution radically changes the entire structure and components of the productive forces, the conditions, nature, and content of labor. While embodying the growing integration of science, technology, and production, the scientific and technological revolution at the same time influences all aspects of life in present-day society, including industrial management, education, everyday life, culture, the psychology of people, the relationship between nature and society. (14)

Note that this definition emphasizes that the STR is essentially a fundamental transformation of the scientific-technical and human "productive forces" of society. This conceptualization leaves open for theoretical development the likely and desirable effects of the new productive forces on "the social relations of production" (e.g., authority, property, or class relations) and on the "superstructure" (e.g., the political culture, laws, and institutions) of different societies (socialist, capitalist, and

Third World). Also, there is room for much more analysis of
the reciprocal influences of a nation's superstructure and production relations on its changing productive forces.

In general, Soviet theorists view the STR as a crucially
important means of achieving higher forms of "developed socialism" - and eventually "communism." The STR is to be
"mastered," and to do so, the nature of the opportunities and
obstacles it presents must be better understood. Soviet
authors have made concerted efforts to clarify their thinking
about key concepts such as "science," "technology," and "revolution" and about the interrelationships among these and other
elements of the STR.

Many Soviet writers distinguish carefully between "technique" and "technology" and are devoting increasing attention
to the theoretical implications of alternative definitions.
"Technique" most frequently refers to specific mechanical innovations and labor- and energy-saving devices and the tools
essential to their efficient use in accomplishing a specified
goal; "technology" is a broader and less precise concept that
usually includes knowledge of the regularities of physical and
social phenomena, sensitivity to the values and purposes to
which scientific and technical instruments, methods, and capabilities can be effectively applied, and responsiveness to the
social organization, as well as to the scientific-technical bases,
of the processes of labor, production, and management.(15) A
"technical revolution" is a major set of advances in technique
that constitutes a part of the present-day transformation of
the productive forces. A "production revolution" is a cluster
of significant changes in technology that can help generate,
but without a thoroughgoing "social revolution," cannot establish, new production relations. Sometimes a distinction is made
between technical, technological, and social "modes of production" - the first two referring to methods of linking elements
of the productive forces (techniques and techniques, man and
techniques, respectively) and the third to ways of harmonizing
the productive forces and production relations. It is argued
that "technological relations" must be carefully distinguished
from and do not necessarily produce changes in production
relations.(16)

A recent Soviet study identifies six central components of
the STR and offers a lengthy categorization of phenomena that
express or reflect these respective elements. The six fundamental (or defining) characteristics are:

1.   The merging of the scientific revolution with the technical
     revolution, predominantly influenced by developments in
     science (manifestations are the "scientification" of tech-
     nique and the "technification" of science)
2.   The transformation of science into "a direct productive
     force," which makes possible the scientification of produc-

tion (reflected in changes in the tools of labor, the "materialization" of the objects of labor, sources of energy,
technological applications of science in production, human
capabilities, and management and organization of production)

3. The organic unification of the elements of the production
process into a single automated system whose actions are
subordinated to general principles of management and
self-management

4. A qualitative change in the technological basis of production, signifying changes in man-machine relations that are
stimulated by increased use of materialized knowledge and
by enhanced human capabilities to manage and control
production processes

5. The formation of a new type of worker who has mastered
scientific principles of production and can ensure that the
functioning of production and its future development will
be based on the achievements of science and technique

6. A major shift from "extensive" to "intensive" development
of production, such as broader and deeper application of
scientific and technical advances, more efficient use of
natural resources, and sharply increased labor productiv-
ity(17)

Soviet officials and scholars have begun to elaborate on
the meaning and the intellectual and practical implications of
these and other general propositions. One of the most significant maxims is General Secretary Brezhnev's injunction in
1971 "to combine organically the achievements of the scientific-
technological revolution with the advantages of the socialist
economic system."(18) This major policy pronouncement is
chiefly an appeal to develop and implement ideas about the
modernization of the Soviet political and economic systems
under conditions of the STR. Fundamental goals and characteristics (for example, socialist democracy and public ownership of the means of production) are to be preserved and
enhanced - and in some cases reconceptualized - in light of
the rapidly changing scientific-technical environment in which
they must function. Secondary aims and features of the Soviet
system may undergo considerably more significant changes,
depending on the political leaders' evolving views about scientific-technical and socioeconomic progress and societal guidance, and on their will and capacity to mobilize bureaucratic
support for innovative policies and policymaking and administrative procedures.

Top CPSU leaders seem to understand clearly that party,
state, and economic officials must adapt old principles, such as
centralized economic and social planning, and "democratic centralism," to dramatically changing scientific-technological conditions. That is, most Politburo and Secretariat members
apparently believe that attitudinal and administrative changes

are necessary in order to create and take advantage of new opportunities for economic and social progress. Such changes could also forestall new problems associated with the complexities and interdependencies of the STR and with the possibility of an increasingly unfavorable competitive position vis-a-vis the industrialized nations of the West. The idea is to modify and update traditional Soviet practices and precepts in the hopes of contributing to and benefiting from the worldwide STR.

Soviet spokesmen have offered a variety of ideas about how best to "combine" the achievements of the STR with the advantages of socialism. Differences in the views of Brezhnev, Kosygin, and other top leaders notwithstanding, their analyses have been characterized by an increasing attentiveness to the interconnections between ends and means and between domestic and international politics. Some ideological innovation, cognitive reorientation, and conceptual search are clearly taking place. In contrast to the utopian theorizing of the Khrushchev years, contemporary Soviet authors focus on the processes, not on the end results, of social change. That is, descriptions of a developed socialist society are now consistently linked to the analysis of the transition to developed socialism and communism. Consequently, the prescription and evaluation of goals and methods and the continuous reassessment of domestic and international conditions are more closely intertwined.

This does not mean, however, that contemporary Soviet theorists have abandoned the traditional Marxist-Leninist "goal culture." On the contrary, they argue that the broadening of worker participation in the management of society, the elimination of differences between city and country and between intellectual and physical labor, the optimal distribution and use of natural and human resources, and even "the withering away of the state" will all be significantly enhanced in the course of the STR.(19)

Soviet analysts differ about the extent to which these and other goals can be realized under the present STR, and some have suggested that important social and economic goals cannot be achieved even with the full automation of production. A small but growing number of Soviet writers envision a "new" STR, which will begin after the contemporary STR has run its course in perhaps 75 to 100 years. This idea is closely associated with increasing Soviet concern about the environmental problems posed by the STR and about the need to develop more constructive relationships between man and nature in socialist, as well as in capitalist, societies. Julian Cooper, a British scholar, observes that Soviet theorists more and more regard the current STR as "a transitional phenomenon, a final upsurge of an historically limited 'industrial' mode of production, to be superseded by an 'ecological' mode of

production brought about by the reorientation, or 'ecologization,' of all the sciences and technology. [G. S.] Gudozhnik
and other writers stress that this reorientation will not occur
automatically: ecologization must be consciously pursued and
may entail considerable transitional problems."(20)
Cooper concludes:

> Taking the [Soviet] literature of the last ten to
> fifteen years as a whole, there is no question that
> there has been a significant change in the general
> appreciation of the role of scientific and technical
> progress in the development of socialist and com-
> munist society. The boundless optimism of even the
> fairly recent past has been yielding to a more
> realistic, constrained, and anxious assessment.
> While there is evidence of pessimism and even of
> eschatalogical sentiments, the mainstream Soviet
> approach to science and technology is still distinctly
> more positive than that prevailing in the West. The
> new, increasingly dominant theme is that science and
> technology must be reoriented if ecological disaster
> is to be averted and socialist goals are to be
> attained: only an "ecologized" technology can form
> the appropriate technical basis of a communist
> society. There is now a greater humility in the face
> of the natural and biological factors of human exis-
> tence, but, nevertheless, a firmly held conviction
> that solutions to the threatening problems of society,
> generated in part by the STR itself, can only be
> found through the further development of science
> and technology. . . .
> What then is the current state of the theory of
> the STR? One cannot speak of any generally ac-
> cepted understanding. Instead, there is a coexis-
> tence of diverse theories with ecologized variants
> increasingly displacing the more traditional con-
> ceptions, although the latter still sometimes appear
> in virtually unchanged form.(21)

On one fundamental theoretical and ideological proposition
there has been and almost certainly will be no public debate in
the USSR. This is the contention that, despite inevitable
"nonantagonistic contradictions" between the productive forces
and production relations of socialist countries, only in such
societies can scientific-technical and social progress proceed
simultaneously and further each other's development. G. N.
Volkov states: "The use of the positive results of the STR and
the neutralization of its negative consequences are possible
only in a society that is not divided into antagonistic classes -
a society in which the products of human endeavor do not

resist their creators by taking the form of an alienating and ruling force above them, but are subject to centralized social control, under which the fundamental interests of society as a whole and of the individual person do not diverge but coincide."(22)

Soviet modernizers (more so than conservatives) affirm that it is the social and organizational context in which the achievements of the STR are used, not those in which they are generated, that will decisively shape the purposes served, and hence determine the effects on people's values and human relations. On this basis, Soviet analysts explain the confidence of Lenin, Khrushchev, and Brezhnev (and even Stalin during the first Five-Year Plan from 1928 to 1933) that the importation of certain types of Western technology will not have harmful socioeconomic consequences. Soviet theorists found their position on numerous conceptual distinctions between the purportedly value-free and value-laden components of systems of labor, production, and management. For instance, capitalist "forms" of production are to be imbued with socialist "content." Or again, technique is considered value-free; technology has some values inherent in or associated with it; and socioeconomic production relations are the dominant sources and bearers of values.

It is then assumed or argued (with varying degrees of disdain for Maoist ideas on the subject) that techniques – and even systems of technology – can be imported from Western nations at little or no sociopolitical risk or "cost." Soviet spokesmen confidently anticipate that selected foreign technology will help to implement national party leaders' conceptions of "scientific," "rational," and "efficient" management of industrial, organizational, and social processes. Conservatives especially view the information and expertise embodied in certain techniques and technologies as "capitalist" or "socialist," and modernizers acknowledge that the importation of Western technology sometimes transmits or fosters "technocratic consciousness." Most frequently, scientific discoveries and technological innovations generated in the West are seen as valuable means of serving socialist ends – and sometimes even as a welcome form of cultural diffusion (e.g., labor productivity).

Much of the foregoing thinking is summarized in one of the most basic theoretical propositions developed by Soviet analysts: "History shows that a technical revolution can sometimes precede a social revolution, but a production revolution can begin only after a social and technical revolution."(23) That is, the dialectical relationships between the dynamic new productive forces and the production relations of present-day capitalist and socialist societies can spur production revolutions only in socialist states. Soviet writers maintain that there are no technologically determined or necessary connections among technical, technological, and social relations. Commentators then argue that relations among men must be governed by collectivist norms in order to develop and use scientific-technological advances for socially significant purposes and to enhance man's interrelationships with his technologies and natural environment.

Hence, theorists of the STR emphasize the need for "radical" change in certain cognitive processes and production relations, but at the same time affirm that once a socialist "cultural revolution" has been set in motion, the dominant values and social-economic-political relationships are relatively impervious to retrogressive change. The STR is thought to be bringing another production revolution to the USSR, which, by transferring more and more physical and mental work from men to machines and to automated systems of management and control, will eventually create "fundamental social trans-formations in society." But these changes will speed the evo-lution of socialism to communism, it is argued, because scientific-technical and economic accomplishments will ac-company - indeed, be stimulated by - the development of socialist property and interpersonal relationships and of "the new Soviet man." Soviet analysts conclude that "it is possible to construct communism only by fully utilizing the opportuni-ties the STR presents to society - [and only by] mastering the revolution itself and learning to manage it."(24) In capitalist societies, on the other hand, the current STR will allegedly not be able to run its full course before generating sufficient societal pressures for a socialist revolution, which in turn will create the preconditions for an eventual production revolution.

THE STR AND THE HISTORICAL COMPETITION BETWEEN
ADVANCED CAPITALISM AND DEVELOPED SOCIALISM

Soviet leaders and theorists view the STR as a universal pro-cess that is characteristic of mature productive forces.   As V.I. Gromeka states, "The development of productive forces has its own logic, its own internal laws, which to a certain extent are independent from production relations.   Thus, the main lines of development in the STR. . . are identical in both socialist and capitalist countries."(25)

Under capitalist conditions, the STR is an objective force creating "state-monopoly capitalism." This advanced form of capitalism has emerged in response to two basic pressures. First, the monopolization of production has been established to provide the economic base for the development and marketing of modern technology.   Second, the growing role of the ca-pitalist state has developed in response to the mounting production and consumption needs that have to be met by the capitalist system, such as the funding of large-scale research and development (R&D) projects. As Gromeka notes: "The STR leads to a situation in which the capitalist state takes on the function of leadership and organization of scientific, industrial, and technical construction work."(26)

The government has become a central actor in state-monopoly capitalism, according to Soviet analysts. In the era of the STR, the long-range interests of capitalism cannot be served by market competition among the corporations. The state adjudicates conflicts among the corporations. In order to protect the long-range interests of capitalism, political institutions occasionally come into conflict with individual monopolies that overzealously pursue short-term profits. In a word, the state begins to plan. "[State] programming aims primarily not at the satisfaction of the interests of individual monopoly groupings, but at the solution of the difficult problems of monopoly capital as a whole."(27)

Nonetheless, the basic character of capitalism blocks the capacity of the state to exercise genuine comprehensive planning, which is the only kind of planning adequate to meet the needs of the STR. In fact, the STR accelerates the inherent contradictions within capitalism, such as the contradiction between the private ownership of the means of production and the public needs to be met by the STR. As Inozemtsev puts it, "The STR does not help to perpetuate capitalism but tends to reproduce its inherent social antagonisms on an ever greater scale and with increasing bitterness."(28)

Soviet theorists contend that an advanced society possesses a highly developed productive base and sophisticated organizational forms to manage the productive base. Both advanced capitalism and developed socialism must confront new productive forces and the challenges of managing them. Material progress, especially in the advanced stage, is universal in nature. Progress in the material sphere creates common problems of nurturing, directing, and coping with modern productive capabilities. The goal of material prosperity also generates pressures for creating internal and international structures and relations appropriate to deal with the universal forms of science and technology.

Indeed, the universal character of the advanced productive forces places competitive pressure upon the Soviet leadership and spurs efforts to develop further the effectiveness of the Soviet economic system. A team of Soviet researchers concludes: "Today, in the competition between the two systems under the conditions of the STR, it is necessary to use more fully the advantages of socialism through a more rational or efficient application of material and human resources and by improving the systems of planning and management, etc. Increasing the effectiveness of social production has become a basic problem whose resolution is critical for further social progress."(29)

Soviet analysts view the STR as an objective force that makes possible the construction of a more developed socialist society. Developed socialism is defined as the conjunction of the STR with the advantages of socialism. Socialization or public ownership of the means of production is the core meaning of socialism in its initial phase. Nevertheless, the emergence of the highly powerful productive base of advanced society accelerates the development of socialism. As A.S. Akhiezer argues, "The STR requires that the whole of human practice . . . should be transformed into a scientifically grounded and guided process. This is possible only in a society capable of considering its development as an object of its own activity, that is to say, under socialism."(30)

The development of socialism in advanced conditions is rooted in the socialization of the processes of expanding human material power. Socializing the STR requires much more than establishing and maintaining the basic structures of public ownership. The meaning of socialization itself is extended on two levels. First, greater socialization refers to the increased effectiveness and efficiency of the Soviet economic system. "The high level of the socialization of production in the stage of developed socialism is manifested in the growth of the concentration, specialization, and cooperation of production sectors, in the extensive production ties between sectors of the domestic economy, and also in the framework of socialist collaboration on the basis of an international socialist division of labor."(31) Second, socialization refers to an ability to extend planned control over the STR and its social consequences. According to Fedoseev, "the creation of the material and technical basis of communism contains an organic implication for ever greater social orientation of scientific and technological progress in the mature socialist society."(32)

Briefly stated, a developed society retains the basic social and political institutions of socialism and adapts them to the challenges of the STR. This process is "guided" by the CPSU, especially by its national policymaking bodies. Soviet writers contend that centralized planning and direction are necessary to ensure that socialist values are expressed in feasible policies and are successfully implemented, and that all party, state, and public institutions fulfill their potentials by responding to the opportunities and problems presented by the STR. V.I. Kas'ianenko avers: "The achievement of a mature level of development of the productive forces and production relations allows society to use more fully the advantages, objective laws, and potentials of socialism in all spheres of social life."(33)

Soviet perspectives on social change are stage-oriented. In an advanced society heavy industry has been built; the work force has become largely skilled; mass education has been established; and urbanization has become the dominant mode of life influencing the population. The industrialized stage must be completed before an advanced stage of development is possible. The STR can result in a higher stage of industrialization only when it is merged with the productive forces of a highly industrialized society. Societies in a lower stage of development (e.g., the Third World) can use components of science and technology, but cannot forge an STR. In contrast to the position of Maoist voluntarism, Soviet theorists argue that a stage of development cannot be transcended, but must be passed through. It is possible, however, to shorten the period of change by means of a socialist revolution.

Soviet theorists have identified four stages in the social development of the USSR.(34) The first stage, from 1917 to the Stalin constitution in 1936, was the period of the formation of the basic institutions and values of socialism. The second stage, from 1936 to 1967, was the period of the consolidation of these key structures. The third stage, "developed socialism," began in 1967 and is to continue indefinitely. In this stage the further broadening and deepening of socialism in response to the STR is the central task. The fourth and final stage, "communism," is a classless and stateless society of material abundance and personal fulfillment.

Thus, developed socialism is a transitional period between the consolidation of a socialist order and the establishment of socioeconomic and political communism at home and throughout the world. Developed socialism thereby embodies the ideas of continuity in the basic characteristics of socialism and change in terms of the policy and managerial initiatives and responses necessary to reach communism. As Fedoseev summarizes the process: "The developed socialist society is a law-governed stage in the formative period of the communist system, signifying that socialism has finally triumphed and been fully established in every sphere of social life, and that the premises have been created for the full and all-round manifestation of the potentialities and advantages of the socialist system and for the realization of practical steps in the gradual transition to the higher phase of communism."(35)

The transition from a traditional industrialized economy to an advanced industrialized economy rests upon the growing significance of scientific discoveries and technological innovations. The former increasingly influence the latter, according to Soviet writers. In turn, advanced technological development is viewed as the key to increased labor productivity in the modern manufacturing and service economy. An authoritative Soviet text asserts:

The most important characteristics of the economy of a developed socialist society will inevitably have their distinctive features in every socialist country.

These features will depend on the specific internal and external conditions of socialist construction in the various countries, on the level of development of their productive forces, on the branch structure of the economy, on environmental conditions, on the use of the achievements of the STR in the development of the economy, and on the scale, forms, and methods of participation in economic and scientific-technical cooperation and economic integration with fraternal countries and in the international division of labor.(36)

Kas'ianenko has extensively reviewed the economic litera-ture dealing with developed socialism. On the basis of his investigations, he has identified eight dimensions of the economic foundations of a developed socialist society. First, there is widespread socialization of production. Second, there is a highly developed productive base, especially in heavy industry. Third, industry is to be developed in a comprehen-sive manner and productivity increased by the STR. The latest scientific findings and their practical applications are to be promptly used throughout the economy. Fourth, the mate-rial-technological basis of production in the future communist order is being built. Fifth, the cooperative forms of property in the agricultural sphere are being transformed into state-run and highly mechanized farms. Mechanization creates the ob-jective possibility for the emergence of the industrialization of agricultural labor. Sixth, there is a shift from extensive to intensive methods of economic development, with an increasing level of complexity and interdependence in economic production and management. Seventh, there is a sharp increase in the use of collective goods and services to meet a greater diversity of human needs. Eighth, there is greater cooperation and integration between the Soviet economy and other socialist economies. Kas'ianenko underscores the significance of mature economic forces for developed socialism as follows: "A high level of maturity in the socialist mode of production (in the productive base as well as in the production relations), and a comprehensive, all-round development of the basic spheres of social life, are equivalent to the essential characteristics of developed socialism."(37)
A major distinction between capitalist and socialist modes of production focuses on the human needs to be met by scien-tific, technical, and economic achievements. Soviet writers stress the importance of enhancing economic growth, the tech-nological level of the economy, and labor productivity, on the one hand, and of improving the social and economic well-being of the entire population, on the other.(38) This is not just a question of meeting already existing needs with economic goods. Rather, needs under socialism are to be reconcep-

tualized in conformity with the new opportunities created by economic progress.(39) Both advanced capitalism and developed socialism provide for increasing material prosperity, but capitalist production relations create and use material wealth for consumerism or "commodity fetishism." Socialist production relations are defined with reference to the ability to use science and technology to meet public, as opposed to private, needs, and to distribute material, sociopsychological, and cultural benefits more equitably among the population.

Even under socialism, however, there are conflicts between evolving opportunities to define new needs to be met by the STR and past definitions of the uses of economic power. That is, there are differences between the needs to be served by technology in industrial society and the needs that are generated and can be fulfilled by the growing economic power of an advanced industrial society. The resolution of such "nonantagonistic contradictions" between different stages of development is central to progress in industrialized socialist states. As Kas'ianenko asserts, "Social progress under socialism occurs dialectically through the overcoming of contradictions and difficulties."(40)

A central contradiction shaping the fundamental characteristics of developed socialism is that between the universality of the productive forces of highly industrialized nations and the antagonistic quality of capitalist and socialist production relations. On the one hand, the common problems of modernization in advanced capitalist and developed socialist societies create mutual interests. Hence, peaceful coexistence or detente are both possible and necessary for the exchange of material goods and for the continued development of the entire industrialized world. On the other hand, the antagonisms between advanced capitalism and developed socialism limit the levels of exchange and exacerbate conflict. As Inozemtsev notes, "The STR opens up unprecedented opportunities to mankind for the most efficient use of natural resources in the interests of mankind and of progress."(41) Cooperation is essential to solve "a series of global problems whose resolution demands collective effort."(42) But cooperation cannot eliminate and does not necessarily even reduce the competition between capitalism and socialism. The fact that the STR has been led by a group of highly developed "imperialist" powers "is latent with real danger that these [new] opportunities may be used against the vital interests of society."(43)

The historical competition between socialism and capitalism in the context of advanced modernization focuses upon the ability of socialism to use its inherent advantages to master the new productive forces more effectively and efficiently than capitalism, Soviet theorists maintain. These advantages inhere in the basic values, property relationships, and institutions of socialism, which must shape and respond to the rapidly evolving productive forces. In other words, the advantages of socialism cannot be realized "automatically" or without creative political-administrative efforts and accomplishments. Hence, the superiority of socialism in the historical struggle with capitalism must be demonstrated through the ability of developed socialism to carry out a more successful strategy of advanced modernization than is possible through the socioeconomic and political structures of advanced capitalism.

"The correlation of forces" is shifting in favor of socialism, however, and East-West competition is profoundly affecting this shift in the spheres of science, technology, and production. Competitive advantage rests in large part upon the respective dynamism of the socialist and capitalist systems. A. Vakhrameev asserts:

> Marxists have never sought to reduce the balance-of-forces problem to its military-strategic aspects, but have always believed that it has various other ramifications: economic, scientific and technical, political and ideological. [These ramifications] cover not only the whole aggregate of present-day international relations, but also the state of affairs in the various individual countries, mutual relations between classes and parties in these countries, and social processes going forward in the modern world.(44)

Hence, the global "correlation of forces" can continue to shift in the favor of socialism only if developed socialist societies strengthen their capability to accelerate and to manage the universal productive forces of the STR. The STR is an open-ended and somewhat malleable process that is unfolding under both advanced capitalist and developed socialist systems that are having an increasing influence upon one another.

Paradoxically, East-West competition is taking place in a more and more interdependent setting. The STR is an objective force for the internationalization of problems and opportunities. In his major work on peaceful coexistence, A.O. Chubar'ian comments: "The STR significantly influences the development of international relations, broadening and deepening economic, scientific, and technological ties between countries, especially those with different social systems."(45) But interdependence does not reduce competition, Soviet analysts emphasize. Rather, developed socialist societies must be capable of competing in new and, if possible, less confrontationist ways in a dynamic international division of labor. Developed socialism must be competitive in the international arena in order to establish and maintain advantageous political, economic, and military relations with other nations, and to influence as much as possible the policies and polities of capitalist, Third World, and other socialist states.

In short, Soviet analysts perceive that developed socialism in the USSR is evolving in the context of a rapidly changing international system. Advanced modernization under both capitalist and socialist conditions creates the need for greater cooperation between the two types of societies. But technological advances produce qualitatively different and increasingly intense forms of competition as well.

2 "The Scientific-Technological Revolution" and the Contemporary "General Crisis of Capitalism"

THE DYNAMISM OF DETENTE

According to Soviet analysts, contemporary East-West relations are being forged in the context of dynamic changes in international politics. Detente is part of world historical development, not merely a component of a balance of power between the superpowers. I.A. Sovetov asserts that "detente is a global process and cannot be confined to bilateral relations, however important."

> If international detente is regarded not as a static phenomenon that has taken shape for a given period, but as a continuous process involving the establishment of peaceful cooperation among nations, the extension of the scale and forms of their mutual understanding, and the formation of a lasting basis for universal peace, it is obvious that it cannot have any simple, fixed, and immutable features. International development has its own logic and unfolds in accordance with definite laws. . . . This is what, in the final count, determines the motive force behind international detente, which is not a subjective but an emphatically objective process.(1)

On the one hand, Soviet writers contend that the dynamism of detente is intensified by the evolution of the USSR. The Soviet people are constructing a more developed socialist society whose economic priorities are the "enhancement of the efficiency of the economy and the boosting of the productivity of living and materialized labor." These priorities require the USSR to participate more extensively in the world economy.

In order to improve Soviet economic performance, it is necessary to establish "external economic ties and a policy of the
most active involvement in the worldwide division of labor,"
N.P. Shmelev argues.(2)   That is, greater economic interdependence with capitalist and other socialist countries is
thought to promote economic progress in the USSR.   G.A.
Arbatov, Central Committee member and head of the Institute
of the USA and Canada, declares: "Though the problems are
differently solved in different societies, and differences in
social systems provide different opportunities for such solutions, common to all societies is a growing concern for concentrating more resources, and perhaps attention, on internal
affairs."(3)
      On the other hand, Soviet theorists affirm that the dy-
namism of detente is spurred by the deepening "general crisis
of capitalism" in the contemporary period.(4)   While many
Western nations are extending political, economic, and even
military detente with the East, these capitalist nations are
undergoing crises in their development that are associated with
detente itself.   "The general crisis" is rooted in the structural
dynamics of advanced capitalism - conditions that also promote
the internationalization of economic life and the strengthening
of East-West economic ties.
      The intersection of detente and "the general crisis of
capitalism" helps to create "the material prerequisites for
socialism" in the West.   These conditions are generated by the
very processes that speed the internationalization of the world
economy and of detente.   I.P. Faminskii asserts: "In the process of the internationalization of economic life that is occurring in the epoch of the STR in both socialist and capitalist
states, the technical-economic prerequisites for the formation
of the future international socialist economy are being
forged."(5)   Moreover, such developments provide the basis
for the internationalization of polities, societies, and cultures
under conditions favorable to socialism.   According to V. Zagladin and I. Frolov, there is a "dialectical" interconnection
between detente and internationalization.   The emergence and
resolution of global problems accelerate detente and the restructuring of international relations.   "An approach to the
solution of such [global] problems in itself becomes a factor
promoting peaceful coexistence, since it presupposes intensive
economic, scientific, and technical cooperation between states
with differing social systems, thereby promoting detente."(6)
      Because of the "dialectical" link between detente and the
internationalization of economic, cultural, and scientific life,
the current phase of "the general crisis of capitalism" impacts
significantly upon the nature of the detente process itself.
Indeed, Soviet analysts perceive the development of advanced
capitalism to be especially significant for detente, because the
modernization and internationalization of the productive forces

are the "historically progressive mission of capitalism."(7)   As
O.T. Bogomolov, director of the Institute of Economics of the
World Socialist System, puts it, "The socialization of labor and
production, including their internationalization, is one of the
major historical results of the development of the capitalist
mode of production."(8)

Fedoseev also reduces the complex interconnections between the advanced productive forces of industrialized
capitalism and the advanced production relations of developed
socialism to a "dialectic" of socioeconomic development.(9)
That is, he views the worldwide STR as a factor critical to the
modernization of both socialist and capitalist countries.   The
STR is "an inalienable component of the material prerequisites
of communist society.   Revolution in the productive forces
prepares the material and technical basis needed for the
communist mode of production.   And here, too, we can see the
inseparable organic unity of the historical process of our
time."(10)

But this "dialectical unity" of global productive forces
and socialist production relations obscures a serious practical
problem.   Should a primary influence on Soviet foreign policy
be the pull of common interests created by the productive
forces of advanced industrialization, or should it be the
common interests created by socialist production relations?
Should the Soviet Union's chief immediate objective be greater
interdependence with the advanced industrialized countries of
the West, or should it be the consolidation of the state
socialist camp and the drawing of the Third World into that
camp?   Is the competition with advanced capitalism to be
conducted primarily in a cooperative and regularized manner in
the economic spheres associated with the STR, or in a confrontationist and unstable manner in the military spheres also
associated with the STR and in the political spheres associated
with the cold war, the need to maintain socialist unity, and
the collapse of the West?   Succinctly put, does "the general
crisis of capitalism" create a favorable climate for East-West
interdependence, or does "the general crisis" limit or preclude
such interdependence?

In presenting our own and Soviet responses to such
questions, we will focus upon Soviet analyses of contemporary
capitalism and detente.   The first section of this chapter will
provide a general overview of the Soviet interpretation of the
present-day "general crisis of capitalism."   The basic or
consensual Soviet view will be articulated here, leaving for the
final section and later chapters an analysis of significant differences in Soviet perspectives.   The second section will examine some of the general propositions developed by Soviet
researchers to understand the nature of the STR and the
growing internationalization of economic life occurring in the
West, including Japan.   The third section will focus upon

Soviet analyses of the changing "correlation of forces" among advanced industrial states. The emergence of "three centers of imperialism" - the United States, Western Europe, and Japan - will be underscored as central to Soviet thinking about international economic relations. The fourth section will explore the impact of the STR upon the division of labor between the developed capitalist countries and the developing countries, with special attention devoted to the role of the multinational corporation (MNC). In the fifth section, Soviet perceptions of the impact of "the general crisis of capitalism" upon the detente process will be discussed. We will contend that conflicting Soviet interpretations of detente emerge from different Soviet views about the nature, direction, and scope of the present-day problems and performance of capitalist societies.

THE CONTEMPORARY "GENERAL CRISIS OF CAPITALISM": INITIAL CONSIDERATIONS

Soviet theorists consider the problems of capitalism to be manifestations of a disintegrating social system. "The general crisis of capitalism is the period of the revolutionary collapse of capitalism as a social structure, of the internal decomposition and collapse of the world capitalist system."(11) But since capitalism's death rattle has yet to be heard even with the "ascendency" of socialism in the twentieth century, Soviet analysts view the collapse of the West as a prolonged and debilitating malady. That is, "the general crisis of capitalism is a chronic and incurable illness of a social structure doomed by history."(12)

The "illness" of capitalism is thought to be rooted in the continued existence of antiquated production relations that circumscribe the possibilities inherent in the progressive and rapid growth of the capitalist productive forces in the post-1945 period. As I. Kuzminov notes, "The progressive weakening of capitalism is based on the deepening contradiction between the productive forces, which have been acquiring an ever more social character, and the narrow framework of the obsolete capitalist relations of production. The STR is an important factor in aggravating this contradiction."(13)

Capitalist production relations provide the basis for the unity of class interests in the West, but at the same time they limit capitalism's historical appeal to the forces of social progress in the socialist and Third World countries. The advanced capitalist productive forces associated with the STR provide an objective base for the growth and development of capitalism, but these changes ultimately outmode and transcend capitalist production relations. Hence, even though capitalism's production relations are fatally flawed, its productive forces provide the basis for continued strength in the West. Brezhnev noted at the Twenty-fifth CPSU Congress: "It is farthest from the communists' minds to predict an 'automatic collapse' of capitalism. It still has considerable reserves."(14) That is, the powerful productive forces of advanced capitalism have provided the West with room for maneuver, but the production relations of capitalism constrain the opportunities for choice. Iurii Shishkov adds: "A society doomed by history has indeed no desire to change anything; needless to say, this does not mean that the present crisis has brought capitalism, as a system, to the brink of destruction and that it will collapse at any moment."(15) In short, the productive forces of capitalism induce change, while its production relations limit change, and internal tensions or "contradictions" ("antagonistic" and "nonantagonistic") mount. Capitalism is characterized by conflicting tendencies toward stagnation and decay, on the one hand, and toward rapid growth and technological innovation, on the other.(16)

In its contemporary "crisis," capitalism's economic and organizational growth creates pressures for greater regulation of the scientific-technical and socioeconomic spheres and for the internationalization of goals and policies. Both tendencies press upon the narrow boundaries of the production relations of private capital. As Skorov argues, the development of the world's productive forces finds "the Procrustean bed of international capitalist economic relations much too small."(17)

The present-day or "third stage" of capitalism's decline is characterized by the adaptation of capitalist institutions and policies to the STR, by the response of the world capitalist system to changing international conditions, and by changing interrelationships between these internal and external environments. Especially important new circumstances are the internationalization of economic life, the increasing assertiveness of independent Third World countries, and the challenges posed by developed socialism.(18) The complex interaction between the domestic and international elements of advanced capitalism has led I. Kuzminov to argue that a new fourth stage of "the general crisis" is emerging. Kuzminov states that "the general crisis of capitalism is designated as 'general' precisely because it is a comprehensive crisis of the whole capitalist system, from its foundations to its superstructures; it is a crisis of the very foundations of private capitalist ownership in every form and at every level, because the modern productive forces have long since outgrown their framework."(19)

Domestic Factors

Soviet analysts contend that a fundamental problem of capitalism is the structural weakness of its "economic mechanism."
An economic mechanism, as characterized by Shishkov, is "a
system of instruments regulating the reproduction process on
the basis of the objective economic laws of the given social
system."(20)   Because of the extensive private ownership of
the means of production in capitalist systems, market forces
predominate.   Under classical capitalism, the economies were
based entirely on market relations.   But under the pressures
of the economic crises of the twentieth century, state interference with the laws of supply and demand has been required.   Capitalist economies are "no longer able to function
without constant correction of the market mechanism by the
bourgeois state.   However, this correction, naturally, cannot
push aside the market, which remains the basis for the regulation of capitalist reproduction as long as capitalism exists
as a system."(21)   Hence, one of the basic contradictions of
contemporary capitalism is the conflict between spontaneous
market forces and state-monopoly intervention in the economy.
"An unremitting struggle takes place between these two different elements, and in the course of that struggle a certain,
albeit extremely precarious, balance is established in each
country."(22)
    "State-monopoly capitalism" refers to the cooperation
between powerful monopolies and governmental institutions for
the purpose of controlling the production and distribution of
economic wealth.   Under state-monopoly capitalism, the state
takes over the capitalist economy in the most diverse ways.
"The state becomes a big industrialist, merchant, and banker.
State regulation extends to all the most basic aspects of capitalist reproduction."(23)
    The material basis for state intervention in the capitalist
economy is provided, first of all, by selective state ownership
of the means of production.   There is great variation in the
scope of state ownership in the advanced capitalist world.
State dominance over industrial and agricultural production
ranges from one-seventh in the United States to two-fifths in
France and Austria.   Together with direct state ownership,
quasi-state ownership is exercised through governmental subsidies to key enterprises.   Also, the state budget has become a
critical economic tool for intervention.   State funds are spent
in three basic ways: to support military forces and the state
bureaucracy; to finance the social infrastructure for economic
development (e.g., education and science); and to maintain
aggregate demand for domestically available goods and services.(24)
    State-monopoly capitalism is relying more and more on
administrative techniques of regulation rather than on market

techniques. With the growing significance of governmental controls, a structural crisis has emerged. According to A. Anikin and V. Kuznetsov, "Traditional methods of state regulation influence the economy mainly through the use of market and financial levers. But the possibilities of such influence, especially over the monopolized sector, are exceedingly limited. In particular, the state cannot solve many questions concerning the structural development of the economy."(25) Hence, planning has emerged as an important element of advanced capitalism. Because of the growth of the productive forces and the objective need to expand the state's economic activities in the era of the STR, the problems associated with capitalist planning are of increasing political significance.

Soviet theorists acknowledge that the advanced capitalist state possesses the building blocks for effective planning. First, economic science is at the disposal of the state. Second, computer technology, coupled with the systems management concept, facilitate dynamic, centralized intervention.(26) Third, the state budget and its controls have become vital to the growth of the capitalist economy and society. Fourth, the West European states, especially Great Britain and France, have nationalized many key industries. Fifth, the science of prognostics is developing at the service of the state.

Capitalist countries have used these instruments to guide economic and social development.(27) But state planning is indicative or voluntary. Corporations are not compelled to follow the state's programs. These economic "plans" merely suggest directions for corporate policy and hence function as guidelines for the expansion of monopoly capitalism.(28)

Soviet analysts view capitalist planning as the antithesis of genuine planning. Capitalist plans are voluntary; socialist plans are compulsory. Capitalist plans focus almost exclusively on the economy; socialist plans encompass economic and social goals. Capitalist plans often concentrate on individual sectors of the economy; socialist plans are comprehensive. Capitalist plans embody the interests of private capital; socialist plans express the general will of the farsighted elements of society. Capitalist plans leave the key investment and distribution decisions in the hands of the corporations and the market; socialist plans allocate scarce resources authoritatively and justly, in accord with the purposeful and "progressive" transformation of society.

The political leaders of Western nations are incapable of planning for national, as distinguished from particularistic, purposes. The means of production remain in private hands. The monopolistic corporations limit state power. A unified planning center cannot emerge. "By its very nature state-monopoly capitalism cannot combine in one center for planning and management the ability to direct the development of science, technology, labor resources, capital growth, education, culture, and public health."(29)

The rise of state-monopoly capitalism promotes "meta-socialization."(30) That is, the gradual expansion of the public sector, on the one hand, and the centralization of the economic means of production, on the other, produce a highly concentrated form of economic power. Although this accumulation of power falls short of the socialization of the means of production, the trend is in this direction. Inozemtsev argues that "the growing state-monopoly tendencies, the spread of state property, and the increasing state interference in the economy have not strengthened but have weakened the very pillars of capitalism, because they ultimately tend to intensify the socialization of production."(31)

Metasocialization is a new stage in capitalist development that confirms the appropriateness of identifying a new or fourth stage of "the general crisis of capitalism." Anikin and Kuznetsov state: "In the contemporary stage of the general crisis of capitalism, the active use of programming by separate governments not only fails to liquidate difficulties but leads in fact to a further deepening of contradictions."(32) In short, metasocialization introduces two important new kinds of "contradictions."(33)

First, there is a contradiction within the capitalist regulatory process itself. The central problem that state intervention in the economy and state planning seek to resolve is the cyclical and uneven development of the domestic and world capitalist systems. Governmental control has had a decisive effect on this problem by reducing "the amplitude of fluctuations in the volume of production, incomes, and prices."(34) S. Menshikov argues that this does not signify the weakening of the contradictions of the capitalist economic mechanism, but merely a shift in their nature and effects.(35) Governmental intervention alleviates economic crises through state spending to maintain aggregate demand. But this very success creates significant new problems. "State stimulation of the economy promotes inflation, undermines the competitiveness of the goods of a given country on the world market, and creates an unstable, at times critical, balance of payments."(36) Menshikov ominously concludes that "Sooner or later these contradictions lead to an explosion."(37)

Second, metasocialization does not enable the state to govern in the general interest. The advanced capitalist state cannot use scientific and technological achievements to improve the economic or socio-psychological quality of life of the masses. The STR develops the material prerequisites for socialism throughout the capitalist world, but this does not change the purposes for which the new material power is utilized. Zagladin argues that there is a "high degree of maturity of the premises of socialism in the developed capitalist world."(38)

This maturity, however, is not the result of altruistic motives. The bourgeoisie seeks to maintain its strength by resorting to "nationalization and to state regulation in various spheres of the economy, although this ultimately clashes with the very substance of private property and inflicts considerable harm on capitalism as a system."(39)   Hence, the development of the material prerequisites for socialism has not been accompanied by a concomitant development of the spiritual life of people or of nonexploitative interpersonal relationships.   Nor is class conflict sufficiently intense to make socialist revolutions imminent.   "In the developed capitalist countries the ripening of the objective premises of socialism and the .objective premises of socialist revolution tend to be highly contradictory processes, with the latter lagging far behind the former."(40)

Soviet writers nevertheless contend that the socialization of the means of production requires a social revolution.   In the absence of such a revolution, the state embodies the "false consciousness" of a public interest.   Adjudicating conflicts among corporations, the state claims it is acting in the public interest.   But, without a social revolution, the true welfare of the nation can never be served.   "It often appears that the current needs of individual monopoly groupings clash with the basic interests of finance capital as a whole.   In this event, the state will subordinate the first to the second, even at the risk of the dissatisfaction of some financial groupings.   All this means is that the monopolies themselves need the state's autonomy to secure their vital interests."(41)

In short, Soviet analysts view Western governments as central actors in state-monopoly capitalism, but not as the dominant ones.(42)   The most important forces in capitalist society are still the monopolistic national and multinational corporations.   Their pursuit of profit dominates economic life, their drive for power dominates political life, and their materialistic values dominate social and cultural life.

However, the long-range interests of capitalism cannot be furthered by unbridled competition among corporations, especially in the era of the STR.   The state's role is to mitigate conflicts among the corporations and to ensure the stable sociopolitical, economic, and fiscal environments (e.g., law and order, reliable markets, favorable tax policies) in which the corporations can thrive.   The state may occasionally come into conflict with particular firms that ignore goals other than immediate profits.   But, in order to prolong the existence of the capitalist system and to distribute its benefits fairly equitably among the major corporations, the federal government must assume a more and more active role.

Some capitalist states have nationalized major industries. Soviet commentators view this development as an innovative type of linkage between governmental and business interests, rather than as the domination of the latter by the former.

More important, the capitalist state is becoming increasingly involved in economic planning and regulation. Western political leaders are more concerned than business executives with resolving the general problems of their economies, such as unemployment, recession, and inflation.(43) The contradictions of advanced capitalism, however, preclude the success of these efforts.

International Factors

The first external major component of "the general crisis of capitalism" lies in the relations among the highly industrialized capitalist countries. Soviet theorists contend that international developments are exacerbating the domestic difficulties of state-monopoly capitalism. The regulatory process in advanced capitalism is becoming much stronger on the national level than on the international level. The need for international state-monopoly regulation is accentuated by the internationalization of production. There is a growing tension between the rising level of the international socialization of production and the confinement of state-monopoly regulation to the jurisdiction of the national bourgeois state. In the world economy, "anarchic market forces" prevail over the regulating mechanism to a much greater degree than they do within the domestic economies of capitalist states.

The internationalization of production and the incapacity of national state-monopoly institutions to control this process is a central contradiction of advanced capitalism. Shishkov poses the problem as follows:

> The need for greater regulating interference in the world economic process grows steeply under the impact of the STR. The rapid development of the international division of labor and of industrial, scientific, and technological cooperation between countries; the swift growth of foreign trade; the intensification of the export of capital; the perceptible expansion and complication of credit relations . . . ; and the unprecedented development of international transport and communications represent a qualitative advance in the development of international socialization of production. Most of the capitalist countries, chiefly the industrialized nations, are today finding themselves so closely bound to each other that any significant economic development in one immediately affects the economy of the others.(44)

Shishkov identifies five spheres in which the interdependence of the international capitalist economy has increased.

First, there has been a significant expansion of trade among highly industrialized capitalist nations since 1945. As a result, capitalist economies are more and more dependent on market conditions in the other capitalist countries. Second, there has been a greater flow of capital among advanced capitalist economies. Third, there has been considerable internationalization of the credit and banking systems. Fourth, capitalist nations are increasingly interdependent in monetary relations. Devaluation in one country's currency system has immediate effects on the economies of the other advanced capitalist states. Fifth, there have been additional and closer production ties among contemporary capitalist economies, especially with the development of the multinational corporation (MNC).(45)

The result of the growing interdependence among advanced capitalist states is that "the national economies are being intertwined into the single fabric of the world economy, and not one of them is any longer able to function in isolation," Shishkov argues.(46) The basic contradiction within an advanced capitalist economy is between the productive forces that are becoming more international and the production relations that are failing to manage adequately the internationalization of production. To date, the failure of attempts to develop new cross-national and supranational methods of regulating the advanced capitalist economies has become "one of the most important sources of economic instability and of collosal difficulties experienced by capitalism."(47)

Because scientific and technical change and the internationalization of the world economy are central to the relations among the major Western powers, we will devote the entire next section of the present chapter to this subject. Suffice it to say here that the internationalization of production impinges upon the advanced capitalist world in two contradictory ways, according to Soviet analysts. On the one hand, internationalization necessitates interdependence and creates pressures for the integration or consolidation of advanced capitalism. Hence, K. Mikulskii argues: "Highly developed state-monopoly capitalism has become a necessary condition for the operation of the complex systems of international specialization and cooperation within the capitalist world at the present level of the productive forces and capital concentration. The increasing capitalist international division of labor to an ever greater degree occurs by means of state-monopoly regulation."(48) That is, the internationalization of productive forces will intensify the need and enhance the ability of state-monopoly capitalism to expand on the international level.

On the other hand, the internationalization of production exacerbates the competition among developed capitalist states and strengthens "interimperialist contradictions." The shift in "the correlation of forces" against the United States and in favor of Western Europe and Japan has resulted in the emergence of "three centers of imperialism" and has aggravated the contradictions among these power centers.(49)   That is, the internationalization of production has coincided with the decline of American hegemony and of coordinated policies in the West. We will also elaborate on this theme in the next section.

The second major international element of "the general crisis" is taking place in the relationships between the advanced capitalist states and the Third World. One of the elements of the present stage of capitalism is the disintegration of the European colonial system. The traditional imperialist exploitation of the colonial world rested upon the use of overtly political means of domination to ensure a steady flow of raw materials from the colonies to Europe. The present stage of capitalist development is characterized by the complete elimination of the possibility of political colonialization.   As V. Solodovnikov puts it, "the virtual liquidation of the world colonial system is an expression of the current sharpening of the general crisis of capitalism."(50)

The central development in relations between the advanced capitalist and Third World states is the strengthening of "neoimperialist" methods of domination. Even though the Third World has been freed from "direct colonial dependence," these countries now suffer from "neocolonialist exploitation in its various forms," S.P. Novoselov declares.(51)   The advanced capitalist nations use economic controls and the achievements of the STR to sustain an asymmetrical economic division of labor with Third World nations.(52)   This neocolonialist division of labor, according to Mikulskii, further concentrates the "productive forces in the industrial and trade and transport centers located in the most developed states. This trend is to the detriment of economic progress in the less developed countries and regions and hampers the use of labor and national resources over a large area of the world."(53)

The developing nations are increasingly dissatisfied with the capitalist international division of labor, Soviet authors contend. The role of the Third World in the capitalist international division of labor and impact of the STR upon the division of labor will be analyzed in detail in the next-to-last section of this chapter. We will merely note here that the movements within the Third World against neocolonialism and neoimperialism intensify the third stage of "the general crisis of capitalism" and legitimize the conceptualization of a fourth stage. K.N. Brutents, deputy chief of the International Department of the Central Committee, writes: "The massive nationalization of monopoly property and the collective actions for a new economic order mark the beginning of a new stage in the relations between the liberated countries and imperialism, one which in its implications is comparable to the collapse of the colonial empire."(54)

The third broad international factor in "the general crisis" is the growing significance of socialism for world historical development. On the one hand, the construction of developed socialist societies and the metasocialization of production in the West represent a substantial growth in the scope and importance of the socialization of the productive forces in the contemporary world. The economic performance and potential of developed socialism represent a competitive challenge to advanced capitalism to enhance its forms of metasocialization. This challenge, in turn, provides the basis for the economic "materialization" of detente.(55) On the other hand, the Third World is becoming more of an independent or a "free-floating" historical force, which increases the possibility of further reducing the capitalist predominance in the international division of labor. Two Soviet analysts assert: "The developing countries, being simultaneously components of the world capitalist economy and of the worldwide economy, have been active allies of the socialist countries in the struggle to shape a new system of international economic relations based on equality and mutual advantage for all those involved."(56)

The changes associated with the internationalization of economic life among advanced capitalist states and between advanced capitalist and Third World states create an historical challenge for developed socialism. Soviet spokesmen have described that challenge as follows:

> The new system of international relations currently being formed cannot be viable if it includes economic inequality and, as before, economic pressure. For this reason the Soviet Union, other socialist countries, and all truly progressive forces view as one of their most important international tasks the creation and development of new economic relations between states with different social systems, and also in the global economy. The liquidation of inequality in the sphere of international economic relations eliminates one of the sources of conflict between states and peoples, and makes the structure of the contemporary world more secure.(57)

The impact of the internationalization of production upon the interdependence of advanced capitalist states is the subject to which we now turn. Such economic interdependence creates a most significant challenge to developed socialism. And the effort to meet this challenge is one of the central components of the Soviet policy of detente in the Brezhnev period.

THE STR AND THE INTERNATIONALIZATION OF THE
ADVANCED CAPITALIST ECONOMIES

We will begin by presenting the basic Soviet interpretation of
the effects of the STR upon the advanced capitalist division of
labor. Special attention will be devoted to the major work of
I.P. Faminskii, which provides an exhaustive synthesis and
analysis of the Soviet literature on the subject.

The STR and the International Division of Labor

The division of economic labor that emerged in the nineteenth
century in the capitalist world was oriented toward the bipolar
axis of the developed countries of Europe, on the one hand,
and the colonies of Asia and Africa, on the other hand. The
former was the locus of industrialization; the latter, the source
of raw materials and foodstuffs.
    This classic division of labor has been undercut by four
critical developments, according to Soviet writers. First,
decolonialization and the growing struggle for economic independence have led Third World countries to begin to indus-
trialize. No longer are underdeveloped states merely the
suppliers of raw materials to the imperialist powers.(58)
    Second, the processes associated with the STR have
broadened and deepened ties among the advanced capitalist
nations themselves. Production interdependence is increasing
among the highly industrialized states. "In the conditions of
the STR the international division of labor becomes ever deeper; the development of forms of socialization within production
sectors closely binds the main branches of industrial production in the advanced capitalist countries."(59)
    Third, the STR has decreased the dependence of the
industrialized world on certain raw materials from the Third
World. The advanced economies now use many synthetic,
rather than natural, materials. Also, because of the mechanization of agriculture, the industrialized countries have become
the major producers of agricultural surplus in the world, and
they no longer rely upon the Third World for foodstuffs.
Indeed, many developing countries are highly dependent on
advanced capitalist nations for basic food products, for the
technologies to extract and utilize their natural resources, and
for the markets to sell their raw materials and manufactured
goods at reasonable profit.
    Fourth, the STR has increased the dependence of the
advanced world on the Third World in one significant area -
energy. The burgeoning worldwide demand for fuels has
improved the prospects for detente. But the scientific and
technical capabilities of the industrialized nations are becoming

even more formidable in responding to adverse conditions. "The energy crisis has generated a further STR in energetics" in the advanced world, Faminskii notes. (60)

Soviet analysts debate whether independence or dependence is more significant for understanding the developed world's relationship to the developing world. (61) They generally agree, however, that the STR has produced a "new type of division of labor" founded upon production specialization. (62) "Specialization in certain fields is not merely based on the utilization of natural resources [as in the past], but on the results of scientific activity and on industrial specialization among the developed capitalist nations." (63) International specialization is especially salient in the most advanced industrial sectors. The chemical, aerospace, and electronics industries, for example, are characterized by high levels of R&D investment, high levels of competition within the capitalist world, and a high degree of dependence on foreign markets for profitability.

The STR underscores the growing importance of the economies of scale. The further mechanization of industry is most profitable if large amounts of more specialized goods are produced. But the expansion and specialization of production require sources of supply and markets broader than the national ones. Hence, economic growth and specialization transcend national borders and attain an international character, thereby increasing the volume and altering the nature of production ties among advanced capitalist nations.

The growing specialization of production within an advanced capitalist nation is oriented toward satisfying foreign as well as domestic needs, in the view of Soviet analysts. The external market is of growing profitability for the economies of industrialized capitalist nations. Exports are significant for national economic growth and productivity. Imports are also becoming more and more important in meeting internal economic needs, both in terms of finished goods and of components for the production process. Hence, the volume of foreign trade among advanced capitalist countries has increased throughout the post-1945 period as a percentage of overall GNP.

Correspondingly, the growth of specialization has enhanced the quality of industrial and agricultural products. The price of items has become only one dimension of international economic competition. Indeed, the desirability and marketing of goods have become critical elements in determining competitiveness within and among sectors - for example, in advanced technology fields such as computers and electronics, and in the choice between purchasing grain to feed domestic livestock or purchasing meat products from abroad.

Faminskii declares: "The place of a country in the international division of labor and the level of its specialization are determined by two factors: (1) its economic potential and consequently the size of its internal markets; and (2) its level of economic development."(64) The United States, with its extensive, complex, and highly developed internal markets, is less dependent on the world capitalist economy than are Japan or West Germany. But, even in the United States, "the level of dependence is growing with the development of the pro- ductive forces and of the complexity of modern produc- tion."(65) Soviet writers consider it significant that the two capitalist countries with the highest growth rates in the post-1945 period - West Germany and Japan - are also the two most active in foreign trade.(66)

Faminskii adds: "The deepening of the international divi- sion of labor and the growing dependence of the economies of advanced capitalist countries on foreign economic ties lead to a strengthening of the internationalization of production."(67) This development establishes "close and more or less stable productive ties between enterprises of diverse countries, and, as a result, the productive process in one country becomes a component of the productive process on an international or worldwide scale."(68) Internationalization is a manifestation of the growing scope of the "socialization of production" within and among advanced capitalist economies.

Faminskii concludes: "The internationalization of produc- tion constitutes the objective basis for the development of all forms of international economic relations and, as such, in- fluences all other forms of international relations (political, cultural, etc.)."(69) Specifically, the modern forms of production have led to the internationalization of capital, the development of the MNC, the growth of capital flows among Western and Third World nations, the migration of the skilled work force from the less developed to the more developed countries, and the establishment of collaborative forms of state-monopoly capitalism, such as the Common Market.

The Internationalization of Capital

Soviet writers affirm that the objective basis for the interna- tionalization of capital is provided by the internationalization of production, the deepening of the international division of la- bor, and the growing interdependence of enterprises in vari- ous countries. This new stage in the development of the productive forces is a worldwide phenomenon that must find expression in the social forms of organizing production. Growth in the scale of production in capitalist countries leads to the concentration of capital. And the socialization of pro- duction leads to the exchange of capital on the international level and to the emergence of the MNC in the capitalist world.(70)

The older international cartels were oriented toward the transfer of raw materials from the colonies to the European centers. The newer MNCs are primarily engaged in economic dealings among the advanced capitalist nations and secondarily in neocolonialist relations with the Third World.(71) Faminskii asserts: "In contemporary conditions, when the production linkages among the economies of the developed capitalist countries are growing stronger, the nature of the internationalization of capital changes. The expansion of the spheres of activity of the largest companies, because of the establishment of enterprises in the other highly developed capitalist countries, is itself a form of the adaptation of capital to the demands of the contemporary stage of the development of the productive forces, the contemporary STR."(72) Hence, the MNC has emerged in response to objective elements of the advanced productive forces.(73) "The inclination of giant companies to create enterprises in different countries has its basis in the objective tendency toward the internationalization of production and the growing interdependence of production in various countries."(74)

The STR has created "the material prerequisites" for the MNC in a number of ways. The establishment of global transportation networks binds countries more closely together. The development of global communication systems links segments of the production process more efficiently, which in turn strengthens the technological preconditions for managerial control. And the emergence of modern managerial science enhances organizational capabilities to seize global opportunities and to cope with global problems. Also, the development of science-based industries requires a high degree of capital investment. It is no accident that science-based industries are by and large MNCs and are heavily subsidized by capitalist governments.

The STR and the internationalization of production are greatly affected by the flow of capital among industrialized Western nations, according to Soviet spokesmen. The sheer volume of capital export has substantially increased in the post-1945 world. Most of the capital exported consists of direct investments, which provide the financial basis for the exercise of control over foreign factories by the MNC. Also, there has been a major shift in the geographical locus of capital investment away from the developing to the developed world. "The flow of capital toward imperialist states has been significantly increased."(75) Moreover, the sectors with considerable capital investment flows have changed. Investments were previously concentrated in raw material industries and in the plantation economies of the colonies. In the contemporary period, the MNCs primarily invest in the manufacturing industries of the developed and developing economies.

Soviet analysts perceive considerable diversity in the present-day institutions and operations of international capital, but they stress the importance of several characteristics of the MNC.(76)

First, the MNC was developed initially by the American
business community to maintain and expand its economic predominance over the capitalist world in the 1950s. The great
majority of MNCs are still U.S.-controlled, but West European
and Japanese MNCs are of ever increasing significance.

Second, the MNCs tend to be concentrated in the most
dynamic sectors of advanced capitalist production, such as oil
and gas, automobiles, chemicals, aeronautics, and electronics.

Third, one of the main ways MNCs are developing is
through diversification. This tendency leads to a sharp
struggle among them for preeminence in world markets.

Fourth, science-based industries tend to be MNCs, or
conversely, MNCs largely control R&D in the commercial
sphere.

Fifth, the major innovators in management are the MNCs.
Precisely because of the scope of their enterprises and the
diversity of functions to be directed, the MNCs must innovate.
Management has been restructured in order to control, direct,
or cope with (in descending order of preference) the entire
sweep of production, financing, and marketing activities. The
MNC is a unified management center that is creating a new
stage in the international concentration of capital and production.

Sixth, MNCs are promoters of corporate planning. This
is especially important because MNCs create and satisfy market
demands, and - often with government support - develop new
technologies.

Seventh, the MNC has stimulated the growth of international banking. International financial groupings have emerged
as highly influential participants in the shaping of capitalist
forms of interdependence.

In short, Faminskii concludes that "the growing internationalization of production is [closely] connected with the
further monopolization of the world capitalist economy in the
hands of a few MNCs."(77)

Nonetheless, the development of the MNC has introduced
significant lines of conflict in the advanced capitalist world
economy.(78) MNCs have increased "interimperialist contradictions." The MNCs struggle for control of portions of the
world market and induce their governments to help them compete with other MNCs. "In conditions of the growth of state-
monopoly capitalism, the state becomes an important tool in the
hands of national monopolies, defending their interests both in
the internal and external markets."(79) Moreover, the structure and objectives of the MNCs are not congruent with individual domestic economies, and this asymmetry provides the
MNCs with ample opportunities to evade government regulation
of their activities. "The growth of the internationalization of
capital and the development of the MNC are taking place together with the preservation of the current role of the national

economies. . . . [Hence], there is not only a contradiction
between the socialization of production on the global level and
the preservation of the capitalist mode of appropriation, but
there is also a contradiction between the internationalization of
production and capital and the state's management of the
national economy."(80)

The STR and the Development of New Forms of International
Economic Ties among Advanced Capitalist States

According to Soviet writers, the STR has broadened the scope
and depth of interactions among advanced capitalist states.(81)
Economic interdependence has become especially evident in
three major domains: the flow of capital, the structure and
patterns of trade, and the expansion of scientific and technical
ties.

Capital Flows

Capital flows in the international economy have shifted from
the developing to the developed worlds. Responding to this
trend, Western powers have increasingly penetrated each other's economies for the purpose of capital investment.(82)
     The United States has invested heavily in Western Europe
and Canada.(83) American economic interests in Europe have
been stimulated by a desire to hide behind the trade barriers
established through the common tariff of the European Economic Community (EEC). U.S. investments have been more and
more resented by the Europeans who fear an "American challenge" within Europe itself. The American investment "invasion" and the European reaction to it have stimulated a
"counterinvasion" of the American market by the Europeans.(84)
     Soviet analysts offer several critical reasons for the in-
creased ability of the Europeans to enter the American economy. The frequent crises of the dollar have increased the
value of European currencies. Also, the long period of fighting the Vietnam war placed great inflationary pressures upon
the American economy. These pressures reduced the competitiveness of American goods on the world market and further
devalued the dollar. Moreover, the increasingly unfavorable
balance of trade has reversed the outflow of "surplus" capital
generated from trade, and has spurred foreign investments in
the American economy. Furthermore, the Europeans have
increased their investments in R&D and have simultaneously
enhanced their capabilities to compete in the science-based
industries worldwide.
     The Japanese rapidly accelerated their investments abroad
beginning in the 1960s.(85) The Japanese have invested pri-

marily in the United States but increasingly in Western Europe as well. Serious conflict has developed between Japan and Western Europe over the issue of capital investment flows, because the Japanese have resisted outside investments in their economy. A key source of conflict within the advanced capitalist world is the continued existence of such domestic barriers to international capital investment.

The Japanese favor a higher degree of investment in the developing countries than do either the Americans or the West Europeans. This is due to Japan's very considerable dependence upon raw material imports, as well as to its geographical proximity to South Korea and Taiwan.

The shifting levels and nature of capital investment among advanced capitalist economies are significant for various reasons. Foreign investment tends to flow to the most advanced sectors, especially to the science-based industries. The "American challenge" of the 1960s stemmed from the fact that U.S. investments in Western Europe have been heavily concentrated in the machine building, automotive, electronics, and chemical industries. The "American sectors" of European production are frequently the most advanced sectors of the European economy. The Europeans have not responded to this aspect of the American challenge by resorting to protectionism, because this would limit the advantages to be drawn from the internationalization of production. Rather, Western Europe has responded to the United States in kind. Since the 1960s, the Europeans have begun to invest heavily in American industry, and, like their American counterparts in Europe, they are investing in the most innovative fields.

European investments in advanced American industries have yielded an important benefit besides the high rate of return on those investments. For example, "British monopolies that have invested in the American economy are not only making great profits, but, with the help of direct foreign investments, are also trying to strengthen their position in the competitive struggle to overcome the 'technology gap' with the U.S."(86) Hence, foreign investment in science-based industries is a major conduit for the transfer of technology and R&D knowledge.

The capital investment process as a whole has contradictory effects upon the economies involved in capital exchange. For the exporting nation, the outflow of capital strengthens the domestic economy by expanding trade relations abroad and by expanding the scientific and technological capacity of the country. But a negative consequence is the balance of payments problem. In many countries the state must regulate the export of capital to deal with this difficulty. Also, there is a contradictory effect upon the country that imports capital. On the one hand, foreign investment is a key source of capital for technological innovation and for the reconstruction necessary

to modernize industry. On the other hand, dependencies are
created and leverage for foreign intervention in the domestic
economy is increased.

Soviet analysts conclude that greater international investment flows increase the economic interdependence of
advanced capitalist nations. "The main result of the contemporary export of capital is the strengthening of the internationalization of the production of capital and the significant
growth of trade among developed capitalist countries."(87)
The increased flow of capital among advanced capitalist states
has stimulated trade, and vice versa. Hence, Soviet observers
perceive a close link between capital investment and commerce
in advanced capitalist economies. This linkage has not been
well developed in East-West economic relations to date, and its
absence is a significant barrier to increased East-West industrial trade, as we will discuss in the following chapter.

Trade Patterns

The basic structural change in trade among capitalist nations
has been a reduction in the exchange of foodstuffs and raw
materials and an increase in the exchange of manufactured
goods. Production machinery and equipment in the advanced
capitalist world have played an important part in the expansion
of the division of labor. To broaden and diversify its assort-
ment of machinery products, an advanced capitalist country
specializes in those products it can most efficiently manufacture and market. This specialization nurtures innovation,
because each country strives to create new markets or to
capture its corner of existing markets. "A high tempo of
growth in the trade of the newest types of equipment is dictated by the demands of scientific and technological progress."(88)

There has also been a tremendous growth in the international exchange of licenses. The broad trade in licenses based
on patents and "new methods" has led to the formation of a
world capitalist market for the fruits of R&D. Moreover, licensing is a major area of market competition. The MNCs
especially use new licenses as a means to penetrate a particular foreign market, or to try to corner a worldwide market.

Licensing represents an R&D savings for the importing
firm or country, and it can also serve as an important stimulus
for technological innovation. Among advanced countries, in
clear contrast to the developing countries, a strong domestic
R&D base is complemented, not undercut, by the licensing
trade. In addition to providing savings and an incentive for
growth and productivity, licensing provides the foundation for
specialization in R&D activity. R&D specialization for the
world market becomes a significant part of the development of
domestic industry. Soviet writers consider Japan to be a

notable case study in the use of licensing. After 1945, the Japanese modernized their industries largely through the purchase of foreign licenses. But after attaining a higher level of development, Japan began to invest heavily in R&D both to increase its foreign market competitiveness and to promote its national independence.

Scientific and Technical Ties

Faminskii declares: "In the conditions of the STR, the most important factor of progress is the possession of new knowledge that allows the organization of the production of the newest products and the mastery of the newest technology. In these conditions a basic characteristic of the world capitalist economy is the broadening exchange of scientific-technical knowledge among countries." (89)

Licensing is not the only important form of scientific and technological cooperation among advanced capitalist economies, according to Soviet researchers. There have been interfirm agreements on the development of a new process or product - for example, the extensive cooperation among microbiological firms. Also, joint scientific research programs have been created to deal with specific scientific or technological problems on the level of the MNC or the national state, as in the case of the development of the British-French Concorde. Moreover, there has been broad participation in some international efforts to coordinate R&D, such as the emergence of EURATOM or the European space program.

Furthermore, coordination of state R&D policies has been improved to avoid duplication of effort and to draw upon the advantages of specialization. This task is extremely difficult. "But if in conditions of capitalism it is difficult and sometimes even impossible to create a unified conception of scientific development in a given country in light of the diversity of monopoly interests, how much more difficult is it to do on the international level? The diverse goals and needs of various monopoly groups and states hinder even the best and most long-term international projects." (90)

The need for greater international scientific and technical ties is rooted in the shift from extensive to intensive forms of R&D. The extensive form of R&D refers to the quantitative growth of science and technology, particularly the number of scientific and technical personnel and the number of laboratories. The intensive form of R&D refers to the more efficient management of human and material resources, in order to gain greater benefits from a given quantity of investment. "The scale of R and D investment in a whole series of areas is so large that it cannot be done even by a large firm or by a single state." (91) Hence, there is a need to develop new forms of international scientific and technological ties to spur the intensive development of R&D.

The STR and State-Monopoly Capitalism

Faminskii states: "The internationalization of economic life that is manifested in the deepening international division of labor, the formation of giant multinational corporations, and the intensification of various forms of international economic ties must inevitably be reflected in the processes of state-monopoly capitalism, the development of which is the most basic characteristic of the contemporary capitalist society."(92) Faminksii is referring to the development of the domestic form of state-monopoly capitalism, as well as to the emergence of new forms of international state-monopoly capitalism.

State-Monopoly Capitalism on the Domestic Level

One of the most basic ways internationalization is affecting state-monopoly capitalism is by increasing the need for governments to make their economies more competitive in world markets. "With the increased dependence of the [domestic] economy on the world market, the national mechanism of state-monopoly regulation has as its most significant task the raising of the level of international competitiveness of 'its' monopolies."(93) In fact, under the conditions of the STR, "national competitiveness has become one of the most basic factors in the struggle of monopolies for foreign markets."(94)

A fundamental goal of capitalist governments, then, is to increase the amount and profitability of their countries' participation in the world economy. First, steps are being taken to encourage the accumulation of capital and the renewal of fixed capital. "The intensification of the processes of the accumulation of capital creates the foundation for increased labor productivity and for the establishment of new fields and types of production."(95) Second, measures are being designed to stimulate technological innovation in production. Third, direct state financing of R&D is being instituted and programs are being developed to encourage the introduction of the results of R&D into production.

The modern capitalist state supports "its" MNCs as a means of improving the domestic economy. "The growth in the concentration and centralization of capital in the international arena has become a basic tenet of national state policy, in terms of encouraging the concentration and centralization of national capital for the purpose of strengthening its position in the world market."(96)

State-monopoly regulation becomes oriented toward encouraging production for export. There are state subsidies for fields of production capable of entering the export market. Also, state credit mechanisms have been created to finance activities in the export area.

State intervention in the economy to protect the interests of the MNCs has become increasingly significant in another way

as well. Although advanced capitalism has removed many of
the direct obstacles to international trade, many hidden trade
barriers exist for the primary purpose of aiding the competitive positions of the indigenous MNCs. Procedural regulations
and administrative standards have been an important impediment to foreign penetration of domestic markets. Japan provides an excellent example of this trend.

     In short, domestic forms of state-monopoly capitalism
remain central to the process of interdependence in the
advanced capitalist world. "Despite the growing internationalization of capital, the national state remains an important instrument in the hands of the monopolies in the capitalist
countries. Sensing the danger from foreign competitors in the
domestic economy, national monopolies always resort to the
defense of 'their' state."(97)

State-Monopoly Capitalism on the International Level

Faminskii contends that "the objective basis for the development of international forms of state-monopoly capitalism is
created by the influence of the STR upon the internationalization of the economic life of capitalist states and the
internationalization of production and capital, i.e., by the
growing socialization of capitalist production on a worldwide
scale."(98) The further development of the STR and of international economic relations underscores the central contradiction of advanced industrialization under capitalist
conditions. "As the internationalization of economic life grows,
so does the sharpness of the contradiction between the socialization of production on a worldwide level and the narrow
limits of the national states. The new forces of production
require a broader space for their development than the capitalist national state will allow."(99)

     The growing internationalization of production undercuts
the effectiveness of economic regulation by the capitalist state.
This is especially true of economic programming. It is impossible to regulate domestic production effectively when, as in
Western Europe, from one-fifth to two-fifths of the domestic
production is oriented toward the export market. Hence, the
objective need for international economic regulation is intensifying.

     Soviet analysts affirm that the many forms of state-
monopoly capitalism operate in different ways in the international system. Advanced capitalist states vary tremendously in
the degree of state regulation of the business community.
Considerable conflict among capitalist nations stems from the
different kinds of state-monopoly regulation.(100) At the same
time, the universal need for some form of "highly developed"
regulation creates the possibility of international economic
controls.(101) Such controls would coordinate the "activities

of the imperialist states in the international arena in the interests of international monopolies and in the interests of preserving the capitalist structure."(102)

A minimal kind of international coordination is "negative" regulation. This refers to bilateral or multinational "agreements that deal with a particular barrier to international trade, the export of capital, the migration of the work force, etc."(103) The single most successful form of capitalist regulation on this level has been the General Agreement on Trade and Tariffs (GATT). Trade liberalization, in the narrow sense of the removal of tariff barriers, has been basically achieved in the advanced capitalist world.(104)

A more ambitious type of international coordination is the attempt to carry out "positive" international regulation. This refers to "actions that lead to the solution on the international level of specific problems, such as the stabilization of trade markets and the creation of world prices. . . . The establishment and implementation of joint policies are much more complex and more developed forms of state-monopoly capitalism."(105) A key example of the attempt to establish "positive" international regulation is the Organization for Economic Cooperation and Development (OECD). This organization, which was established in 1960, provides a forum for consultation among advanced capitalist states. But, because the OECD institutions do not have supranational power to broaden or deepen positive regulation, only the coordination of policies is possible.(106)

The most ambitious form of international economic coordination is integration. Integration on ascending levels of complexity can aim at creating a free trade zone, a tariff union, an economic union, or a political union. Of course, the most successful capitalist attempt at integration has been the EEC. West European integration is a reaction of advanced capitalism to the objective and progressive tendencies of the internationalization of economic life.(107)

West European economic integration has been shaped by two conflicting tendencies. On the one hand, there has been "the necessity to create a broader space for the development of the productive forces, which the largest monopolies are especially interested in and which are inducing the bourgeois states to take new steps in the direction of economic and even political unification. New national forms of economic regulation and new supranational organs are emerging."(108) On the other hand, a sufficiently large number of capitalists in the different European states are "interested in preserving control over 'their' national state," and are undercutting supranationality in many ways. "Each capitalist country tries to receive maximum advantages from integration without losing its economic sovereignty."(109)

The process of European integration has had several "rational" effects on economic development, according to Soviet observers.

There has been an increase in the effectiveness of production. This has been achieved by economies of scale and by the concentration of capital on projects benefiting all EEC members rather than individual or small groups of European states.

There has been a vast upsurge of international specialization and cooperation within the EEC. Such specialization has, in turn, further encouraged the growth of the trade flows within Europe.

Although its agricultural policy has encountered many difficulties, the EEC has encouraged the more rational development of agricultural specialization within Europe.(110)

Conditions have been created that nurture greater capital reinvestment within Europe and encourage capital investment from outside of Europe. These developments have encouraged the technological modernization of production, which, in turn, has spurred the competitive quality of European products on the world market.

The rapid growth of the most advanced sectors of the economy (e.g., aerospace) has been encouraged by common policies, or by the encouragement of R&D cooperation within Europe.

In short, the successes of the EEC have made possible the emergence of a multinational center of capitalism as one of the three foci of power within the advanced capitalist economy (the United States and Japan being the other two centers).(111)

However, cooperation has primarily benefited the huge monopolies, the form of capitalist organization most suited to take advantage of the economies of scale. Small- and medium-sized enterprises within Western Europe have suffered. "Integration has accelerated the process of destroying small enterprises not only in the agricultural sector but in other economic fields as well, especially in the trade and service sectors. All of these processes have resulted in the increase in the proletarianization of the population."(112)

Several other negative social consequences have flowed from the integration processes and from technological advances: the unemployment of unskilled workers, the exploitation of foreign laborers, the social dislocation of the farmers, and the increasingly uneven development of backward and advanced regions of Europe.(113)

The objective limits of the capitalist form of integration are thereby evident in the West European experience.(114) The economic role of the nation-state has been strengthened, not diminished. National monopolies have preserved their central role within the state and have derived the majority of

the economic advantages from the EEC. Unplanned and dis-
jointed economic development have continued and sometimes
have been exploited by the monopolies to protect their advantages against a weak supranational authority. "The uneven
economic development of the EEC countries is an objective
basis for sharp contradictions among them, which in turn
strengthens the interest of the monopolies of each country in
preserving political power over their internal market."(115)

Hence, the growing interdependence of the capitalist
economies is unable to remove the basic contradictions within
capitalism and the basic contradictions among the imperialist
states. It is to the nature of the "interimperialist contradictions" in the era of the STR, and to the changing "correlation of forces" within capitalism that stem from the
internationalization of economic life, to which we now turn.

THE STR AND THE CHANGING "CORRELATION OF FORCES"
AMONG ADVANCED CAPITALIST STATES

According to Soviet writers, the changes in economic life associated with the STR provide the "objective" basis for changes
in relations among the advanced capitalist states.

First, the rising economic power of Japan and Western
Europe has eroded American hegemony in the West. The Atlanticist doctrine of the early postwar years was rooted in an
economic situation in which the American economy, despite its
autarkic or isolationist tendencies, was overwhelmingly predominant in the capitalist world. With the decline in power of the
American economy vis-a-vis Western Europe and Japan, the
Atlanticist doctrine is no longer viable. Economic equality
precludes deference to American interests on the part of Japan
and Western Europe.(116) Also, greater competitiveness among
the major capitalist nations puts pressure on the United States
to seek global markets and to integrate its economy more effectively with those of other Western, socialist, and Third World
countries.

Second, the EEC was initially formed under conditions of
American support for the "two pillar" approach to the Atlantic
community.(117) America and Europe would be partners in
economic, cultural, and military affairs. But as Western
Europe developed its scientific, technological, and economic
potential, it has competed with and even threatened American
economic interests. American support of the EEC has thereby
been reduced, producing a growing European concern for the
strength of the EEC in the world capitalist economy. The
growing scientific and technical potential of Europe has made it
a formidable adversary to the large-scale American corporations, even in fields such as aerospace, which the United

States has dominated throughout the postwar period. American
predominance rested in part upon the economies of scale,
which gave it a distinct advantage over individual European
countries. But the emergence of the EEC as a viable economic
entity has produced a similar economic advantage for Europe,
and the United States is just beginning to feel and to meet
this competition.

Third, Japanese economic development was founded upon
the acquisition of foreign technology to nurture its own innovative and productive capabilities. But Japan has developed
a strong R&D base that it is using to its commercial advantage. The Japanese have become the second largest economic
power in the capitalist world, due to their ability to compete
more effectively than the United States or Western Europe in
the world economy as a whole. The managerial skills, indus-
triousness, and creative capacity of the Japanese have provided the basis for the emergence of a nation unwilling to
subordinate its economic or political interests to an American
definition of those interests, especially through an Asian form
of the Atlanticist doctrine.(118)

Fourth, "three centers of imperialism" have emerged,
rather than a cohesive Western camp whose unity is enforced
by American dominance.(119)   American foreign policymakers
have attempted to reassert U.S. leadership through a "trila-
teral" approach, but the objective basis of economic change
does not permit the United States to maintain its predominance
in the world economy.(120)   Many American analyses of interdependence merely reaffirm the principle of American hegemony
in changing economic circumstances, rather than conceptualize
new coequal relations among the three imperialist powers.(121)

Fifth, with the growing equality of "the three centers of
imperialism," American foreign policymakers are attempting to
exercise leadership on the military front as a means of
preserving economic dominance.   Inozemtsev notes that an
important aspect of the contemporary situation is that "the
changes running against the United States in the economic and
political positions of the leading West European countries and
Japan have been taking place in the context of tremendous
U.S. military superiority."(122)   In other words, the United
States has not been able to use its military dominance to sustain its economic and political dominance.

Sixth, the high level of scientific and technological
potential in all "three centers of imperialism" increases competition among them as the internationalization of economic
production proceeds.   The conflict between West Germany and
the United States over the German sale of nuclear technology
to Brazil is symptomatic of the growing competition in
science-based industries.(123)

Seventh, the impressive scientific and technical capabilities of Western Europe and Japan enhance their ability to

wage a modern war of the advanced conventional or nuclear
type. On the one hand, nuclear proliferation is a growing
danger. A European nuclear force might emerge as a significant and perhaps independent part of the Western arsenal.(124) On the other hand, the scientific and technological
resources of Western Europe and Japan are important components of the West's collective warmaking capacity, spearheaded
by the U.S. military forces. Inozemtsev observes: "In present-
day conditions, the military strength of any state is especially
closely bound up with its economic, scientific, and technical
potential, with the level of education and the availability of
highly skilled personnel in every sphere of activity. This is a
fact which the capitalist powers increasingly reckon with in
their policy."(125)

In brief, "the correlation of forces" in the imperialist
camp has shifted away from the United States in favor of Western Europe and Japan. This redistribution of power has increased the quantity and quality of "interimperialist" contradictions. As O. Bogdanov argues:

> With the change in the balance of strength between
> the chief centers of imperialism, the capitalist powers
> tended gradually to substitute "polycentrism" for
> "U.S.-centrism" in their economic and political lines.
> This involved abandoning the scheme of international
> economic relations resting on U.S. supremacy. U.S.
> economic and political overlordship clashed with the
> weakening of the U.S. position in the world capital-
> ist economy. As a result, foreign economic relations
> tend increasingly to become an important area of
> interimperialist rivalry within the triangle of the
> U.S., the EEC, and Japan.(126)

The detente policies of the Western powers express these interimperialist contradictions. Detente has provided Western
Europe with greater opportunities to reduce its dependence on
the United States, and to transform its increased economic
power into political influence that enables West European countries (individually and collectively) to reconceptualize, pursue,
and fulfill their own interests. Awareness of these possibilities has considerably strengthened West European support for
the policy of detente.(127)

At the same time, interimperialist contradictions are atten-
uated by the common class interests of the Western governments. The internationalization of production, which creates
greater polycentrism in the West, also creates the objective
basis for greater cooperation among the industrialized capitalist
nations. Inozemtsev maintains that "the economic prerequisites
for joint action by the monopoly bourgeoisie of various countries are in a sense much greater than ever before."(128)

Soviet analysts explain the mix of conflict and collaboration produced by the internationalization of economic life in the West as follows. These phenomena are largely the results of a contradiction between the disintegration associated with capitalism as a sociopolitical system and the economic and organizational growth stimulated by the STR. Hence, Inozemtsev argues that "one of the key problems in analyzing the strategy of contemporary capitalism is to discover the balance between its centripetal and its centrifugal tendencies, between integration and disintegration."(129)

According to the Marxist "law of uneven economic and political development," the spontaneous or unregulated sociopolitical character of capitalism prevents it from carrying out coordinated and balanced economic policies. Despite concerted efforts toward cooperative problem solving, competition among Western powers will remain a serious barrier to economic progress. The unevenness of economic development among advanced capitalist states ensures that the internationalization of production will not stimulate or be accompanied by the internationalization of political action in the West.(130) Inozemtsev concludes: "The operation of the law of uneven development creates the material prerequisites for continued changes in the balance of strength."(131) The main lines of such changes are those identified above - namely, the weakening of the U.S. position in the global capitalist economy and the strengthening of the positions of Western Europe and Japan.

The uneven economic development of advanced capitalism produces a series of significant contradictions among the leading capitalist powers.(132) These contradictions form the objective situation within which Soviet detente policy operates and will continue to operate in the forseeable future. In particular, Soviet industrial trade policy with the West must be formulated and carried out within the framework of pressures for the internationalization of economic life and of mounting economic competition among the Western powers. We will examine such developments and their political implications more fully in the third chapter.

SOVIET PERSPECTIVES ON NORTH-SOUTH RELATIONS IN
THE ERA OF THE STR

According to leading Soviet officials and foreign policy analysts, the worldwide STR has influenced the relationship between the industrialized capitalist nations and the countries of the Third World in three major ways.

First, advanced capitalism has devised a strategy of "neo-imperialism." This strategy is founded on the West's organizational superiority in the form of the MNC; its economic superiority in terms of capital resources, marketing skills, and fiscal controls; and its scientific and technological superiority, which makes possible a "one-way" transfer of manufactured products and licenses from the developed to the developing world. Industrialized countries are the center of science-based production. The Third World is a raw materials and labor-intensive reserve for the United States, Western Europe, and Japan. This division of labor promotes the transfer of natural resources and semimanufactured products from the Third World to the industrialized capitalist states. In the process, advanced technology and capital flow from the Western nations to the developing countries. Foreign capital plays a key role in the economic growth of the Third World and economic development is oriented toward the foreign market under such a division of labor.(133) Hence, Western neoimperialism strives to create asymmetric dependencies in the developing states and to forestall the very real possibility of reverse dependencies (e.g., excessive reliance on Third World oil).

Second, the STR creates particular demands unique to the late twentieth century. For countries that began to modernize in the nineteenth or early twentieth centuries, scientific advances and the use of science-based technology for development were not central. But this is no longer the case. Given the dynamism of the STR in advanced capitalism, the Third World dooms itself to a position of even greater economic inferiority if it does not attempt to gain from and actively contribute to the worldwide STR. In other words, development in advanced capitalist countries is cumulative and exponential, and the ability of the Third World to "catch up" depends on its capacity to borrow and effectively to utilize the scientific and technological accomplishments of the West. The establishment of an adequate indigenous scientific base, in order to participate in the STR, is a critical component of a strategy for modernization in the Third World. Formulating and implementing a domestic strategy for development is vital to a Third World country's ability to benefit from the STR and to engage in a mutually advantageous division of labor with the advanced capitalist world.(134)

Third, the STR and the internationalization of production make possible a shift from an exploitative to an advantageous division of labor. These developments will increasingly enable Third World countries (some more than others) to exert pressure upon the advanced capitalist states. The concentration of science-based and technology-intensive industries in the West increases the dependency of the industrialized Western nations upon the raw materials and the energy resources of the developing countries. Because raw material commodities chiefly flow from the Third World to the prosperous capitalist nations, the potential for economic leverage is expanded.(135)

The struggle to replace asymmetric dependence with mutually advantageous interdependence lies at the core of "the general crisis" of relations between the Third World and advanced capitalism.(136) We will first examine Soviet perspectives on the nature of the asymmetrical dependence between the West and the Third World, and, in the two following parts, assess Soviet views on the prospects for "genuine" interdependence and for the creation of a "new international economic order."

The Dependence of the Third World on Industrialized Capitalist Nations

Soviet spokesmen contend that the Third World is most dependent on the advanced capitalist world in the areas of science and technology. The vast "technological gap" between the developing and advanced capitalist countries is rooted in vast differences in the scope and depth of capital investment in R&D, as well as in significant differences in the quantity and quality of personnel trained in the natural, social, engineering, and managerial sciences.

Neoimperialist policies utilize these gaps to strategic advantage. As two Soviet commentators argue, "Imperialism attempts to use the technological weakness of young states in order to tie them more closely to the scientific and technological potential of the world capitalist economy."(137) The Third World represents a new market for technologically advanced goods, and Western nations compete to penetrate these markets.

Nevertheless, neoimperialism is "dialectically contradictory." In order to expand the scientific and technological capabilities of the industrialized capitalist states, the Third World must be able to buy new goods and to assimilate them within their own production processes.(138) The contradictory essence of neoimperialism is the attempt to help the Third World become a consumer of science-based production, while preventing the Third World from becoming a producer of scientific and technical knowledge and thereby a competitor of advanced capitalism. V.G. Solodovnikov asserts: "Life taught the neocolonialists that economic stagnation cannot be a real alternative to neocapitalist development. They learned that steps must be taken to develop capitalism in the former colonies and semicolonies, to form the mechanism of expanded capitalist reproduction, to develop new spheres of monopoly capital investment, and to create an infrastructure meeting the requirements of the STR."(139)

But the development of the Third World through an asymmetrical division of labor with advanced capitalism creates a situation in which the STR is having largely negative results

in Third World countries. On one level, the STR has stimulated the production of synthetic materials that are increasingly
undercutting the competitive position of the Third World's
natural resources. A team of senior researchers from several
institutions of the USSR Academy of Sciences concludes: "The
developing countries' specialization in raw materials and
foodstuffs has resulted in [the fact] that, under the conditions
of the revolution in science and technology, their position in
the world economy began to worsen."(140)

On a second level, the better wages and professional
opportunities in the advanced capitalist states have siphoned
off domestically and foreign-trained Third World specialists who
are absolutely essential to the creation of a scientific and
technological potential in their own countries. This "brain
drain" has a demoralizing impact upon the Third World intel-
ligentsia, and, by fostering condescension or indifference
toward Third World cultures, further blocks indigenous scientific and technological development. The Academy of Sciences
research team elaborates: "The native scientists are brought
up as cosmopolitans, indifferent to the destinies of their own
countries, skeptical of the possibility of building real modern
centers of science and education, and imbued with the idea of
the superiority of all things foreign and of 'Western civilization.'"(141)

In short, the STR has resulted in the creation of more
sophisticated forms of dependence. Economic growth in the
Third World is rooted in the capacity of a given state to
become closely linked with the advanced Western scientific and
technological communities, in order to accelerate its own
development. But Third World leaders and businessmen too
often equate the expansion of foreign trade with scientific and
technological dependency, which they in turn view as a pre-
condition for rapid economic growth. Central Committee official
Brutents affirms that "neocolonialism's strategy remains essentially the same; the only alteration is with an eye to the
opportunities opened up by the STR. It is now setting its
sights on a higher level of economic development of the liberated countries and more sophisticated forms of dependence."(142)

A second dimension of asymmetrical dependence is associated with the activities of the multinational corporation. The
MNCs are the critical "commercial-political organizations"
through which capitalism is changing the global division of
labor and creating innovative forms of dominance vis-a-vis the
Third World. N. Sergeev asserts: "In their strategy of keeping the developing nations in the orbit of capitalism, the
state-monopoly apparatus of the West is using the international
systems of the super monopolies on a growing scale to spread
and reinforce their political influence in the new nations."(143)

Soviet analysts recognize that the MNCs promote economic development, but they contend that this development is based on exploitation and vulnerability. First, technological innovation in Third World nations depends heavily upon the patent and licensing operations of the MNC.(144) Second, the MNC deliberately creates an incomplete production cycle in Third World economies, in order to take advantage of the cheaper labor resources and to avoid the dangers of nationalization. A group of Soviet researchers affirms:

By building enterprises to produce certain types of equipment, units, and components in the developing countries, the monopolies seem to be helping these countries toward industrialization and diversification of their economy. The construction of such projects does, indeed, increase employment somewhat, expand exports of finished products, and promote industrial development in general. However, such enterprises do not, as a rule, become an integral part of the industrial-economic complex of the countries concerned, as they are bound by many strings to the head enterprise . . . outside the country, often being its technological extension.(145)

Briefly stated, Soviet officials and theorists maintain that the MNC blocks the equitable interdependent development of the Third World economies. As Sergeev puts it: "By establishing subsidiaries, the transnational corporations wrest key sectors from the economy of the new nations . . . and include them in their international complexes. The development of these sectors is subordinated to the interests of the monopolies and in many cases comes into conflict with the interests of the countries where these subsidiaries operate."(146) Under such conditions, it becomes difficult for the Third World nations to plan for economic development. The MNC curtails the ability of the developing states to achieve the economic independence necessary to become a participant in a "mutually advantageous" division of labor.

A third dimension of asymmetry lies in the unequal and unfair trade relations between the advanced capitalist and Third World countries. Soviet writers stress several aspects of this relationship:

World prices for raw materials have not kept pace with the prices for industrial manufactured goods. The lower level of growth in raw material prices compared to the rise in prices of industrial goods signifies that the STR is having an important negative effect on the trade relations of the developing world. As A. Elianov characterizes the dilemma: "The developing countries are compelled to import most, if not all, of the new equipment and production technologies. At the same time, on the world market their exports, which are practically the only source of paying for their imports, encounter obstacles difficult to surmount, obstacles which are also largely the result of the revolution in science and technology. Among them are, first and foremost, the relative drop in demand and a downward trend in prices of raw materials which are predominant in local exports."(147)

The lower level of labor productivity in the Third World means that developing states must sell their industrial production at world prices that are lower than the national cost for production.

Third World states tend to be producers and exporters of a single commodity or industrial product, which makes them extremely vulnerable to foreign market fluctuations and limits their ability to respond flexibly to changing world market conditions.

The advanced capitalist nations virtually monopolize the transportation systems used by the Third World in international trade.

The imperialist states have maintained quasicolonial influences over trade relations with their former colonies and with "their" representatives in these Third World countries. In the colonial period, each imperialist state created monopoly control over economic dealings with its colony. Even after political independence, the former colonial powers have to a large extent retained their role as the primary suppliers of industrial and other goods to their liberated colonies. Various methods are used to perpetuate dependence, such as the establishment of mutually complementary markets and the cultivation of certain tastes, attitudes, and consumption habits among Third World elites. Soviet analysts conclude that "dependence is maintained on the basis of carefully preserved economic and other conditions carried [over] from the past."(148)

A fourth asymmetry consists of the fiscal relationships between the advanced capitalist and Third World countries. The credit and currency systems prior to the oil crisis in 1973 were completely dominated by advanced capitalism. Even with the emergence of petrodollars as an important influence in the global currency system, the advanced capitalist nations use fiscal tools to maintain and extend dominance over the Third World.(149) For example, the debts of developing nations provide a major opportunity for the exercise of economic leverage against them. As V.S. Baskin notes, "Capitalist creditors seek to take advantage of the difficult financial situation of a debtor country and use the concessions they have . . . as an instrument by which they can impose upon the latter the kind of domestic financial policy they want and strengthen their own economic positions."(150)

In addition, foreign "aid" is designed to draw the Third World more closely into the international capitalist division of labor. There has been a steady decline in sizable uncommitted grants-in-aid, which provide maximal flexibility for a Third World state to use this aid in its own interests. Increasingly, aid is given for specific purposes and is "tied" to concrete economic demands by the donor country. The recipient of such aid must buy products only in the donor nation. "For capitalist states, the tying of credits serves as a powerful means of accelerating the export of goods and services."(151)

Finally, the asymmetrical international dependencies are reflected in the nature of domestic development in the Third World.

There is an incomplete production cycle in the industrial sector and foreign management of "local" manufacturing. The integration of production is under the aegis of the MNCs, and not of the Third World government or of some of its corporations.

Third World strategies for development rely on foreign involvement, which nurtures domestic economic growth through integration in the international capitalist division of labor.

Attention is thereby shifted away from the primacy of domestic developmental needs to foreign market demands, which often do not stimulate those sectors of the domestic economy most important to industrial growth and productivity.

Two economies emerge within the Third World state. One economy is "modern, fully or heavily dependent on foreign capital, and producing for export, and the other traditional, the two being not inherently interconnected (or hardly so). The creation of a single economic organism requires enormous effort and radical redistribution of resources, changes in the economic mechanism and, above all, time."(152)

The growth of domestic scientific and technological potential is stunted in favor of foreign technology trade. The emergence of a domestic market for advanced technology and for the products of science-based industries is blocked. This, in turn, lowers the opportunities for overall economic development in the Third World.

In brief, the current international division of labor provides a critical strategic advantage to the advanced capitalist world. The Academy of Sciences researchers conclude:

> The production and technological subjugation of developing countries to the monopolies, based on the "new international division of labor," allows them to influence both the general economic and sociopolitical development. In these circumstances the developing countries' efforts to organize on their own the manufacture of industrial goods for export to advanced capitalist countries come up against the resistance of the monopolies.(153)

The Struggle for "Genuine" Interdependence

The Third World's struggle for "genuine" interdependence requires the reversal of all basic asymmetries with the industrialized capitalist states. To eliminate the exploitative nature of this relationship, a developing nation must above all build up its own scientific and technological capabilities and launch a domestic "national liberation movement."

Scientific and Technical Progress

Soviet analysts affirm that a Third World country can achieve genuine interdependence through the enhancement of its scientific and technological capabilities, through control over the activities of the MNC, through the creation of more advantageous terms of trade and credit, and through the realization of a strategy for development that maximizes the benefits to be drawn from foreign economic involvement and that minimizes dependence.

   First, Soviet writers stress that a Third World nation's ability to formulate and implement a domestic scientific and technological policy is critical to the processes of genuine interdependence. National autarky in scientific development is viewed as neither possible nor desirable under contemporary conditions. To benefit from the worldwide scientific revolution, a country must create its own effective scientific base.

   The authoritative collective work of the Academy of Sciences devotes considerable attention to the developing nations' formulations of science policies adequate to the opportunities and pitfalls of interdependence. The problem is one of striking a correct balance between "the national effort in setting up an effective research sector and the use of foreign science and technology."(154)   Ties with international science must be forged and deepened. But "one should recognize the need to establish a national research base capable of meeting national development demands."(155)

   Among the main dimensions of an adequate national research base are: the training of research personnel and the provision of material and political support for scientific progress; the creation of an effective state institution to plan scientific research; the establishment of policy guidelines for scientific planning; the careful integration of the scientific research plan with the national economic development plan; and an appropriate balance between pure and applied science.

   Above all, the national research effort of a Third World country must select "priority research fields strictly in keeping with the short- and long-term socioeconomic targets set by short- and long-range development plans."(156)   Given the scarcity of resources that a developing state has to commit to a national R&D effort, the productive utilization of scientific

and technical knowledge and of material and human capabilities
is a critical task. "Vital areas of concern for the developing
countries are concentrating resources in spearhead efforts,
making rational use of the limited resources available, avoiding
duplication of research domestically . . . [and] carefully
selecting imported technology."(157)

It is also necessary for the Third World government to
develop a comprehensive technology policy. The chief priorities for economic growth and productivity must be identified,
and the native and foreign technology appropriate to meet
these priorities must be generated or selected and then applied
to existing or newly created institutions and relationships.
The purchase of advanced technologies can serve domestic
economic needs only through careful planning and the meshing
of technical choices with economic priorities. The development
and use of new technologies must be "geared to serve the
internal needs of the developing countries and, at the same
time, contribute to a changed international division of labor."(158)

Second, control over the activities of the MNC has become
a central problem for Third World states. One form of control
is the establishment of mixed ownership or joint decisionmaking
between the MNC and the Third World nation. Another form is
the creation of "a full production cycle on an up-to-date scientific and technological basis," A. Kodachenko contends.(159)
By so doing, Third World leaders can tap the resources of the
MNC in ways conducive to national development. Solodovnikov
notes that Third World countries, "while not rejecting the
services of the international corporations, [must] at the same
time seek to eliminate discrimination and institute controls on
their activities."(160)

Third, more advantageous terms of trade involve the need
to receive higher prices for raw materials and to establish a
more stable relationship between raw material prices and the
prices of industrial goods. The oil crises of the mid- and late
1970s vividly demonstrated the power of a single commodity
group or cartel.(161) Securing better prices for raw materials
is highly correlated with coalition building among the producers of the same and different commodities. In fact, collective
action and regional cooperation in the Third World are needed
to establish a free-trade area among the developing nations.
Most important, a united front must be created against the
advanced capitalist world, in order to obtain higher prices for
raw materials and to avoid numerous kinds of dependencies.
The significance of stable price relationships has been underscored by the developing countries' demand for administrative
regulation ("indexing") of the prices of raw material commodities produced in the Third World and for greater influence
over the prices of industrial goods manufactured in the advanced capitalist world.

Fourth, the creation of more favorable terms of finance rests upon the ability of a Third World country to obtain aid through international agencies, rather than through bilateral institutions and relationships. Soviet writers acknowledge that this goal is extremely difficult to achieve, however, because of the asymmetries in levels of development and the exploitative nature of neoimperialism.

Fifth, the need to formulate a domestic strategy for development is enhanced by the increasing impact of the STR and of the internationalization of production upon the Third World. The Academy of Sciences researchers maintain: "In the current situation, the developing countries seeking to overcome economic backwardness and dependence, and [striving] to bring about an improvement in the conditions of the masses, must stand committed to widescale use of scientific and technical achievements in the economy. That, in turn, is only possible if a long-term policy of deepgoing social transformations and cultural upsurge of the masses is mapped out."(162)

"National Liberation Movements"

Leading Soviet officials and social theorists view the development of Third World countries primarily as a political challenge to indigenous leaders who have gained or are capable of gaining the support of the masses. In order to achieve genuine interdependence and socioeconomic progress, a contemporary "national liberation movement" must emerge and be completed. Soviet writers often refer to national liberation movements as the national liberation movement. The Soviet purpose is probably to suggest that the efforts of Third World countries to free themselves from their colonial legacies are part of a cohesive or unified global effort.

According to Soviet analysts, national liberation movements have gone through two phases since 1945. The first phase was the political liberation of colonies from imperialist rule. Consequently, the newly independent nations of the Third World are no longer the political bailiwick of imperialism. The second phase is the struggle for economic independence and socioeconomic development. This current phase is anti-imperialist in essence and involves an intense struggle against continuing neoimperialist exploitation, dependencies, penetration, and constraints on socioeconomic progress. Brutents asserts that the economic basis of present-day national liberation movements "consists of the conflict between the requirements of independent economic development and the sway of the imperialist monopolies, a conflict involving the whole system of the international capitalist division of labor. What is more, this conflict is a part of the overall contradiction between the requirements of development of the productive forces in the capitalist world and the narrow framework of the socioeconomic relations of imperialism."(163)

New states oriented either toward capitalist or socialist development must now struggle with the problem of economic independence. For capitalist states, the local bourgeoisie comes into conflict with the MNC over the question of the scope of the benefits to be obtained from their mutual relationship. Much of the impetus for control over the MNC in the Third World comes from the local capitalist elite, which hopes to conduct business with the MNC in order to benefit its class. More and more, this indigenous elite's orientation is antiimperialist and objectively promotes some degree of economic restructuring of the international capitalist division of labor.

New states inclined toward socialism, however, struggle to combine involvement in the international division of labor with control over the central levers of economic development, in order to guide the process of social transformation. The objective is to augment economic wealth while at the same time redistributing it more equitably among the population. That is, the task is to combine involvement in the world economy with the forging of a socialist breakthrough in development. This, as Soviet officials fully recognize, is an extremely difficult challenge.(164)

Hence, the restructuring of international economic relations is founded on the growing antiimperialist sentiment of Third World capitalists. As Brutents argues, "Despite the efforts of the neocolonialists, who are looking to the class solidarity of the local bourgeoisie in the former colonies and semicolonies, no solid or extensive compromise has yet been reached between that bourgeoisie and imperialism. Such an arrangement has been hampered above all by the objective antiimperialist tendencies in the development of independent national capitalism in the countries of Asia and Africa at the present phase."(165)

But, as a social class, the local capitalists are oriented only toward those reformist measures that promote domestic economic independence. The antiimperialist orientation must be deepened by the development of a revolutionary democratic movement that, by peaceful or coercive means, assumes power in the Third World state. Such a movement must establish a revolutionary polity and society in which there is "a concentration in the state sector of the commanding heights of the national economy, in order successfully to combat foreign capital and create a national economy [based on] the practice of drawing up development plans."(166) Such a state would use its economic leverage to carry out a "marked enhancement of the living standards of the people in order to expand the domestic market for developing industry and agriculture."(167) The new state would also carry out the transformation of the cultural infrastructure, thereby helping to "muster the social energy of the masses for national construction."(168)

In short, a Third World country's commitment to the restructuring of its international economic relations will depend heavily upon the scope and depth of its commitment to domestic socioeconomic transformation. As Skorov succinctly notes, "the deeper and the more radical the anticapitalist transformation of the domestic life of liberated countries, the more rapid will be the restructuring of the system of the international capitalist division of labor."(169)

The Creation of a New International Economic Order

Even though the commitment to social change varies considerably in the Third World, the current phase of national liberation movements has impelled developing countries to call for the creation of a "new international economic order."(170) The demand for such an order is antiimperialist in essence, and it creates an important pressure for genuine interdependence in the world economy. Bogomolov writes: "The program of reforms advanced by the developing countries to create the new international economic order is aimed at making the capitalist system of international economic relations more democratic . . . and establishing equitable participation by all states in solving world economic problems. The implementation of this program, which objectively has antiimperialist overtones, would be a step forward in restructuring the present system of worldwide economic ties."(171)

In the Soviet view, there are numerous "progressive" objectives underlying Third World demands for a new international economic order: to establish complete national sovereignty over natural resources; to improve radically the terms of international trade; to receive very substantial financial assistance and to alleviate the problem of Third World debt; to control more effectively the activities of the MNC; to gain better terms for the purchase of new machinery and know-how; to end the "brain drain"; to reform the international monetary system; to obtain special concessions for the poorest countries; and to strengthen ties among the developing nations as a means of increasing their economic leverage in world economic policy.(172)

These basic components of the "new international economic order" would, if implemented, go a long way toward establishing an equitable form of interdependence. According to Skorov, the progressive changes in the global economy depend on

> the creation of a new mechanism for the redistribu-
> tion of the world social product in favor of the lib-

erated nations, through financial compensation for
economic losses caused by the fluctuation of prices
of raw materials and the growing inflation in the
capitalist countries, and also through a substantial
expansion of economic assistance [and] the granting
of unilateral preferences and other concessions,
giving the developing nations better terms in foreign
economic relations. It is thus a matter of [making]
a major correction in the operation of the uncontrolled market forces of the capitalist world economy.(173)

From the Soviet perspective, the current "general crisis
of capitalism" is deepened by the pressure for genuine interdependence and by the emergence of economic levers that the
Third World can use against the industrialized capitalist world
as the internationalization of economic relations progresses.
The demise of capitalism is also promoted by mounting competition among the United States, Western Europe, and Japan in
their struggle for raw material and manufacturing markets in
the Third World. For example, even in the context of a common energy crisis, the West has been unable to develop a
coordinated energy policy. Rather, competition for available
natural resources has intensified.(174) In fact, the deepening
of interimperialist contradictions has greatly increased the
Third World's economic and political leverage vis-a-vis the
industrialized countries of the West. Brutents concludes:

> The coordination of action by the imperialist powers
> in the national liberation zone has, perhaps, tended
> to decline, owing to the general aggravation of the
> interimperialist contradictions. But this has also
> been caused to some extent by the fact that against
> the now obvious prospect of a protracted struggle to
> determine the orientation of the young states' devel-
> opment and the difficulties facing the progressive
> forces in some of these countries, each imperialist
> power has tended increasingly to look to its own
> interests. Meanwhile, the forces of national liber-
> ation have greater opportunities than ever before to
> make use of these contradictions.(175)

Soviet Policy in the Third World

Soviet analysts contend that the USSR's policy of detente is a
major factor exacerbating conflict between advanced capitalist
and Third World nations.
First, the recently achieved military parity between developed socialism and advanced capitalism underscores the

futility of armed intervention to resolve conflicts in the imperialists' favor. As Brutents affirms, "[Capitalism's]
opportunities for resorting to sheer violence and armed suppression against the national liberation movement have been
sharply curtailed."(176)

Second, the atmosphere of detente allows the Third World
states to solicit aid, trade, and credits from developed socialist
and/or advanced capitalist powers. For example, Soviet commentators maintain that under conditions of detente, the Third
World can trade on more advantageous commercial terms with
both the advanced capitalist and developed socialist states, and
can obtain aid and credits more easily.(177)

Third, the common interests of the Third World and the
USSR in establishing better trade relations with the West increase pressures for the creation of the genuine interdependence that detente requires. Soviet spokesmen note that in a
developing country's struggle with the West, "The task of
utilizing the possibilities of the contemporary international
division of labor in the national interest is one of the most
important tasks of economic policy."(178) Of course, this is
the same goal the Soviet Union has established for itself in
pursuing economic detente with the West. Like a Third World
country, the USSR depends upon advanced technology imports
and raw material exports. Like Third World states, the USSR
wishes to enforce "indexing" in the exchange of raw materials
and industrial goods, and it attempts to do so through compensation agreements with Western trading partners. And,
like Third World nations, the USSR wants to control the selection and use of foreign technologies and products. Two
Soviet writers declare: "The developing countries, being simultaneously components of the world capitalist economy and of
the worldwide economy, have been active allies of the socialist
countries in the struggle to shape a new system of international economic relations, based on equality and mutual advantage
for all those involved."(179) In other words, Soviet analysts
perceive the economic interests of both the Third World and of
developed socialism to lie in the restructuring of the international division of labor to their mutual advantage.

One important example of congruent interests between the
USSR and the Third World concerns relations with the MNCs.
A "leftist" critic of Soviet detente policy might ask why a
developed socialist state has any dealings at all with a capitalist MNC, which is exploitative by its very nature. The official
Soviet response to such a challenge is twofold. For one thing,
the MNC is a manifestation of the organizational requirements
of the STR, and not just of capitalist production relations.
For another, the Soviet Union, by establishing mutually advantageous ties with the MNC, sets an important example for
Third World nations. Accordingly, R.S. Ovinnikov argues
that "agreements between MNCs and the Soviet Union and

other socialist states have already 'created problems' for these companies in their relationships with developing countries. . . . [Closer East-West economic relations thereby] help developing states to deal with MNCs on an equitable basis."(180)

Fourth, Soviet observers contend that detente accelerates social transformation in the Third World. By demonstrating developed socialism's economic compatibility and competitiveness with advanced capitalism, together with the more equal distribution of material goods among the classes and strata of socialist societies, detente increases the prestige of socialism throughout the Third World. The historical alternative of noncapitalist paths of socioeconomic development is strengthened by the force of this example.

Fifth, to the extent to which detente increases the economic capabilities of the Soviet Union, and to the extent to which the internationalization of economic life enhances Soviet scientific and technical potential, the USSR is in a better position to provide material aid to the Third World nations pursuing noncapitalist strategies of development. Brutents maintains that "Direct and indirect support from world socialism has an immediate effect on the development of the national liberation movement."(181)

In short, Soviet analysts conclude that detente promotes the internationalization of scientific, technological, and economic life, which, in turn, improves the chances of achieving genuine interdependence. North-South interdependence need not retard social transformation in the Third World. Rather, equitable and productive forms of interdependence can become critical accelerators of socioeconomic progress in both the Third World and in the socialist states.

"THE GENERAL CRISIS OF CAPITALISM" AND SOVIET PERSPECTIVES ON DETENTE

Soviet theorists and officials affirm that "the general crisis of capitalism" affects the nature and scope of detente in at least nine significant ways.

First, the very existence of a "general crisis of capitalism" makes detente possible. Military intervention by the West in socialist and Third World countries becomes a less viable option. The process of detente signifies that "the capitalist West has fewer possibilities for conducting a 'from positions of strength' policy, to say nothing of the use of armed force in its relations with the socialist countries, and also that its more realistically minded circles have adopted a more cautious and restrained stand and have come to appreciate the need for settling acute international issues by way of constructive negotiations rather than war."(182)   Prudent Western policymakers recognize that advanced capitalism is only one of the three significant sets of actors in the world today; developed socialist and Third World states are becoming increasingly powerful, individually and collectively.

Second, establishment of "the three centers of imperialism" has increased the possibilities for the further development of detente.   There has been and will continue to be competition among the United States, Western Europe, and Japan to garner the fruits of cooperation with the socialist world. Detente, which was launched by the Soviet Union and the West Europeans in the late 1960s, sparked American interest in such cooperation in the early 1970s.   West European interpretations of detente, because they are more similar to the Soviet than to the American interpretation, either will weaken substantially the Western alliance or will pressure the Americans to take a similarly "realistic" view of East-West relations.

Third, the process of detente increases domestic and international conflict in the West.   "Realistic" Western groups are in intense competition with the reactionary forces that oppose detente.(183)   The conflict between realism and reaction in a Western nation is at once a manifestation of the crisis of capitalism and of social progress within a declining socioeconomic system.   "The materialization of the detente and its investment with concrete content is bound to proceed in acute struggle between the forces promoting and hampering implementation of the principles of peaceful coexistence, and this will be an expression of the struggle between the two social systems, between the different class forces in the world arena."(184)

Fourth, "the three centers of imperialism" and their different detente policies increase the socialist nations' bargaining opportunities.   This is especially evident in the economic sphere, where American dominance has eroded. Soviet analysts have begun to think in terms of a European-oriented, rather than an American-oriented, technology trade policy.(185)   But they clearly recognize that American predominance and technological virtuosity continue in the military sphere.   Hence, Soviet specialists are cautiously assessing the complex interaction between economic and military capabilities in the West.(186)

Fifth, "the three centers of imperialism" and the growth of economic detente with Western Europe have important political implications for East-West relations.   Increased involvement in the Western economies provides the USSR with opportunities to gain diplomatic advantage, especially from mutual dependencies in trade.   Former Prime Minister Kosygin stated in 1979:

In trade and other international exchanges we see an effective means of enhancing detente and trust between states. At the same time, everything that undermines trust cannot promote international trade either. This means first and foremost a buildup of military preparations, interference in the affairs of other peoples, and encouragement, in particular by arms supplies, of the peace-endangering course of those forces pursuing a policy of expansionism and subversion of international detente. All of this cannot but cloud prospects for economic links with relevant countries. And we shall to an even greater extent orient ourselves to cooperation with those who do not jeopardize long-term interests for the sake of dubious benefits in the immediate situation.(187)

Sixth, the unilateral political benefits of dependency are limited by the mutual economic benefits of interdependence and by the internationalization of contemporary economic life. The West has been unable to solve the problem of economic insta-bility in its foreign trade cycles.(188) To the extent to which the Soviet Union involves itself in economic detente, developed socialism "imports" economic instability into its planning pro-cesses. The USSR does so by depending on capitalist prod-ucts and on foreign markets for Soviet industrial goods and raw materials. Furthermore, the USSR opens itself up to the conscious intervention by capitalist states in the Soviet economy and to less manipulable external economic forces, such as inflation. Mikulskii argues: "Despite their immeasurably im-proved economic potential, the socialist states still face the task of strengthening their technological and economic in-dependence from the capitalist world, of reliably protecting their economies from the anarchy of the world capitalist market and imperialist political maneuvers."(189)

Seventh, the contemporary "general crisis of capitalism" reveals the resiliency of the West, as well as its weaknesses. The STR, the internationalization of economic relations, and the emergence of "highly developed" forms of state-monopoly capitalism vitalize Western productive and organizational capacities. Zagladin notes: "The considerable development of the internationalization of production and exchange, signifying a further growth in the premises of socialism on a world scale, simultaneously creates a new objective basis for even closer cohesion between the forces of monopoly capital in their fight against the [socialist] revolution. . . . This is not just some objective tendency, it is also actual political practice."(190)

Eighth, "the general crisis" in relations between devel-oped capitalist and developing nations is caused by neocolo-nialism and by the struggle of Third World states against it. Neocolonialism rests upon the use of the powerful scientific and technological potential of advanced capitalism to create asymmetric dependencies with the Third World, rather than "genuine" interdependence. However, detente provides the international environment in which Third World countries can struggle most effectively against this form of oppression by advanced capitalism.(191)   Because of the rapid pace of the STR, the highly industrialized capitalist nations possess greater opportunities to convert scientific and technological superiority into political power vis-a-vis the Third World.   But East-West detente promotes North-South detente, and both increase the likelihood that capitalist governments and MNCs will curtail somewhat their exploitation of Third World states, especially of the less vulnerable ones.

Ninth, international forms of state-monopoly capitalism will remain weak because capitalist governments are unable or unwilling to socialize production relations.   New production relations are essential to keep pace with the socialization of productive forces, which stems from and nurtures both the STR and the internationalization of economic life.   The need to plan on an international scale is becoming central to the processes of directing the productive forces of advanced modernization.   Faminskii declares: "The widespread socialization of production, which is occurring in the epoch of the STR on the international level, demands planned organizational direction. Capitalism is trying to adapt to these new conditions."(192) To the extent to which state-monopoly capitalism expands throughout the world, the material prerequisites for a global socialist economic system are created.   Hence, the West's growing awareness of worldwide problems, whose resolution requires international planning, is at the same time a means for strengthening detente and socialist tendencies on the global level.(193)

CONCLUSIONS

The nine elements of "the general crisis of capitalism" and their impact on detente represent the basic parameters of consensus among Soviet analysts.   But the question of emphasis within this general framework is of considerable significance.   There are two distinct Soviet interpretations of "the general crisis" and detente.   The first underscores the interdependencies that emerge from detente and the opportunities for improving the growth and productivity of the Soviet economy through selective cooperation with the still formidable industrialized powers of the West.   The second underscores the possibilities for exacerbating "the general crisis" that are inherent in detente and that would promote the independence of socialism from the degenerating capitalist systems.   The first orientation stresses the cooperative elements of detente and the vulnerabilities generated by East-West confrontation.

The second orientation stresses the adversarial elements of detente and the vulnerabilities generated by East-West collaboration. Both orientations emphasize continuing East-West competition.

The "modernizing" or interdependent tendency underscores the centrality of the STR and the internationalization of economic relations for the development of detente and of socialism itself. Soviet "modernizers" perceived the Helsinki agreements of 1975 to confirm the idea that "in view of their growing economic interdependence, [all] states have to take ever more effective joint action to solve the world's major economic problems."(194) Or, as Shmelev asserts, "The need for further deepening detente, radically improving the international political climate, and for broad cooperation between the socialist and capitalist countries, is dictated by the objective requirements of the STR, by the deepgoing processes under way in the system of the global division of labor. In its turn, economic, scientific, and technical cooperation between states with different social systems strengthens and broadens the material basis of the peaceful coexistence policy."(195)

Soviet proponents of East-West interdependence perceive the STR to be creating global problems, such as environmental pollution, and a mutual interest in regulating "anarchic" market forces in the world economy. Significantly, Soviet modernizers consider international management and problem solving to be part of the "shift in the correlation of forces in favor of socialism." As Shmelev argues: "In their fundamental logic, the internationalization of production and scientific and technological progress are closely bound up with a further consolidation of the material premises for the socialization of labor on the scale of the whole world, and with the requirement for a greater role to be played by regulating - in contrast to spontaneous - factors in the shaping of the basic trends in international exchange."(196)

On balance, Soviet modernizers contend that the East and West are competing within a framework of nascent interdependence. Inozemtsev concludes:

> The need to observe the principles of peaceful coexistence is dictated by the fact that in the conditions of the unprecedentedly rapid development of the productive forces [and of] science and technology, the interconnection and interdependence of countries and peoples sharply increase, the international division of labor deepens, and economic, scientific-technological, and cultural cooperation between countries on an equal basis acquires growing importance. Mankind is increasingly contending with problems, truly global in scale, whose solution requires the collective effort of different states.(197)

The "conservative" or autarkic tendency stresses ideological competitiveness and national independence, supplemented by highly selective economic ties with the West and by economic and military interdependence within the developed socialist community. Soviet "conservatives" underscore the weaknesses in the West that are engendered by its "general crisis," the opportunities to exploit these weaknesses in the period of detente, the dangers of interdependence for Soviet economic development, and the need to preserve the political, social, and cultural values of socialism in the face of persistent ideological subversion from the West.

This second orientation focuses on developed capitalism's problems with the Third World and not primarily on the relations among advanced capitalist states. Soviet conservatives stress that "the weak link" of imperialism lies in the Third World. The raw materials problem is considered the Achilles heel of advanced capitalism. Mikulskii declares: "At the present stage of world social development, 'weak links' are forming in the world capitalist economic system within the zone of national liberation."(198)

Soviet conservatives argue that in order to exploit these "weak links," the USSR must become stronger economically. They view the scientific and technological capabilities of the advanced capitalist world as a magnet drawing the Third World into the international capitalist division of labor, but they contend that the Soviet Union and Eastern Europe can and must create a more powerful magnet. Conservatives maintain that the majority of Third World nations will not strengthen their ties with developed socialism unless the Soviet bloc contributes substantially more to the worldwide STR and more effectively uses the STR for social and economic benefit at home and abroad. Hence, developed socialist societies must improve their existing centralized institutions. Better use of the inherent advantages of the socialist planned economy, tighter economic integration of the Comecon nations, substantially increased military power, and greater ideological vigilance toward capitalism will continue the "shift in the correlation of forces in favor of socialism." Mikulskii explains: "A growing burden lies today upon the economically more advanced socialist states, whose job it is to work out ways of utilizing the scientific and technological achievements and creating more complex lines of production, not to mention expenditures on strengthening the defense capability of the entire socialist community. Any serious narrowing of the possibilities for [economic progress] in these states would be to the great detriment of each socialist state."(199)

Soviet conservatives emphasize the competitive and diverse elements of the STR's development in socialist and capitalist societies, rather than the convergent or universal characteristics or consequences of the STR. Mikulskii argues:

"The economic coming together of countries in the capitalist world, and especially in the world socialist system, contains immense potential for encouraging economic development and for improving the efficient use of economic resources for each of the world social systems."(200) Conservatives deem interdependence between East and West to be impractical, even dangerous, because "the very attempt at such a coming together could only have an adverse effect on the socialist community. Even the economically advanced capitalist states feel the effect of the harmful aspects of international capitalist economic relations, with their anarchy and competition."(201)

For Soviet modernizers, however, such an argument contradicts the logic of economic efficiency and world historical development. M.M. Maksimova responds to conservatives in the following way:

> The viewpoint is sometimes expressed that, inasmuch as the USSR possesses plentiful natural resources, as well as a powerful industrial, scientific, and technological potential, it is bound to consider external economic ties as something of secondary importance. . . . Of course, the Soviet Union is fully capable of producing any type of output, but it may well be asked: at the price of what efforts, and what expenditures and production costs each definite type of output will entail? It is common knowledge that, as a result of scientific and technological progress, and the greater specialization of industry in recent decades, the range of commodities has been rapidly expanding, new types of output are rapidly ousting the old ones, and many new and hitherto unknown kinds of output have appeared, especially in such branches as mechanical engineering, the chemical industry, and consumer goods. . . . It is natural for even such a country as the Soviet Union to find it unprofitable and sometimes impossible to effect production of the entire range of output necessary for the full satisfaction of its mounting industrial and private demand. This is a problem that economic ties with other countries can help to deal with.(202)

Much more is at stake in the competition between modernizing and conservative perspectives than a narrow or technical interpretation of economic efficiency. At issue are the nature of "the crisis of capitalism" and the future of Soviet development. For the conservative or neoisolationist, the West is in a deep crisis of a fatal, not of a transitional, nature, and the end will come in the not-too-distant future. Socialist unity must be maintained to immunize developed socialism from the

processes of Western decay.(203)   In contrast, the modernizer
or the proponent of interdependence sees the West in a crisis
of transition, because the STR and a changing international
system are promoting, and, in turn, are creating pressures
for change in the forms and content of state-monopoly capitalism.   Hence, the USSR can gain from and contribute to these
processes, thereby strengthening the worldwide socialization of
the productive forces and the "realist" and "progressive"
groups in the West.   Most important, Soviet participation in
the global STR will help to change socialist perspectives on
socioeconomic progress and to accelerate socioeconomic development in the USSR and in the Soviet bloc.(204)

One of the central ways in which Soviet leaders and theorists are attempting to resolve the conflict between these two
tendencies is through "the two spheres" argument.   Arbatov
affirms that in the contemporary international system there are
nonnegotiable and negotiable issues.   The first lie in "the
sphere of social development, which inevitably influences all
international conditions, be they detente, 'cold' or even 'hot
war.'"(205)   The liberation of the Third World is an historical
process, for example, not a subject for negotiation.   In the
second sphere of relations between socialism and capitalism,
however, "highly important issues are . . . resolved: issues
of war and peace, methods of settling controversial international issues, opportunities for mutually advantageous
international cooperation."(206)   Numerous opportunities and
problems arising from the global STR are thus subject to
international negotiation and can and should result in mutually
beneficial interdependence.   Arbatov adds: "To draw a clear
distinction between the two spheres is one of the basic
premises of the Soviet foreign policy of peaceful coexistence."(207)

Soviet analysts contend that the two spheres are distinct,
but an emphasis upon one sphere or the other has critical
theoretical and practical implications.   Some Soviet commentators view "the general crisis of capitalism" primarily in terms
of the linkages among advanced capitalist, developed socialist,
and Third World countries.   Other Soviet observers stress the
significance of developments within the most industrialized
capitalist and socialist societies.   These different foci, in turn,
can and do produce very different judgments about the nature
of the contemporary era and the policies that best express the
general idea of detente.

Hence, there is an ambiguity in Soviet thinking that is of
considerable historical consequence.   This ambiguity is characterized as a "dialectic" central for our times, but the tensions
inherent in these alternative Soviet orientations are to date
unresolved.   A. Narochnitskii affirms: "The main contradiction
of our times - that between capitalism and socialism - is manifested in the conditions of the ever greater involvement of

whole continents and other vast regions of the world in international contacts. The tremendous advances made by national
liberation movements, the emergence of new and the development of long-established national states [are] going hand in
hand with trends toward the ever greater internationalization
of economic, political, and social life."(208)   G.Kh. Shakhnazarov concludes: "It is a distinctive feature of the present
historical moment that the interests of survival, the STR, and
all other objective trends of social development operate in such
a way as to draw peoples and countries closer together and
prompt them to solve the problems of mankind through common
efforts, while at the same time the struggle between the two
social systems continues to unfold."(209)

3 "The Scientific-Technological Revolution," Soviet Economic Development, and East-West Economic Relations

In this chapter we will analyze Soviet perceptions of and policy responses to the predominantly economic elements of the STR. Specifically, we will examine the interconnections among the STR, the development of the Soviet economy, and the economic relations between East and West. Also, we will investigate the ways in which the political and economic dimensions of East-West commerce influence one another, and we will devote special attention to some of the organizational and legal aspects of Soviet-American trade.

Under Khrushchev and especially under Brezhnev, leading Soviet officials have viewed the internationalization of economic relations as an "objective" force that can and must strengthen East-West ties. Many Soviet policymakers and administrators have argued that the domestic development of the USSR is increasingly dependent upon contributing to and benefiting from the international division of labor. Hence, foreign economic relations are perceived to play a major role in meeting what Brezhnev has identified as the central challenge of the current epoch: "organically to combine the achievements of the scientific-technological revolution with the advantages of the socialist economic system."(1)

Although Soviet analysts view the deepening involvement of the USSR in the global economy as a "progressive" manifestation of the development of the STR and of detente, a negative challenge is seen as well. Western nations – some more than others – remain serious military, ideological, and economic adversaries. Capitalist contributions to Soviet modernization must therefore be carefully selected and monitored.

Soviet spokesmen repeatedly stress that East-West economic relations should be "mutually beneficial" and based on "stable" and "long-term" ties. But greater Soviet participation in the international economy provides new opportunities for

influencing Western domestic and foreign policies, socioeconomic
developments, and public opinion. Such advantages must be
carefully weighed against any disadvantages that accrue from
increased Western penetration of the politics, economies, and
societies of the Soviet bloc. The leverage the West gains must
be carefully balanced with counterleverage. Hence, controlling
or balancing dependencies becomes a major policy problem for
the industrialized socialist states and advanced capitalist
states. This problem has been of special concern to the Soviet
leaders in the 1970s and 1980s, because the worldwide STR has
begun to expose the USSR and Eastern Europe to more and
more international scientific, technological, and economic forces
and trends. Indeed, conflicting assessments of the scope and
significance of Western influence upon the USSR and Eastern
Europe have become an important source of debate and competition among the Soviet bureaucratic elites. (2)

To put these policies and administrative disputes in
perspective, recall that influential Soviet analysts insist that
the STR is generating strong pressure for greater East-West
economic interdependence. But even the most ardent Soviet
proponents of detente emphasize that there are important limits
to East-West ties. Describing these constraints in general
terms, V. Iokhin asserts: "The economic cooperation of socialist states with the West is a manifestation of the objective law
of the internationalization of production that has emerged as a
result of the STR, but such cooperation is by no means unlim-
ited, for it is connected at the same time with such objective
laws as the contradiction between the production relations of
the two competing systems." (3)

The tension between the internationalization of economic,
technological, and scientific life under contemporary conditions, on the one hand, and the multifaceted competition
among socialist and capitalist states, on the other, is a
formidable challenge to Soviet economic policy. As Iu. Pekshev argues, "Defining the scale, the basic direction, and the
structure and organizational forms of economic ties with states
of different social systems is necessary for participation [in
the international division of labor], and for the careful
assessment of all possibly negative consequences from such
ties." (4)

In spite of potential difficulties, many Soviet officials
affirm that the domestic and international developments associated with the STR and with the changing preconditions of
economic growth are making it necessary for the USSR to
participate much more actively in the global economy. The
Soviet authors of a major study on foreign trade contend:
"Foreign trade, which connects the Soviet national economy
with the economies of foreign countries, contributes greatly
toward the development of the Soviet economy. The expansion
of foreign economic relations has become an integral part of

our state's general economic policy. As the Soviet economy
develops, our foreign trade, based on the principles of state
monopoly, is becoming an increasingly powerful factor aiding in
the successful resolution of economic and foreign economic
problems facing our national economy."(5) Thus, greater
Soviet participation in the world economy is thought to be a
sine qua non for the development of Soviet society.

THE INTERNATIONALIZATION OF ECONOMIC LIFE IN THE
WEST AND THE DEVELOPMENT OF EAST-WEST TIES

Many Soviet analysts contend that the STR, international
economic developments, and the performance of the Soviet
economy are creating pressures to expand East-West scientific,
technological, and economic links. G.L. Rozanov, in his study
of detente in the 1970s, asserts: "The general process of the
internationalization of economic life is accelerating. In
contemporary conditions, no state can fence itself off from the
changes in production and science that are occurring in the
world. The economic progress of any given state depends on
its participation in the world exchange of material and human
values."(6)
      The STR, an "objective" force, produces changes in
attitudes and beliefs in both the West and the East. These
new attitudes and beliefs concern the legitimacy and feasibility
of broader scientific, technological, and economic exchange.
As Iu. Molchanov comments: "The STR has been exerting
profound influence on the establishment of the principles of
peaceful coexistence. In accelerating the development of the
productive forces and intensifying the interdependence of all
parts of the world, the STR contributes to an awareness of
the objective necessity of peaceful coexistence and multiform
and mutually advantageous cooperation between states."(7)
That is, economic modernization makes greater East-West collaboration possible and desirable and promotes an understanding of this fact in both socialist and capitalist countries.
      Many Soviet analysts, especially economic reformers,
maintain that developments in the Western economies have
created a real and perceived need for the expansion of ties
with the East.
      First, the MNC has emerged as an important proponent of
East-West economic interdependence. As one group of Soviet
international affairs specialists puts it: "In developing economic
cooperation between the socialist and capitalist countries of
Europe, an important role is played by the large industrial
corporation, whose economic interest is oriented toward the
international market. [This economic interest] is a response to
the STR, which prompts such corporations to search for re-

liable partners. It is common knowledge that socialist states provide a stable market. The interest of the large firms is determined by growing energy and raw material needs, which socialist states can reliably fulfill on a long-term basis."(8)

Second, the trends toward the specialization and expansion of production generate a search for new markets for technological goods. The quest for untapped markets induces Western enterprises to pursue opportunities in the East. D.I. Kostiukhin notes that "the development and improvement of production specialization and cooperation [promote] international trade in machinery and equipment and [serve] as a weapon in the monopolies' competition for foreign markets."(9) The competitive drive nurtured by specialization increases the socialist countries' interest in Western markets, as well. S. Pomazanov writes: "The ongoing STR and internationalization of economic life tend to increase the interdependence of national economies. This leads to an increased flow of goods between countries and deepens the international division of labor. Modern industry in the socialist and capitalist countries is coming to grips with the problem of organizing production of many types of goods on a scale for which the markets of individual countries and even regions, such as Eastern and Western Europe, are insufficient outlets."(10)

Third, the organizational capabilities of the MNC enable it to become an active partner in East-West economic cooperation. Because the MNCs and the USSR's large domestic and foreign trade associations have the capacity to manage an extended production cycle, the development of economic detente and the emergence of an international production process reinforce one another. V.N. Sushkov, USSR Deputy Minister of Foreign Trade, declared in 1977: "Since detente has reduced the political risk for the partners, and since scientific and technological progress has made it possible to split up the process of production in space and time, favorable conditions have appeared for all-out development of production cooperation between the firms of the capitalist countries and Soviet foreign trade associations."(11)

Fourth, the increased significance of foreign trade for economic growth and productivity, coupled with the mounting responsibility of the capitalist state for generating and maintaining economic progress, creates a situation in which the advanced capitalist powers are more and more interested in expanding trade with the East. The tradition of long-term economic planning in the socialist economies and the stability of socialist markets are particularly attractive to MNCs. These features of Soviet bloc economies are also attractive to certain Western governments, especially those which have nationalized major industries and have developed comprehensive forms of indicative planning (e.g., France).

Fifth, conflict among "the three centers of imperialism" increases the competitive pressure upon the United States, Western Europe, and Japan to become more involved in Eastern markets. Attempting to heighten Western Europe's interest in economic detente, Iu. Shiriaev and A. Ivanov argue: "West European industries are now operating in conditions of fierce competition, notably with U.S. and Japanese companies. In this struggle, which tends to grow with the advance of the STR, some industries and economic regions in individual West European countries are doomed to stagnation, unless they are assured of fundamentally new opportunities for maintaining and extending production."(12) Greater interdependence with the Soviet bloc economies would of course provide Western Europe with such an opportunity. Shiriaev and Ivanov conclude: "Europe-wide cooperation and the extension of opportunities for industrial cooperation and marketing across the whole continent would probably increase the chances of survival in the competitive struggle for entire branches of industries and large enterprises."(13)

Sixth, the capitalist mode of internationalizing production and the exacerbation of "interimperialist contradictions" provide opportunities for Soviet involvement in the world economy without excessive vulnerability to Western manipulation. As Iu. Kapelinskii notes, Soviet foreign trade strategy is based on "the utilization of economic and political contradictions among capitalist states and groups of capitalists, in order to provide the most favorable trade and political conditions for the activities of our foreign trade organizations, and for the successful realization of the export and import plans."(14)

Seventh, the raw material shortages in the West intensify the pressure upon the United States, and especially upon Western Europe and Japan, to establish long-term and stable flows of natural resources into their economies. As the advanced capitalist economies become increasingly dependent upon science-based industries and high-technology sectors, they become at the same time more and more dependent upon a continuous flow of key raw materials. A. Karenin asserts: "The broad expansion of economic relations among states is one of the basic law-regulated developments of the contemporary world. This expansion is made necessary by the uneven distribution of known reserves of natural resources, especially energy resources, and by the different levels of industrial development of states. These conditions have produced an important global problem that must be jointly resolved by many countries."(15) Or, as V.S. Evgenev argues with respect to Western Europe, "the situation in the world fuel and primary materials markets . . . is unfavorable to the industrialized West European countries."(16) These circumstances, he contends, provide the basis for broad East-West cooperation in Europe.

In short, the STR increases the West's demand for raw materials, especially in energy-intensive industries. Also, the STR expands the science-technology-production cycle across national borders. And the STR is accompanied by increased international specialization and concentration, and by the drive to optimize the scale of production in each industrial branch. As N.P. Shmelev maintains: "the prospects for economic cooperation between the Soviet Union and industrial powers of the West are closely related to further development of the current revolution in science and technology."(17) Hence, the considerable material and scientific-technical power of advanced capitalist economies, together with the perceived neutrality of the productive forces unleashed by the STR, makes the West a desirable - indeed, even a necessary - participant in Soviet development.

Soviet policymakers and analysts recognize that East-West competition is not limited to the quantitative or physical growth of major industrial sectors, but is also related to the emergence of complex new economic growth models. These models emphasize the stimulation of basic scientific research, the technological modernization of industry, and the urgent need to increase labor productivity. V.L. Mal'kevich, head of the main engineering and technical department of the USSR Ministry of Foreign Trade, observes: "The criteria by which the economic development of an industrial country are judged include not only the quantity of its production output but, more and more, the technological level of its economy."(18) Mal'kevich adds that "the growing international exchange of goods and know-how, and the diversity and intensity of international technological and economic ties, not only enable but compel national producers to measure constantly their own costs and efficiency against those of other world producers."(19) Hence, the stimulus of the Soviet Union's growing involvement in foreign markets is a critical component in its continuous but, to date, only moderately successful drive for technological modernization.

Soviet leaders perceive the USSR to be in an inferior position in the qualitative and productivity dimensions of East-West economic competition, and they readily acknowledge the increasing importance of competitive advantage in these spheres. Brezhnev frankly stated in his report to the Central Committee at the Twenty-fifth Party Congress in 1976:

> If we are to accomplish successfully the multifarious economic and social tasks facing the country, there is no other path than rapid growth in labor productivity and a sharp rise in the efficiency of all social production. . . . The orientation of all branches of the economy and of the work of every ministry and enterprise toward a determined increase in efficiency

and quality - this, comrades, is the most important
thing now.
    We interpret the problem of quality in a very
broad sense. It embraces all aspects of economic
activity. High quality means savings of labor and of
material   resources,   the   growth   of   export
possibilities, and, in the long run, the better and
fuller satisfaction of society's requirements.(20)

    Soviet economic modernizers stress that the USSR must
become much more deeply involved in the world economy in
order to become competitive in the qualitative aspects of
economic progress, such as product desirability and reliability,
the intensive use of scientific resources, and the improvement
of management and marketing capabilities. The Soviet Union,
they tacitly acknowledge, has much to learn from the West. In
contrast to the Stalin years, when the USSR borrowed on an
ad hoc basis in order to strengthen its autarkic position,
technological exchange during the STR is a continuous and
open-ended process that leads to long-term interdependent
relationships. Worldwide technological and informational
interchanges are increasingly salient to the planning and
management of the USSR's economic development. As a deputy
minister of foreign trade remarks, "The demands of the STR
and the necessity to keep in step with world technological
progress, and where possible to be in advance of it, constitute
a global stimulus to the continuous modernization of our
industry."(21)
    The perceived neutrality of the productive forces of the
STR makes careful and selective borrowing from Western experience both feasible and legitimate. Foreign economic accomplishments have played an important part in shaping Soviet
perceptions of the nature of technological progress in the
post-Stalin era. Indeed, Soviet conceptualizations of the
advanced productive forces are heavily influenced by their
analyses of Western developments, including many favorable
assessments of American achievements.(22) Hence, Soviet
commentators observe:

    The most urgent tasks [in the context of economic
    detente] include examining and scientifically inter-
    preting the world capitalist division of labor at the
    current stage of capitalist development, and deter-
    mining the causes and motive forces that lead to the
    deeper division of labor. This should result in more
    intense   international   exchange   of   commodities,
    know-how, and services. The identification of these
    causes and processes is the key to finding a well-
    founded and purposeful solution of problems relating
    to economic and scientific and technical cooperation

between the USSR and the capitalist countries, and
to choosing the most promising and mutually profitable trends and forms of this cooperation. The
positive elements of the international capitalist
specialization and the cooperative [aspects] of
industrial production can be usefully applied to
improve our economic relations not only with the
capitalist, but also with the socialist, countries.(23)

In addition, Soviet analysts are carefully studying many
structural and technical elements of international economic
relations, especially East-West trade. Writing in 1976,
Kostiukhin affirmed that, "particularly in recent years, there
has been a considerably growing need to study the organizational forms and methods of foreign trade operations, including
scientific and technical ties. This is connected with the
present relaxation of international tension and the implementation of the Soviet Union's active policy of peaceful coexistence."(24)
  Also, increased knowledge of the foreign economic environment is deemed necessary for the successful adaptation of
the Soviet economy to changing international economic conditions. Kostiukhin underscores the significance of a Soviet
book that assesses the operations of state monopoly capitalism
and their implications for the USSR's foreign economic policy:

  Of great practical value is the authors' exposure of
  the elements of the "policy of growth." This policy
  is turning into a significant new factor in forming
  not only situational, but also long-term trends of the
  world capitalist market and the whole of international
  trade. This feature should be taken in full account
  by Soviet organizations that have to deal with the
  capitalist countries' markets, particularly at the
  contemporary stage when the Soviet Union's foreign
  trade and other economic ties with the capitalist
  countries are increasingly built on a large-scale and
  long-term basis, including delay-compensation agreements.(25)

  In short, leading Soviet officials affirm that the STR is
increasing the economic interdependence of advanced capitalist
and developed socialist nations, thereby creating an objective
pressure for greater East-West cooperation. They argue that
domestic changes associated with the STR and with the emergence of a new economic model are generating pressures on the
USSR to participate in a greatly expanded international division of labor. Participation of this kind is perceived to
strengthen, rather than to undermine, the development of
advanced socialist societies. We will now examine more closely
Soviet perspectives on domestic and international linkages.

SOVIET ECONOMIC DEVELOPMENT AND THE STR

The basic economic strategy of the collective leadership was encapsulated by Brezhnev at the Twenty-fourth CPSU Congress when he called for "combining" the achievements of the STR with the advantages of Soviet-type economic systems.(26)

On the one hand, Soviet analysts in the 1970s and 1980s have emphasized "intensive," rather than "extensive," means of growth. New economic variables - science, technology, and organizational rationalization - have become central to the further development of the Soviet economy. One Soviet economist, discussing the intensive factors of growth, declares: "Progress in science and technology and improvements in the methods of management, as well as in the production and utilization of information, make it possible to overcome the quantitative limitations of productive assets and to increase the capacity of all factors of production much more rapidly than corresponding increases in their physical volume, and even to achieve this when that volume is reduced."(27) Briefly stated, the Soviet economy must respond to the worldwide advances in science and technology, managerial and organizational effectiveness, and the generation, processing, and use of information. All of these challenges are intensified by the international division of labor.

On the other hand, Soviet commentators contend that socialist societies have a major advantage over capitalist societies in the era of the STR. Developed socialist states are said to have the capacity to integrate economic and social planning at the national, regional, and local levels. But it is the function of planning that is important in the context of the STR, not merely the experience of specific Soviet planning institutions, especially those which use outmoded techniques of forecasting and administration. Soviet analysts recognize that planning and management must be adjusted to the new and rapidly changing requirements of economic growth and productivity. Obedience to central ministries by lower-level economic organizations is a necessary but not a sufficient condition for better economic performance. Enterprises and collective farms, and particularly the larger scientific-production and industrial associations, must have a greater influence on the formulation of national economic plans and on the criteria and standards that measure and reward economic achievements. Broader and deeper elite participation of this kind will increase the feasibility of centrally determined aims and the coordinated but differentiated implementation of national economic goals. Above all, Soviet economic performance must be improved to compare favorably with world standards. As Brezhnev declared at the Twenty-fifth CPSU Congress, "Emphasis on efficiency - and this must be said

again and again - is the most important component of our
entire economic strategy."(28)

The benefits of centralized planning and management must
be demonstrated by tangible accomplishments. E.I. Khessina
emphasizes that the advantages of socialist planning must be
reflected in the wise and effective decisions of policymakers
and in the results of the science-technology-production cycle.(29) Economic progress and the equitable distribution of
material goods are made possible by public ownership of the
means of production, but the STR does not "automatically"
fulfill the needs or potential of a socialist society. To do so,
party and government officials must continuously modernize the
theory and practice of planning and management.(30)

There are three major dimensions of planning and management which, in the view of Soviet analysts, must be better
adapted to the STR.

First, the policy planning institutions must become
"rationalized" or "scientifically substantiated." V.N. Kirichenko argues, "In order to increase the scientific level of
planning, it has become necessary to apply research findings
to problems closely connected with the preparation of planning
decisions, and it is possible to involve a broad circle of
diverse sciences and disciplines - sociological, ecological,
technological, medical, economic, etc. The need to integrate
the mass of significant scientific material is becoming a
separate, increasingly essential task."(31)

Second, considerable decentralization must occur in order
to stimulate initiative and provide incentives for innovation at
the middle level. B.Z. Mil'ner writes:

However progressive and scientifically grounded the
decisions taken by central agencies, however perfect
the mathematical and computing apparatus on which
they are based, [there is a need to] take account of
the concrete conditions in which each enterprise has
to operate. That is why the lower echelons are
being allowed ever broader economic initiative, and
greater opportunities for independently deciding the
ways in which they are to implement the decisions
taken by superior agencies, thereby developing an
ever greater economic interest in fulfilling the tasks
set before them with the lowest inputs of social
labor.(32)

In fact, one group of Soviet researchers equates the advanced
forms of the socialization of production with an increase in the
rights and responsibilities of middle-level organizations,
especially those of the production and industrial associations.(33)

Third, decentralization enables the national institutions to plan strategically, rather than to devote large amounts of time to the details of planning and administration and to rushed or stop-gap responses to day-to-day operational problems. Mil'ner asserts: "This kind of approach to the balance between centralization and decentralization provides real conditions for raising the activity of the ministries and departments, the sectoral headquarters, to a new level. In this instance, the emphasis in their activity is switched to the formulation of a coherent scientific and technical policy, prognostication and long-term planning, setting of long-term goals and tasks, solution of sectoral problems, economic regulation and centralized control of the activity of the [economic] associations."(34)

In short, many Soviet analysts view institutional "rationalization" as a means of debureaucratizing the middle-level organizations, so that they make decisions of secondary importance on their own and can provide tactical and strategic feedback to the center, thereby improving the national party and state organs' capacity to conceptualize, choose among, implement, and adjust strategic alternatives. Also, rationalization of the middle entails expanding the size of the intermediate-level production organizations. As I. G. Shilin puts it, "The STR is accompanied not only by a growth in the complexity but in the scale of contemporary production. The more rapid, complete, and economically advantageous assimilation of the achievements of the STR is impossible without a timely increase in the concentration of production to a rational level."(35)

Khrushchev attempted to debureaucratize the center by dismantling major ministries and by establishing regional economic councils in 1957. Brezhnev and Kosygin tried to overcome the bureaucratization of the middle by launching the 1965 economic reforms. When these reforms proved to be less politically and economically viable than expected, the collective leadership created various large-scale science-production and industrial associations and industrial-agricultural complexes in the early 1970s. The scientific-production association, for example, is composed of scientific research institutes, design and technical subsections, experimental plants, construction subsections, and, finally, the individual enterprises. The new associations were expected to exercise a great deal of organizational independence in the pursuit of technological innovation. As was underscored at the Twenty-fourth, Twenty-fifth, and Twenty-sixth CPSU Congresses, one of the most important means of improving the performance of the Soviet economy under conditions of the STR is the gradual adjustment of the structure and functioning of the production and management organs, especially the establishment of intermediate-level associations.(36) A coordinated but flexible science-technology-production cycle is to be created that utilizes the talents of the most innovative managers of the new production and industrial associations. The primary goal is to accelerate technological innovation by overcoming both departmental and psychological barriers to the continuous interaction of modern science and technology with production.

Institutional rationalization involves the coordination of central functions with expanded middle-level organizational responsibilities. On the one hand, the advantage of centralization is the concentration of political power and funds for the purpose of producing technological advances that serve the national interest. S.S. Il'in affirms: "Centrally directed utilization of the state budget to encourage technological innovation is one of the most significant advantages of the planned socialist economic system over capitalism."(37) On the other hand, decentralization provides opportunities and incentives for production units to apply and disseminate new techniques and technologies. Il'in notes: "Industries and associations have become more interested in the growth of the technical level and quality of production. This is connected chiefly with changes in the system of central plan indicators."(38) A shift from administrative to economic indicators of plan control is required in the area of technological innovation.(39)

The expansion of the middle-level organizations' domain of action is rooted in the further diversification or specialization of production associated with the development of the STR. V.G. Marakhov observes: "Combining science with production creates a new social productive force. This productive force emerges as a social factor not only because science penetrates production, but also because of the influence of concentration and specialization, i.e., the natural historical process of the differentiation of labor. Industrial and science-production associations, which are based on the concentration of production, open up the possibility for the more complete differentiation of the production processes and, simultaneously, for the emergence of new social productive forces."(40)

The rationalization of the productive middle also involves the establishment of regional science-production complexes, such as the one in Novosibirsk. These complexes are designed to help plan and manage regional development more rationally - that is, to utilize more efficiently a given region's manpower and material capabilities.(41) For instance, territorial production complexes in the Soviet Far East are to be "the most progressive form of the organization of the economy, because they make possible the efficient use of social labor and the increased effectiveness of production, through the fullest utilization of natural and human resources and the best adaptation to the indigenous natural and human environment."(42)

Territorial production complexes are founded upon the integration of science with the economic management of a specific geographical area. Regional research centers are key components of such production complexes. According to a leading Soviet student of territorial economic organizations, "Regional research centers deal primarily with a systematic study of the full range of productive forces in a given area, and with the identification of optimum paths of economic development from the findings of basic research."(43) Scientized management of this kind requires the creation of a regional administrative organ that is capable of managing the entire territorial-production complex of industrial centers and ensuring the functioning of its infrastructure.(44)

Soviet analysts contend that better central planning and management are needed to encourage initiatives from the production associations and territorial-production complexes. Moreover, they argue that changes in operational style are required, so that scientific and technological contributions to the management of social processes can be used more effectively.

First, new organizational technology and techniques are deemed essential to administrative effectiveness in the era of the STR. For example, a sophisticated computer base is needed to increase the capacity of the center to generate, store, analyze, and respond to vast quantities of diverse information.(45) As Il'in notes: "The growing socialization of production and the high level of the technical base achieved in the course of the STR demand a corresponding development in the material base of planning and management, and in the improvement of their forms and methods. The advantages of the planned socialist system, the opportunity for conscious management of economic and social processes throughout the entire society, allow for the much broader and more effective application of economic-mathematical methods (such as optimal planning, economic-mathematical modeling, balancing, program/goal-setting, etc.) and automatic cybernetic technology than under capitalism."(46)

Second, improved information flows and better data are to be generated by inputs from the policy sciences, such as regional economic planning and systems analysis. This information will provide the basis for more effective participation by national, republic, and local party and state organizations in economic planning and decisionmaking.(47)

Third, a major advantage of socialism is thought to be the center's capacity to view the STR "comprehensively," and to develop and respond to the STR in the national interest. Il'in comments: "The planned organization of socialist industry, based on the social ownership of property, enables the Soviet state to perform the economic and organizational functions necessary to develop and carry out a unified scientific-technological policy, which is a decisive advantage of socialism in utilizing the achievements of the STR."(48)   Or, as the jurist B.N. Topornin argues, if the state and law are weakened,

> the development of the STR unavoidably runs into serious difficulties.   Separate enterprises and institutions do not have at their disposal the resources and means that are needed to promote scientific research, especially fundamental research, in the volume and with the scientific-technical grounding that life demands.   Without a unified state policy in the field of science, without concentrating the efforts of the entire society on the resolution of key scientific and technological problems, and without providing science with an expensive technical foundation, the prospects of the STR are not good. Equally important, without the state it is extremely difficult to replace industrial technology, because this can be accomplished effectively only on a large scale and over a period of time.(49)

Soviet spokesmen contend that central party organs must increase their capacity to initiate and implement policies, not merely to react to forces and events.   In order to "master" the STR and its socioeconomic consequences, it is absolutely essential to maintain and perfect a policymaking system that can produce and adjust integrated, well-informed, and far-sighted programs.   Only by so doing can the Soviet leadership understand better the choices available and make optimal choices among competing alternatives under conditions of rapid change and considerable uncertainty.   M. Rutkevich asserts: "In a developed socialist society, planning is raised to a new and higher stage.   Relying on forecasting, planning is becoming long-range and more universal, and it is encompassing all aspects of the life of society."(50)

The quest for an optimally functioning planning system rests upon the need to increase organizational responsiveness to change.   Marakhov states: "'Combining the achievements of the STR with the advantages of socialism' requires flexibility throughout the entire system of . . . socialist production relations, in order to promote the all-round development of the STR.   This necessitates a search for the forms and processes of combining these achievements with the advantages of socialism, so that the course of this revolution will be optimalized."(51)   Greater administrative flexibility requires planning that is less bureaucratic and directive and more systematic and problem-oriented.   Marakhov elaborates: "In contemporary conditions the most important role in the planning of social production is played by intersectoral, comprehensively integrated, and goal-oriented programs that are shaped by

long-range planning needs. These programs concentrate resources on the solution of the key problems of economic growth
within the parameters of a single plan, thus providing for the
most diverse and yet complete utilization of the achievements of
science and technology."(52)

Furthermore, shortly after becoming General Secretary of
the CPSU in 1964, Brezhnev declared that "The correct blend-
ing of centralization with the rights, initiatives, and responsibilities of the local organs is a question of fundamental
importance, a major policy issue."(53) Recent Soviet discussions of "democratic centralism" stress that this cardinal
organizational principle must be adapted to the problems and
opportunities posed by the STR. V.G. Afanas'ev, the editor-
in-chief of Pravda and a major social theorist, forcefully calls
for the simultaneous strengthening of both democracy and
centralism:

> The development of this principle is now clearly
> displaying two trends. The first - toward further
> centralization - is connected with production concen-
> tration and implementing gigantic projects that
> require the mobilization of tremendous resources and
> coordinated work by a multitude of territorial and
> sectoral management organs. The second - the
> further democratization of management, and transfer
> of decision-making rights "from above" "downward,"
> to an increasingly large circle of people and orga-
> nizations - is caused by the exceptional complexity
> of modern production and all social life and the
> impossibility of decision-making from the center on
> many, let alone all questions. Local initiative and
> enterprise and broad participation in management by
> the masses are now more necessary than ever.(54)

Topornin, summarizing the official Soviet perspective, concludes: "The STR is an argument for centralism, not against
it, but for that kind of centralism in which new social conditions must be reflected."(55)

SOVIET ECONOMIC DEVELOPMENT AND EAST-WEST TIES

Many Soviet leaders and theorists perceive that economic ties
with the world economy are an important stimulus both in the
transition to a new style of centralism and to a new growth
model. G.M. Prokhorov argues that foreign economic activities
are becoming increasingly significant for Soviet development,
because "the Soviet Union and other socialist states are
undergoing a transition to more improved methods of socialist

economics that must use more fully the achievements of the STR, increase the effectiveness of social production, and raise the level of the standard of living of the population. <u>Foreign economic ties are becoming a basic factor in increasing the effectiveness of social production.</u>"(56)

Hence, Soviet analysts maintain that international economic relations in general, and the USSR's ties with the industrialized capitalist nations in particular, are important components of a new strategy of economic development. In support of this viewpoint, economic modernizers offer at least eleven reasons.

First, the expansion of East-West technological exchange is essential to the development of the Soviet economy. Mal'kevich emphasizes that the "expansion of Soviet trade in licenses is part of the strategy set out by the 24th and 25th CPSU Congresses for fusing the achievements of the STR with the advantages of the socialist economic system."(57) However, if technological trade is to be broadened and deepened, the Soviet economy must increase its capacity to absorb scientific discoveries and technological innovations, native and imported. As L.A. Rodina contends, "The basic cause for the slow growth in the export of licenses from socialist states is the relatively slow introduction into industry of progressive techniques and technology."(58) That is, the enhancement of the innovative qualities of the domestic economy is highly correlated with the expansion of trade possibilities, especially in the fields of advanced technology. Rodina adds: "The creation of a more effective branch structure, because of an increase in the proportion of science-based production and the improvement of the quality and technological level of the goods produced by assimilating advanced foreign techniques and technology, promotes the resolution of such urgent problems as expanding the export potential of the socialist countries and increasing the competitiveness of their goods on the world market."(59)

Second, imported technology from the West is a major stimulus to domestic innovation. Quantitative considerations, such as the expansion of the flow of imports, are not the only dimension to be considered. As V.S. Alkhimov observes: "Equally important is the economic effect of introducing advanced machinery and the latest techniques and technological processes which are conducive to intensified social production, higher labor efficiency, better product quality, and lower production cost."(60)

Third, both the import and export of advanced technology accelerate the concentration and specialization of production. These developments create the need to increase the responsibilities of the production and industrial associations. A.M. Voinov argues that in order to increase technology exports to the West, it is necessary to provide associations and enterprises with greater incentives to export their products. These

stimuli must achieve "an optimal combination of centralized
state planning and management with the economic independence
of socialist enterprises, and organically coordinate production
and foreign trade."(61)

Fourth, an increase in the trade of technological licenses
is an important stimulus to technological planning within the
socialist economy. As Rodina affirms: "It is very important
that long-range licensing policies be worked out on the basis
of concepts of technological development of each industrial
sector and of the entire economy. Such technological-economic
concepts will increase the effectiveness of licensing trade as a
whole, and will establish, in turn, one of the most important
means for enhancing the technological level of industry, and
for accelerating technological progress in the socialist
states."(62)

Fifth, there is an increased need for long-range planning
in the domestic economy, and with it a mounting pressure for
the completion of long-term East-West agreements that can be
correlated with the extended range and comprehensiveness of
the planning process. Rozanov comments: "The line of the
25th CPSU Congress regarding long-term trade and scientific
and technical cooperation with capitalist states is determined
by the development of long-range planning of the national
economy, by the CPSU's efforts to promote the intensive development of industry and effective use of capital, and by its
attempt to maximize the satisfaction of the growing needs of
the population."(63) Hence, Soviet researchers, by helping to
formulate the official guidelines for economic and social
development up to 1990, have made comprehensive studies of
questions pertaining to production, to the utilization of the
international division of labor, and to relations with industrial
trade partners. Iu. Shiriaev and A. Sokolov underscore the
emergence of a long-range economic policy that broadens and
deepens foreign economic ties:

> The Soviet Union and other socialist countries are
> today mapping out a long-term economic strategy
> featuring large-scale comprehensive programs for
> periods of 10-15 years. These programs cover fuel
> and energy, metallurgy, leading branches of heavy
> engineering, and food problems. They take into
> account scientific and technological progress at home
> and abroad. This will place economic, scientific and
> technological, and production cooperation between
> socialist and capitalist enterprises on a more
> long-term footing and steadily increase its scale.(64)

Sixth, the USSR's involvement in the worldwide trade of
technological goods spurs continuous and faster modernization
of many interconnected sectors of the Soviet-bloc economies.

Iokhin asserts: "Improving the technical and technological level of industry in the Comecon countries, by cooperating with Western firms, is an important means of promoting the growth of exports of industrial products and, consequently, leads to an improvement in the structure of exports to advanced capitalist states. Industrial cooperation produces a continuous improvement in industry, because changes in the quality and technological characteristics of the products of one partner demand an improvement in the products of the other partner."(65)

Seventh, greater export specialization will improve the quality of products for domestic use. For example, A.K. Kirillov contends that the export of Soviet engineering products "has a positive effect on Soviet engineering enterprises, [because] it encourages them to master the best achievements of world science and technology and improve fundamental and applied research, and it also provides a creative incentive for Soviet engineers and workers."(66)

Eighth, higher growth rates, export specialization, and the diversification of domestic production are becoming closely interrelated. The head of Litsenzintorg (the Soviet foreign trade association that buys and sells licenses) declares:

> We are witnessing a universal STR. The rate of scientific and technological progress is rapidly increasing. . . . Such rapid progress means that no country, not even the most developed, can independently solve its own technological problems. That is why it is important to promote international cooperation in the exchange of inventions, technical ideas, and experience. The very existence of an enterprise, quite apart from its profitability, often depends on the choice of a sound technological policy, equally balanced between local and foreign research.(67)

Ninth, greater participation in the international division of labor promotes the more efficient use of capital. Maksimova declares:

> The CPSU and the Soviet state attach much importance to efficient, rational use of the country's material and financial resources, to saving on investment, and to the need to increase the returns on every ruble invested in the economy. Export specialization and the establishment of large export sectors in a number of industries naturally involve additional investments. At the same time, this enables the country to cut back or even to stop the growth of production capacities for the manufacture

of products which it is more profitable to import
from abroad. Eventually, this enables the country
to concentrate fresh investments in the most effective areas, helping to save funds and stimulating the
establishment of more progressive proportions in the
economy.(68)

Tenth, greater domestic specialization of industrial
production, coupled with an increasing international division of
labor in the manufacturing and marketing of technology, require the development of new forms of economic cooperation
with the West. Mal'kevich, who has been actively involved in
the trade of industrial licenses, asserts:

> The trend toward the international division of labor,
> and the application of international value criteria in
> assessing the expediency of a given large-scale
> program, permit individual countries gradually to
> rationalize the structure of their economy and to
> maximize investment effectiveness. Today no indus-
> trial country needs to develop an entire production
> process from scratch, if, in exchange for its own
> goods, it can acquire an appropriate product or
> license for its manufacture from countries already
> producing it. [A nation] can then more rationally
> concentrate its investments and resources in other
> areas, so as to gain a leading position on specialized
> world markets.(69)

Eleventh, the rapid extraction and utilization of Soviet
natural resources is a prerequisite for domestic economic
growth. The efficient use of capital goods to improve the
processing and distribution of raw materials is therefore a
high-priority national goal. Economic detente enables Western
companies to invest in the search for and development of
Soviet natural resources, and this injection of foreign capital
and expertise will almost surely improve Soviet economic
growth and productivity. According to Rozanov, "The expansion of economic cooperation between the USSR and the capitalist states proceeds from the possibility of a more rational
utilization of the natural resources of the Soviet state, by
attracting the financial means and the material and technical
expertise of Western partners. This permits a more rapid
assimilation of a series of new regions - above all, Siberia and
the Far East - which will enhance many fields of production
and transport."(70)

In short, Soviet economic modernizers make a forceful
case for a strategy of domestic development that is rooted in
the USSR's active participation in the world economy, and that
fosters long-term and mutually beneficial economic interdepen-

dence between the USSR and capitalist, as well as other socialist and Third World, countries. Soviet analysts take for
granted that Western governments and corporations are moti-
vated by self-interest, and that they wish to diversify sources
of raw material supply and meet current and projected shortages in the world fuel and primary materials markets. But
Soviet modernizers especially, and conservatives to a lesser
extent, perceive that the benefits of East-West trade to the
USSR outweigh any accompanying socioeconomic vulnerabilities
or disadvantages, particularly from advanced technology imports. Possible vulnerabilities and disadvantages to the West
are not openly discussed, but Soviet modernizers raise this
issue indirectly by attempting to allay the fears of Western
governments and potential Western business partners (e.g.,
regarding the military applications of sophisticated Western
technologies and the safety of Western capital and equipment
investments under long-term payback arrangements).

THE SOVIET DEBATE ABOUT ORGANIZATIONAL CHANGES AND THE EXPANSION OF FOREIGN ECONOMIC RELATIONS

Since the early 1970s there has been a consensus in the Soviet
leadership about the need to expand and diversify foreign
economic activities. There has also been general agreement
that some of the organizational structures and methods of the
USSR's foreign trade system need to be modified. Most party
and state leaders would concur with the broad conclusions that
the Soviet Union must use the achievements of the STR to
improve the productivity or efficiency of the domestic economy;
that greater economic interdependence with the world economy
is an important stimulus in the transition from an "extensive"
to "intensive" growth model; and that administrative adjustments are needed to take advantage of new economic opportunities and to forestall new difficulties. Sushkov declares:
"Working together with our Soviet organizations to raise
further the economic level of the USSR, Soviet foreign trade
associations have elaborated new forms of economic ties, new
forms of industrial cooperation, which will ensure maximum
economic benefit for our country. They are uncovering additional prospects for combining the advantages of the socialist
economic system with the steadily accelerating world scientific
and technological revolution."(71)
      But what kinds of international economic activities should
be pursued, how extensive should they be, which countries
and foreign business organizations are the most desirable
partners for the USSR, and what changes are needed in the
planning and management of Soviet foreign trade? On all of
these issues there has been ongoing discussion and debate

within and among the Soviet bureaucracies for more than a decade. In posing and responding to such questions, Soviet modernizers advocate a strategy of development that emphasizes foreign trade with industrialized capitalist countries; Soviet conservatives stress tighter integration of the Comecon economies and more extensive trade with Third World nations; and a nostalgic neo-Stalinist minority still favors autarkic patterns of development.

We will now focus on the dispute among Soviet elites concerning the organizational changes needed to cope with the rapidly increasing volume and new types of foreign economic relations. When all is said and done, American observers seem to know very little about the bureaucratic competition within the USSR over the reorganization of the foreign trade system. But we do know that conservative and modernizing positions were publicly articulated, that the struggle between them was for high stakes, and that the conservatives prevailed in the late 1970s.

At the center of the conflict were two key Leninist principles - "the state monopoly of foreign trade" and "democratic centralism" - and their practical applications under contemporary conditions. Specifically, the relationships among at least nine sets of organizations were at issue: Gosplan, the Ministry of Foreign Trade (MFT), the State Committee for Science and Technology (SCST), foreign trade organizations (FTOs), branch ministries, production and industrial associations, large enterprises and firms, Vneshtorgbank (the Bank for Foreign Trade), and foreign banks and companies. The basic feature of this system, as we will elaborate shortly, is that few Soviet customer ministries and "end-user" firms deal directly with Western companies. Not only are Soviet ministries and enterprises legally bound by directives from Gosplan, but they can import and export goods only through the MFT and the FTO responsible for a specific product or service (e.g., machinery, oil, licenses, shipping). Most of the seventy or more FTOs are directly subordinate to the MFT, but some FTOs are subordinate to the State Committee for Foreign Economic Relations, which handles economic ties with Third World countries, and to other institutions, including the SCST and several ministries in the transportation sector.

Examine closely figure 3.1, which, together with the numbered paragraphs below, summarizes the experience of the U.S. Department of Commerce regarding Soviet import procedures.

Soviet modernizers have sought to revise substantially the institutional relationships and procedures described in figure 3.1. In the early 1970s some "radical" modernizers privately appealed for the de facto abolition of the monopolistic position of the MFT over the USSR's international economic activities. Favorably assessing recent developments in Eastern Europe

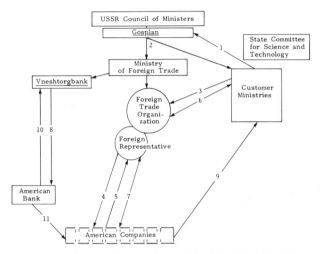

Fig. 3.1. Soviet Procedure for Purchasing in the United States (72)

1. Soviet customers, industrial ministries and other organizations, request that Gosplan include in the annual plan an appropriation to make a specified purchase abroad. American firms may attempt to influence end-user requests by advertising their products and capabilities to FTOs, industrial ministries, institutes, etc. The USSR State Committee for Science and Technology sometimes consults with Gosplan, industrial ministries, and foreign firms on proposed projects.

2. When the Council of Ministers approves the import plan and the plan for supply of imports to the domestic economy or approves a special request, Gosplan notifies the appropriate customer and the Ministry of Foreign Trade. One of the main import administrations of the Ministry of Foreign Trade then authorizes a foreign trade organization (FTO) to make the specified purchase.

3. The Soviet customer, in consultation with a subordinate end-user enterprise or association of enterprises, concludes an agreement with the appropriate FTO, commissioning the latter to make a foreign purchase. The FTO and the customer then consult on the technical requirements.

4. The FTO solicits bids from foreign firms. Sometimes a Soviet customer and a U.S. firm engage in direct technical discussions. (Operations 4, 5, and 7 can be handled directly with the FTO office in Moscow or through FTO representatives abroad.)

5. U.S. firms submit proposals to the FTO. (See #4.)

6. In consultation with the customer, the FTO prepares a draft version of a contract. The customer then approves the contract terms.

7. The FTO and a U.S. firm conclude a contract. When the equipment is ready, the U.S. firm notifies the FTO. Sometimes Soviet personnel inspect equipment at the American plant before shipment. (See #4.)

8. If letter of credit is to be used, Vneshtorgbank (the Bank for Foreign Trade) opens one with a U.S. bank.

9. The goods are shipped to the USSR end-user.

10. Documents are sent to Moscow directly or through U.S. bank.

11. The U.S. firm is paid, through letter of credit or cash against documents. The Soviet FTO then presents a bill to the Soviet customer. Very often U.S. company personnel participate in the installation of equipment at the Soviet plant.

(especially Hungary), Soviet proponents of far-reaching decentralization hoped to establish direct commercial relations between the Soviet branch ministries, associations, and firms, on the one hand, and foreign multinational and national corporations, on the other. The idea was to enhance the decision-making powers of the Soviet consumer and producer organizations by increasing their role in the planning and management of foreign trade.

For example, if the "middleman" FTOs were subordinated to the "end-user" branch ministries (rather than to the MFT), Soviet industrial agencies and enterprises would exercise much greater control over their own foreign economic activities. A similar result would be achieved if the zagranpostavki (the all-union associations that help certain branch ministries distribute Soviet equipment to foreign purchasers and to Soviet-assisted projects in other countries) were empowered to export and import goods without the approval of the MFT.

Such new arrangements would considerably alter the functions and personnel of the FTOs. At present most FTOs are subordinated to the MFT, and the MFT hires and fires responsible officials of their FTOs. If, instead, most FTOs served specific industrial ministries, the current MFT-FTO relationship - and especially its incentive structure and recruitment patterns - would be substantially changed. For even if the FTOs continued merely to trade the goods and services produced and used by other Soviet organizations and their foreign partners, the choice and specifications of these goods and services and the negotiations to obtain them would be much more influenced by consumer and supplier preferences. Quite possibly there would also be more adjustments in the systems of production, management, and information into which imported equipment and techniques are absorbed.

Hence, organizational changes of the kind proposed by the radical Soviet modernizers would considerably enhance the powers of the branch ministries to plan and manage international economic activities. The MFT would lose influence vis-a-vis its superior (Gosplan), its subordinates (the FTOs), and its rival (the SCST). At a minimum, the MFT and its FTOs would be put under considerably greater pressure to be responsive to end-user needs, capabilities, and scarcities at home and abroad.

"Liberal" and "conservative" modernizers - two much larger and more influential policy groups of Soviet bureaucrats and analysts - seek to reconceptualize, rather than reject, the state monopoly of foreign trade. They argue that the legitimation of one institution's domination over foreign trade activity must shift to the legitimation of planned and regularized state intervention in the interaction between Soviet organizations and enterprises, on the one hand, and foreign governmental and private institutions, on the other. As Shmelev affirms, "The

Leninist ideal concerning the state monopoly of foreign trade is not a monopoly of a given organization over all operative behavior; it is above all the right and responsibility of the central planning organs to define the policies and basic directions of foreign trade and thus to control its development."(73)

The chief factors shaping this liberal reformist perspective are the greatly increased volume of East-West trade - actual and potential - and the perceived importance of East-West commercial relations to the growth and productivity of the Soviet economy under a modified but centralized system of planning and management. Iokhin, noting the expansion of the number of participants in the foreign trade process, observes: "The development of new directions of economic cooperation between socialist and capitalist states creates the need to improve the methods of regulating economic ties between the enterprises of cooperating states. Presently such regulation involves a broad circle of institutions and instruments, in order to manage cooperative ties on various levels (governmental, departmental, sectoral, and economic), and in order to stimulate joint business undertakings by various means (economic, juridical, organizational, etc.)."(74)

Moreover, Soviet modernizers seek to develop closer ties between domestic production and global markets and to orient the work of the production and industrial associations toward the world economy. These international connections, they argue, are critical if the USSR is to increase its industrial exports and make better use of advanced technological imports. Maksimova declares that, in organizing its external economic ties, the USSR "faces the crucial task of bringing production and foreign trade activity closer together."(75) V.S. Evgenev adds: "As regards the socialist countries, their industrial and foreign trade mechanisms must interact more closely. Further, they must give more attention to the external market's requirements relative to the quality of goods and to post-sale services, study the Western market more profoundly, and master marketing techniques."(76)

In addition, liberal modernizers join their radical counterparts in stressing the importance of creating "direct" ties between Soviet industrial organizations and the world market, especially in scientific and technological spheres. Rodina summarizes this argument:

> The normalization of international relations and the deepening of the processes of integration in the world economy have produced a qualitative improvement in the development of scientific-technological cooperation with advanced capitalist states, and make possible a transition to more progressive forms and methods of its realization, such as the establishment

of joint research and development, cooperation in solving large and complex scientific problems, patent and licensing exchanges to further production cooperation, the establishment of international institutions, etc. Ever greater significance is attached to <u>direct</u> ties between scientific research organizations, enterprises, and firms in the cooperating countries, and to the development of cooperative relations between them in order to solve pressing scientific and technological tasks."(77)

But modernizers of all kinds are quite concerned about the lack of cooperation and coordination among <u>Soviet</u> organizations, in particular the FTOs and the consumer and producer ministries and enterprises. Closer ties between Soviet importing and exporting institutions must accompany or precede closer ties between Soviet and foreign institutions. Feonova and her colleagues assert: "At the present time, a task of decisive significance is that of fundamentally improving the work involved in the importation of complete sets of equipment for enterprises and installations constructed on Soviet territory, the strengthening of control over the quality of imported equipment, and the expansion of <u>direct</u> ties between foreign trade associations and the construction sites for which this equipment is intended, so that problems connected with the start-up of the equipment can be solved more efficiently."(78)

Liberal modernizers place special emphasis on the role of the State Committee for Science and Technology. They maintain that the SCST must take a much more active part in fostering technological innovation within Soviet industry and in promoting scientific-technological exchanges and trade with the West. Rodina states: "An increase in the effectiveness of the trade in licenses is to a large extent linked with an increase in the responsibility of the branch ministries, associations, and enterprises skillfully to prepare inventions for foreign patenting, to sell licenses, and to conclude contracts. These responsibilities, in turn, necessitate the expansion of the rights of Soviet organizations to establish closer contacts with foreign firms, and the strengthening of the coordinating and verifying role of the State Committee for Science and Technology or other higher leadership organs."(79)

There seem to be notable differences among radical, liberal, and conservative modernizers, however, regarding the appropriate functions of <u>Gosplan</u>. The radical modernizers are most interested in increasing the powers of the branch ministries and firms to help <u>plan</u> foreign trade; the conservative modernizers least so. The radical modernizers are most concerned with providing financial <u>incentives</u> to Soviet ministries, associations, enterprises, and <u>FTOs</u> to produce for the world market and to integrate advanced Western technology into the

Soviet economy; the conservative modernizers least so. And the radical modernizers are most eager to incorporate such incentives into a less centralized and more market-oriented system of planning and management, rather than to lobby for new types of bonuses from Gosplan or "investment credits" from the SCST; the conservative modernizers are least interested in such initiatives.

A lucid discussion of interorganizational relationships and of the centralization/decentralization issue is offered by V.P. Gruzinov, head of a team of Soviet researchers commissioned to conduct an internal evaluation of the MFT in the mid-1970s. Gruzinov, an archetypical liberal modernizer, judiciously but emphatically emphasizes the democratic side of the democratic centralism formula:

> [In practice], a set of centralized planned targets is obtained by the all-union associations from the main administrations [of the MFT], and trading partners are selected and contracts concluded independently.
> The point basically is to achieve a sound and efficient balance in the distribution of powers and responsibilities between the centralized leadership and units further down the organizational ladder, particularly between the central apparatus of the Ministry of Foreign Trade and the all-union associations, so that some initiative and independence can be preserved at the base. . . .
> In the present period, with the economic changes that have been instituted within the country (the transition to the new system of planning and economic incentives in practically all sectors of the economy) and the increasingly complicated internal relationships in the management of foreign trade, the second aspect of democratic centralism is being stressed, namely, greater independence is being given to the all-union associations in their commercial and economic activities. (80)

Gruzinov forcefully argues that this delegation of authority does not constitute the devolution or dissipation of power, let alone the "sacrificing" of the state monopoly over foreign trade. He contends that greater decentralization will increase the capabilities of the center to deal with important long- and short-range questions (e.g., "developing strategies for foreign trade policy and for improving business relations with industry"), thereby enhancing the decisionmaking procedures, decisions, and decision outcomes of the system as a whole. (81) Gruzinov declares: "It should become a hard and fast rule that decisions be made where (i.e., at the level on which) the most information exists about the given question, and where one may be assured that they will be implemented most competently."(82) In Gruzinov's view, such delegation of authority can develop the "creative capacities" of both the top-level managers and their subordinates."(83)

How can the benefits to be derived from organizational decentralization be achieved without abandoning the traditional state monopoly over foreign trade? Gruzinov's response emphasizes the same elements as does the official Soviet approach to democratic centralism in the 1970s and 1980s.(84) Specifically, he calls for "a clearer definition of the respective powers and responsibilities of the different levels of management in the Ministry of Foreign Trade system."(85) He adds: "The effectiveness of delegation of authority depends on the ability of the manager to guide the activity of those under him in the direction needed, and this in turn requires a strict coordination of powers and duties. One cannot require responsibility from a subordinate if he has not been given the powers corresponding to it."(86) Moreover, Gruzinov explicitly calls for the redefinition of the concept of "responsibility" to include work performed and initiatives not taken. This idea is a double-edged sword, because it gives lower-level organs more power to seize opportunities and top-level organs more power to upbraid their subordinates for "missed opportunities" (Gruzinov's term).(87)

The conservative or traditional approach to the management of foreign trade is exemplified by the work and attitudes of the long-time head of the MFT, N.S. Patolichev, and this orientation is perhaps most clearly articulated in the writings of V.S. Pozdniakov, a senior law professor who chairs the legal committee of the U.S./USSR Trade and Economic Council. Pozdniakov, writing at the same time that Gruzinov and his associates were proposing a modest decentralization of the foreign trade system, likewise offered suggestions for improving the planning and administration of foreign economic relations. Pozdniakov's recommendations, however, were based on the presupposition that the key to organizational effectiveness is to strengthen "the unity and mutual coordination of all of the component parts of the system."(88)

The call for "unity" is the hallmark of the conservative perspective on the management of foreign trade, as are the contentions that "departmentalism" and "localism" will subvert the national interest and "very often" lead to the loss of state property."(89) As Pozdniakov asserts, "The close coordination of the foreign activities of all Soviet departments not only prevents possible collisions, but, it is especially important to emphasize, makes possible the resolution of every concrete issue in accordance with the interests of the state as a whole, not just those of a single department. Such coordination also enables various departments to assist one another effectively."(90)

Succinctly put, Pozdniakov stresses the centralist aspects of democratic centralism. Unlike Gruzinov, Pozdniakov maintains that the delegation of decisionmaking responsibilities will result in the dissipation or misuse of power. Without strong national leadership, Soviet ministries and enterprises would pursue "their own personal interests" in foreign economic relations, and the state would be unable to correct many of the harmful effects of these insufficiently informed and parochial actions on other agencies and on the Soviet economy as a whole. Nor would the party-government be able to plan effectively or to maintain close political control over the choice and conduct of foreign economic activities and personnel.(91)

Like Gruzinov, Pozdniakov calls for the clarification of the rights and responsibilities of the many Soviet institutions involved in the planning and administration of foreign economic ties. But Pozdniakov quickly links this appeal to an argument for an even more centralized foreign trade system. Bemoaning "the absence of a unified specialized center for the management of foreign trade at the present time," Pozdniakov recommends that such an institution be created.(92)

One of the chief purposes of this powerful institution would be to "resolve differences that arise between the organs engaged in the management of foreign trade activities." A second primary function would be to assume some of the operational decisionmaking and administrative responsibilities that now "overburden" the Council of Ministers and Gosplan, thereby enabling these bodies to focus on fundamental and long-range issues.(93) Pozdniakov explains:

> This [new] organ would have the following basic responsibilities: the verification of the fulfillment of decrees and instructions of the Council of Ministers on all questions concerning foreign economic relations, the preparation of recommendations for decisions to be made by the Council of Ministers, the direct operative regulation of all of the nations' foreign trade transactions, including the fulfillment of scientific and technical contract work to be exported and imported, coordination of foreign trade activities with Gosplan, transport ministries, the Ministry of Finance, the State Bank and other departments engaged in the management of foreign economic activities, and also with the Ministry of Foreign Affairs. (94)

In essence, this is a blueprint for a considerably strengthened MFT.

Briefly stated, the Soviet leadership has responded to the challenges of the STR by broadening and deepening East-West and North-South economic ties, which in turn have increased the number of Soviet organizations directly and indirectly involved in foreign economic activities and have prompted the debate about the possible organizational changes we have described. We will now discuss the resolution of this debate and its legal manifestations.(95)

SOVIET LAW AND THE MANAGEMENT OF FOREIGN TRADE

The expansion of the USSR's international economic links is an important element of Brezhnev's "grand design" that was articulated at the Twenty-fourth Party Congress in 1971 and reaffirmed at the Twenty-fifth and Twenty-sixth Party Congresses in 1976 and 1981. In the documents of these congresses one finds evidence of both the modernizer and conservative orientations to the planning and management of foreign trade. On the one hand, the Twenty-fourth Congress resolved "to enhance the initiative and responsibility of ministries and enterprises in the development of foreign economic relations that are effective for the national economy."(96)   On the other hand, both Brezhnev and Kosygin stressed the need to eliminate "departmental" approaches to international economic activities by the planning agencies, FTOs, and ministries.(97) Similarly, the Twenty-fifth Congress resolved "To enhance the role and responsibility of branch ministries and departments in developing foreign economic ties."(98)   But Brezhnev (not Kosygin) called for a "comprehensive" approach to international economic relations that would link in "a single center the efforts of all departments and our political and economic interests."(99)

Although a comparison of such pronouncements in the early and mid-1970s suggests serious consideration of the modernizing orientation, the party leadership's decisions about the reorganization of the foreign trade system were still being formulated or were not yet ready for public dissemination (an unpublished Central Committee decree on foreign trade was approved in 1976).(100)

The long-awaited 1977 Constitution did little to clarify matters. Comparing the 1936 and 1977 Constitutions, one finds that the pertinent provisions are quite similar. The former mandates "foreign trade on the basis of state monopoly" (Article 14h), and the latter "foreign trade and other forms of external economic activity on the basis of state monopoly" (Article 73/10, emphasis added).(101)

The somewhat broader new phraseology may help to legitimize readjustments in the structure, administration, and control of the Soviet state's "monopoly" over foreign economic activities under contemporary scientific-technical and socioeconomic conditions. M.M. Boguslavskii might be laying the groundwork for selected readjustments when he observes that "fundamental changes" in the USSR's foreign economic ties, such as the exchange of production and technical services and the sale of patents and licenses, find "juridical acknowledgement and support" in the new constitution.(102) But even conservatives acknowledge that some organizational changes are needed to cope with the rapidly increasing volume and changing composition of Soviet foreign trade. Pozdniakov, for one, observes: "In contrast to 1936, when direct state management of our foreign trade was in fact fully concentrated in the hands of the Foreign Trade Ministry, at present many Soviet departments take part in the direct management of the country's foreign trade activity."(103)

The centerpiece of the legislation that finally sanctioned administrative changes in the foreign trade system is a decree of the USSR Council of Ministers of May 31, 1978.(104) The purpose of this decree was to combine production and trade more efficiently and to encourage the development of foreign economic relations. According to P. Smirnov, the new resolution sought "to improve the effectiveness of the activities of [the FTOs] by strengthening their economic independence, broadening their self-supporting basis, and providing higher material incentives (depending on the final results achieved) for the collective as a whole and for each of its members."(105) D.A. Loeber, a Western scholar, observes: "The objective of the reform is to increase the effectiveness of foreign trade by modernization and rationalization."(106)

Key elements of the 1978 decree and related Soviet legislation have been ably described and analyzed elsewhere.(107) We will contribute to these discussions by assessing the response of the 1978 resolution to the larger issues that Gruzinov, Pozdniakov, A.I. Bel'chuk,(108) and other Soviet officials and analysts have raised.

The most notable provisions in the 1978 decree are efforts to coordinate the work of the MFT, the FTOs, the branch ministries and departments, the industrial and production associations, and the major enterprises. The FTOs are to be headed by newly formed "boards" that are to play an important role in the planning and management of export and import activities. "For the purpose of more extensively involving the branch ministries and departments, and also the large industrial enterprises and associations, in foreign trade activity," representatives of the MFT and other agencies are to participate actively on the new boards (Articles 2, 3 and 19).

For the first time, the chief decisions of the FTO and its component "firms" will be made by a directorate that is "mainly composed of persons who do not work in these organizations but to a large extent represent the state agency under whose jurisdiction these organizations function."(109) Smirnov asserts:

> This [arrangement] does not imply dual subordina-
> tion. It means that the USSR Ministry of Foreign
> Trade is obliged to involve on a broader scale
> sectoral ministries and departments in managing the
> activities of foreign trade associations, and, spe-
> cifically, to map out joint measures to ensure that
> the Soviet side fulfills its export commitments as
> regards goods and services for specializing and
> concentrating export production and the delivery of
> respective goods, curtails the importation of goods
> that can be produced domestically, and imports
> goods that are of a higher quality and technical
> level.(110)

Article 44 reiterates the traditional obligation of the MFT to
"guide" the FTOs and to issue "instructions" to the FTOs
regarding their drafts of five-year and annual plans. Article
52 stipulates that an FTO must develop "with the participation
of respective branch ministries and departments" specific
proposals regarding new products for export. In the section
on imports, however, no obligation is placed upon the FTOs to
consult with the branch ministries and departments.
    A chief aim of the new legislation, then, is to coordinate
better the efforts of the FTOs and the industrial agencies in
the planning and production of Soviet exports. Another purpose might be to prod the ministries, branch departments, and
larger enterprises to make greater use of scientific and
technical advances from abroad. In any case, the assessments
of FTO boards regarding "technological progress," "demand,"
and "efficiency" are to become salient factors in foreign trade
decisionmaking.
    The diverse composition of the new boards of the FTOs,
and the fact that these associations both export and import
goods, services, and information, may improve interorganizational decisionmaking and administration within the USSR
and between Soviet and foreign organizations. It is an under-
statement to say that relations are complex among the myriad
subdivisions of Gosplan, the MFT, the SCST,(111) the State
Committee for Foreign Economic Relations,(112) the Bank for
Foreign Trade, the more than seventy foreign trade associations, and the domestic industrial and agricultural associations
and production enterprises. For example, the legislative acts
empowering Soviet agencies to engage in foreign economic
activities were adopted at different times and for different
purposes in a wide variety of substantive fields. Because
some of these acts were imprecise or inconsistent with one
another, because some major disparities developed between the
powers and duties of particular agencies or departments, and
because the fragmentation of rights and responsibilities
produced tremendous problems of coordination and control,

national party leaders eventually approved the uniform provisions contained in the 1978 decree and in the model charters
for all FTOs.(113)

Yet improved organizational integration and communication, even when buttressed by carefully drawn laws, do not
necessarily reduce bureaucratic conflict or improve administrative performance. In fact, efforts to increase intra- and
interorganizational cooperation may well heighten conflict and
impede performance in the short or long run. The 1978 decree
does not try to resolve the tension between centralizing and
decentralizing forces and between national, middle-level, and
local institutions. Instead, the recent legislation tries to
regularize the competition between centripetal and centrifugal
pressures by clarifying the powers and duties of the many
agencies that are or should be involved in foreign economic
planning, scientific and technological innovation, and other
fields related to international economic activities.

The new Soviet statutes concerning foreign trade clearly
reflect the contemporary official emphasis upon enhancing both
democracy and centralism in the management of the economy.
Soviet analysts talk of expanding the rights and economic
independence of the FTOs, in order to strengthen the state's
monopoly over foreign trade and thereby to increase both the
efficiency and the flexibility of decisionmaking at various
stages and levels. This is not just doubletalk. Enhancing the
powers of the FTOs vis-a-vis the MFT is a modest form of
decentralization. But, given the growing number of agencies,
departments, and production units that are participating or
could participate - directly or indirectly - in foreign economic
activities, the strengthening of the middle-level FTOs constitutes a form of centralization. That is, the capacity of the
top party bodies to plan effectively and to direct the sprawling
ministerial bureaucracy may well be increased by augmenting
slightly the authority of the FTOs and their specialized firms,
while at the same time making the FTOs more responsive and
responsible to producer and consumer organizations in the
USSR and abroad.

If, like the Brezhnev collective leadership, one conceptu-
alizes the centralization/decentralization issue as a non-zero-
sum game, and if one recognizes that "foreign" and "domestic"
policies must be closely integrated in industrialized states,
recent Soviet organizational and legal changes in the field of
foreign economic relations become much more understandable.
After all, the chief purpose of these organizational and legal
adjustments is to enhance the effectiveness of Soviet foreign
economic activities generally and of the FTOs in particular.
"Effectiveness" and "efficiency" can mean different things to
different officials at different times, so the criteria and
standards for evaluating the performance of FTOs will always
be more or less in dispute. But the recent Soviet institutional

and juridical changes are clearly designed to improve cooperative problem solving between the MFT and FTOs, on the one
hand, and the end-user and producer ministries, on the other.
Hence, the new measures may be viewed as a cautious effort to
encourage innovative, differentiated, and comprehensive approaches to the increasingly serious problems of sustaining
economic growth and productivity in the USSR.

The 1978 decree, however, is just as important for the
organizational and legal changes it did not implement as for
those it did.   For one thing, the MFT retains considerable
control over the foreign economic operations of even the
largest domestic production and industrial associations and
enterprises.   For another thing, the ministries and departments still do not play a significant role in the planning of
their own imports and exports.   Hence, the present administrative and incentive structures - and their legal manifestations - still discourage the vast majority of the USSR's
combines and factories from engaging in international commercial activities.

By comparison with their East European counterparts,
Soviet FTOs are still closely tied to the MFT.   As a result,
Soviet domestic associations and enterprises participate in
relatively few cooperative undertakings with Western corporations (e.g., the sharing or coordination of tasks between the
partners, and the joint use or operation of equipment or fixed
installations - in research and development, communication of
scientific and technical data and transfer of property rights
for these data, industrial construction, manufacture, and
marketing).(114)   Briefly stated, the USSR's industrial ministries and SCST still lack the powers vis-a-vis Gosplan, the
MFT, the FTOs, and the Bank for Foreign Trade that the
Soviet modernizers have sought to attain.

There is little question that the Soviet conservatives
bested the modernizers in the struggle over the reorganization
of the foreign trade system in the 1970s.   Patolichev remained
head of the MFT, and a member of the Central Committee;
Dzhermen Gvishiani remained deputy head of an SCST whose
influence declined in the late 1970s (not head of the MFT, as
some modernizers had hoped); Pozdniakov continued to be an
authoritative spokesman on the legal aspects of foreign trade;
and Gruzinov was demoted to a relatively minor position.

Whether the conservative victory will be long-lasting
depends on many factors, including the effectiveness of the
recent organizational and legal changes.   To date, there are
numerous unanswered questions about the nature and extent of
the implementation of the 1978 decree.   According to Smirnov,
the reorganization of the FTOs was completed in the middle of
1979, and 288 specialized firms were created to replace the
existing "offices" within the 45 FTOs of the MFT.(115)   Each
new firm exports and imports a limited number of products,

whereas the former offices usually exported or imported products. The FTOs, but not their firms, are "legal persons." Although the basic obligation of the firm is to carry out the plans the FTO assigns to it, the firm has the right to help design specific projects and to sign contracts in the name of the FTO. (116) In a word, "the firms will have more independent power than the offices did." (117)

Likewise, the powers of the zagranpostavki of the industrial ministries also seem to have been modestly increased as a result of the 1978 legislation. Zagranpostavki "are not empowered to conduct import-export operations, being mainly engaged in helping to organize supplies for the export of machinery and equipment, including equipment and materials for the projects built abroad with the technical assistance of the USSR." (118) Nonetheless, the zagranpostavki are legal persons that may "sign contracts concerning specialization and cooperation of production of particular kinds of goods," although "such contracts do not create obligations to supply specialized goods." (119)

The new boards of the FTOs are the most important administrative innovation in the 1978 decree. If the modernizers influenced this decree in any way, or if the decree constitutes a compromise between modernizer and conservative viewpoints, the results are reflected in the unambiguous call for the creation of these horizontal coordinating bodies.

But how many of these boards have been formed? What is their composition? How active are they? Do they merely legitimize informal relationships already well established? The most that can be said is that the new boards consist of roughly equal numbers of officials from the MFT, FTO, and industrial ministries, or as much as 50 percent representation from the domestic industrial and production organizations. (120) Some of the new boards are dominated by the general director of the FTO; others are not. Some of the boards are quite active; others are not. Some have considerably raised the managerial and marketing efficiency and the technical expertise of FTO personnel; others have not. Some are forming new decisionmaking and administrative relationships; others are not.

From what little we know about the boards, zagranpostavki, and firms of the FTOs, it seems that the 1978 legislation is functioning more as "a disseminator of leading experience" than as an enforcer of specific administrative practices or legal obligations. Uniform structural and operational changes have been recommended to spur foreign trade and production officials to formulate more feasible plans and to carry them out more effectively and efficiently. But flexibility and differentiation, together with better intra- and interorganizational coordination and more precisely stipulated rights and responsibilities, seem to be the hallmarks of the recent modifications in the Soviet foreign trade system.

In short, the conservative 1978 legislation fits in well with three important characteristics of the present-day Soviet approach to economic growth and productivity in general, and to foreign economic relations in particular.

First, as Scott Bozek argues, "Soviet planners seem to have chosen two interrelated strategies for intensifying the development of foreign trade":

> Further expanding ties to world markets through such measures as compensation agreements, joint-stock companies in the West, special export industries, and increased numbers and activities of Soviet organizations in foreign trade; and
>
> More closely linking and better compensating Soviet organizations - especially FTOs and industrial enterprises - that have responsibilities for producing and marketing Soviet exports and purchasing and absorbing foreign imports.(121)

Second, the strengthening of the FTOs was in keeping with the trend throughout the Soviet bloc to increase the powers of intermediate-level organizations and to solidify branch monopolization.(122) The first production and industrial associations were formed in the USSR in the early 1970s, as we have discussed. New and existing FTOs were given greater and more clearly defined powers in the late 1970s. And, perhaps most significant, conservatives and modernizers have both come to recognize the importance of integrating the work of the domestic and foreign trade associations. A primary purpose of the 1978 legislation was to coordinate better the planning and management of the USSR's industrial production and foreign economic activities, thereby trying to improve the quality of the former by expanding the latter.

Third, the reorganization of the FTOs was an excellent example of the Brezhnev administration's penchant for incremental administrative changes, rather than dramatic systemic reforms. Institutional adjustments were legitimized without altering the essentials of the planning, pricing, and incentive structures. The spirit and substance of the Soviet approach to foreign economic relations in the early 1980s are encapsulated in the basic guidelines for the Eleventh Five-Year Plan (1981-1985):

> To carry out the further development of foreign trade and economic, scientific, and technical cooperation with foreign countries. To make rational use of the international division of labor and the possibilities of foreign economic ties in increasing the efficiency of social production. . . .

To improve direct ties among branch ministries, production associations, enterprises, and organizations of the USSR and of CMEA member-countries participating in cooperative endeavors. To enhance the responsibility of ministries, production associations, enterprises, and organizations for the fulfillment of commitments in the field of foreign economic relations. To introduce uniform standards and norms more widely.(123)

Not surprisingly, the goals and organizational forms of Soviet foreign economic ties are evolving. The Brezhnev administration has sought to expand a sphere of activity that it perceives to be increasingly important to the shift from "extensive" to "intensive" patterns of development. Most Soviet modernizers would agree with the Western analyst who concludes:

The Soviet foreign trade monopoly, though providing the Soviet economy with many advantages [e.g., in the planning, bargaining, protection, and control areas], reveals a number of disadvantages [e.g., excessive centralization with resulting bureaucratic problems, and harmful separation of the foreign trade function from the production function] that could be eliminated without loss of the monopoly's advantages. Most important, greater reliance should be placed on the individual Soviet enterprise, and on contractual relationships rather than administrative or "command" relationships.(124)

Significantly, even Soviet conservatives are moving toward this assessment, with emphasis (as we have seen) on decision-making by production associations rather than enterprises, on improved coordination of domestic and international economic activities, and on clarification of organizational roles and relationships and legal responsibilities.

The modest scope of the Soviet Union's institutional and juridical responses to the STR to date may be the result of a compromise between conservative and reformist approaches to modernization. More likely, the incremental decisions reached and the statutes promulgated in the late 1970s constituted a rather decisive conservative victory that will endure to the end of the Brezhnev administration at the very least. The cautious but carefully conceived organizational and legal adjustments we have examined in this chapter are a reflection of the CPSU leaders' confidence in the traditional elements of the Soviet polity and economy and in the adaptability of these elements to new and rapidly changing domestic and international political, economic, and scientific-technological conditions.

Also, the recent administrative and juridical modifications of the Soviet foreign trade system may be expressions of the aging party leaders' efforts to mobilize technical and manageri- al elites to alleviate the increasingly serious economic difficulties of the USSR; to broaden and diversify international economic activities that can be centrally controlled; or merely to postpone hard choices.

Whether the organizational and legal adjustments of the late 1970s and early 1980s will help to resolve the mounting economic problems of the USSR, and whether the conservatives will continue to prevail over the modernizers in their ongoing bureaucratic competition, are difficult to predict. The performance of the Soviet economy and the vicissitudes of the Soviet debate regarding East-West economic relations depend upon political and military, as well as economic, considerations. We will address these larger issues and their interconnections in the following sections and in the final two chapters.

THE LIMITS OF EAST-WEST COOPERATION

Precisely because the broadening of ties between the Eastern and Western economies increases the number of Soviet orga- nizations in direct or indirect contact with the West, CPSU leaders feel confronted with the problems of controlling these institutional, professional, and personal relationships and minimizing "negative" foreign influences. Regulating the expanded interdependence between the Soviet and Western economies and societies, in the context of detente, poses some hard choices concerning "the two spheres" of East-West inter- action.

On the one hand, Soviet analysts reiterate that cooper- ation with the West is "objectively" required by the interna- tional forces of science, technology, and production. Iu. Shiriaev states: "The development of contemporary productive forces, which are ultimately global forces, the varying avail- ability of natural resources, and the broad opportunities for exchanging the latest machinery and technology constitute the objective premises for an extension of mutually advantageous economic ties between countries belonging to the two social systems."(125)

On the other hand, Soviet writers affirm that the histor- ical confrontation with the West continues. D. Tomashevskii declares: "There can be a question, not of an end to the historic confrontation between socialism and capitalism, but only of its new forms, of a shift in emphasis in the class struggle on the international scene from military-political confrontation between states [with different] social systems, to competition in solving the problems of economic and social

development."(126) Hence, economic detente legitimizes East-
West industrial cooperation, but this "relaxation of tensions"
does not mean a reduction in, let alone an end to, political and
economic competition. Instead, changes are taking place in the
nature of the competition and in the ways it is conducted.
"The growing importance of the economic, scientific, and
technical aspects of the competition between the two systems is
a formidable and long-term problem," Tomashevskii concludes.(127)
      Soviet theorists maintain that peaceful coexistence in
general, and economic detente in particular, contain elements
of both cooperation and conflict. These diverse components
are thought to influence one another reciprocally in an ever-
changing process. Iu. Molchanov argues that "peaceful coexistence is a form of relations between states with differing
social systems, in which class confrontation and varied and
mutually advantageous cooperation exist dialectically and are
intertwined. From this viewpoint, peaceful coexistence is a
dialectical unity of opposites."(128) Managing these competing
tendencies and fulfilling changing systemic needs are thus
critical policy problems for the Soviet leadership.
      Leading Soviet officials perceive limits to cooperation
between the USSR and the West, and these constraints channel
and curtail the USSR's interest in East-West rapprochement.
      First, the divergent forms of property ownership limit the
scope of cooperation. I. Saviolova asserts that "radical differences in the partners' forms of ownership draw specific
social and economic bounds that vary according to the inherent
trade exchange relations."(129) The sharply contrasting capitalist and socialist attitudes toward private enterprise impact
directly upon the extent of production cooperation that Soviet
analysts perceive to be legitimate. Saviolova identifies three
basic types of industrial cooperation. Vertical cooperation
involves exchanges of technology between separate organizations. Horizontal cooperation involves mutually beneficial
participation in a production process that generates new
capabilities. Complex cooperation involves joint ownership and
more or less equal responsibility for the design, operation,
and output of a production process. "In their industrial
cooperation with Western companies, socialist organizations
strive for vertical or horizontal forms of cooperation with their
partners. This kind of cooperation is promising because,
while involving partners with the most varied economic potentialities and interests, it does not distort their independent
functioning within their own economic systems."(130) Only in
1978 did a Soviet writer first present an ideological justifica-
tion for "joint ventures" between the USSR and Western nations.(131)
      Westerners often contend that the private ownership of
productive capabilities and economic performance are closely

linked, and that a formidable impediment to profitable economic cooperation with the USSR is the latter's insistence on the inalienability or indivisibility of the public ownership of the means of production. Soviet spokesmen respond that Western, and especially American, disdain for this fundamental socialist principle undermines the opportunities for fruitful but less extensive forms of cooperation. The Soviet aim is to broaden East-West industrial cooperation without jeopardizing the property rights and economic decisionmaking power of the socialist states - that is, without reducing the authority of the centralized management organs to plan and direct their economies. Hence, Brezhnev argued at the Twenty-fifth CPSU Congress that the USSR must promote "new forms of foreign economic relations that go beyond the framework of conventional trade, greatly expand our possibilities, and, as a rule, yield a very great effect. I have in mind, among other things, compensatory agreements under which new enterprises, belonging wholly to our state, are created in cooperation with foreign firms."(132)

Second, a major limit on the scope of cooperation is the substantial buildup of the USSR's military potential. This preference or perceived need is highly correlated with maintaining the isolation of the USSR's scientific and technological community, and with concentrating human and material resources on military projects. The wisdom of such policies is a contentious issue among Soviet officials, as we will see in the next chapter. Conservative proponents of a strong national defense capability minimize the benefits of economic detente, stressing instead the USSR's growing dependence on foreign suppliers in the civilian sectors. In response, Soviet modernizers agree that military needs can be fulfilled without foreign economic ties, but they argue that such ties strengthen the overall political-economic power of the Soviet system. Maksimova asserts: "The Soviet Union's defense capability and military potential are not dependent in any direct way on its foreign economic ties. Whatever the level of these ties - low, as before, or fairly high, as today - the Soviet Union has always met all the requirements of its armed forces in defense facilities, including armaments, on the basis of its own large industrial and scientific potentials, which serve to maintain the country's defense capability at an adequate modern level."(133) Maksimova goes on to affirm that participation in the international division of labor is a prudent strategy, especially because of the USSR's military strength, and because increased foreign economic relations improve the growth and productivity of the Soviet economy.

Greater Soviet involvement in the world economy carries with it the need to increase the level of specialization of the domestic economy, which in turn means that Soviet industry must become competitive in exporting manufactured goods. At the Twenty-fifth CPSU Congress in 1976, Kosygin called for the development of a special sector of export-oriented production. "Since foreign trade has become a major branch of the national economy, the problem arises of setting up a number of export-oriented industries to meet the specific requirements of foreign markets."(134) This appeal is quite significant, because it is based on the idea of creating a sector of the economy that would compete for high technology resources with the military. As John Hardt and George Holliday comment, "Such attention to the requirements of the export market might be a step toward establishing export branches of Soviet industry that might even rival the Ministry of Defense as a claimant for high quality inputs."(135) But even more significant than Kosygin's proposal is the fact that there has been virtually no public discussion of his suggestion since 1976, let alone implementation of any such programs.

Third, a limit on cooperation is imposed by the Soviet desire to ensure that the increasing sensitivity of the Soviet economy to global economic forces does not turn into vulnerability.(136) Vulnerabilities enable foreigners to manipulate dependencies in Soviet industry and agriculture for their own purposes.(137) Nonetheless, Soviet modernizers minimize the risks of participating in the world economy, "One should always bear in mind that this is a two-way street," Maksimova contends. "The Soviet Union's foreign partners are equally dependent on the deliveries of the appropriate products from the Soviet Union (say, on the deliveries of gas and oil in exchange for pipes or of electric power in exchange for atomic reactors). Consequently, there is no question of the Soviet Union's unilateral dependence on any other country; the partners here have mutual interests."(138)

Fourth, a limit on East-West economic ties is the increasing Soviet exposure to the instability of the world economy. The USSR was hurt by the recession in the mid-1970s. Soviet leaders and analysts became much more cognizant of the advantages of insulating the USSR's economy from oil embargoes and other disturbances on international markets. To be sure, the USSR benefited considerably from the inflated prices of oil and gold in the late 1970s. But the disadvantages of fluctuating world prices and markets, to say nothing of the political vagaries of East-West trade, have been very much on the minds of the Brezhnev administration. In a word, the optimism of Soviet modernizers in the early 1970s has been tempered by a more conservative assessment of the costs and benefits of extensive participation in an unstable global economy.

Fifth, a limit on East-West cooperation is the Soviet conservative view that some "circles" in the West seek to use detente to their strategic advantage and must be curbed. L. Vidiasova articulates this concern: "Some Western politicians

would like to see in detente a sanction to interfere in the
domestic affairs of socialist countries, and use the establishment and development of cultural ties as a channel for the
spread of bourgeois ideology and the bourgeois way of life in
the socialist world."(139)

Sixth, a limit on East-West ties is imposed by the broadening and deepening of the East-West ideological struggle in
the context of the internationalization of economic relations,
improved radio and telecommunications, increased interpersonal
and cultural links, and, perhaps most significant, intensifying
superpower rivalry in the Third World. Soviet analysts maintain that the USSR's greater involvement in the global economy, coupled with the USSR's increased capacity to deter
military aggression by the West, signals that ideological
competition is heightening. Iu. Zakharov observes: "As contacts intensify, cooperation expands and becomes more diverse,
and this gives rise to new points of contact and, consequently, to clashes of views. . . . As a result, the ideological
struggle spreads to new spheres of activity, processes, and
phenomena."(140) Iu. Davydov, in a major study of the relationship between detente and ideology, underscores the growing importance of political competition in the context of
detente. "The less imperialism in its struggle with socialism
can count on military force [and economic and political pressure as well], the more significant becomes the logic of social
development [as a competitive factor]. . . . The more relationships with socialist states become normalized, the more
dependent [the imperialists] become upon ideological methods of
influence [within socialist states]. And this objectively leads
to the magnified role and significance of ideological struggle in
the international arena."(141) D.V. Ermolenko notes the
growing importance of ideological subversion as a "global
danger" emerging from the worldwide process of the STR.(142)

Furthermore, there are limits to East-West cooperation
other than those publicly or even privately acknowledged by
Soviet officials. A significant example is American displeasure
over Soviet military activities in the Third World, especially
the use of Soviet occupation forces, as in Afghanistan, and
the use of Cuban proxy forces, as in Angola. But there are
many much less well known constraints on East-West collaboration. In the strategic arms limitation talks, for example,
Soviet reluctance to provide data about their own capabilities
surely helped to undermine the SALT II process. And, in the
economic sphere, some important aspects of the generally
sophisticated Soviet foreign trade system are in serious need
of modernization.

For instance, Soviet commercial decisionmakers continue to
emphasize bilateral trade balances. Individual foreign countries must buy from and sell to the USSR roughly the same
value of goods, and the USSR trades in a similar way with

both Western and Comecon countries. That is, a rise in the quantity or price of Soviet exports to a given country increases correspondingly the amount or value of the products, commodities, and natural resources that country may export to the USSR. Conversely, the inability of the USSR to sell its manufactured items in the West reduces the opportunity for those countries to garner Soviet markets, however much Western industrial and consumer goods are in demand or could be profitably utilized in the Soviet economy. Hence, if bilateral balances are preserved, they are likely to limit considerably the growth of Soviet foreign trade in the foreseeable future. In turn, insufficient trade with highly industrialized Western nations, notably the United States, will reinforce many of the traditional weaknesses of the Soviet economic system, such as resistance to technological innovation and chronic deficiencies in the quality, quantity, and mix of manufactured products and raw material exports.

In short, although the STR and the development of a world economy induce cooperation, Soviet officials perceive definite limits - and there are other limits as well - to East-West political and economic ties. As Zakharov declares: "The fact that socialism and capitalism are entirely different unquestionably places a boundary on the volume and mainly on the depth of the mutual political, economic, scientific, technical, and cultural relations between socialist and capitalist states. Even given the most favorable conditions, these relations cannot pass the limit beyond which they begin to exercise a direct influence on the character of the social system in the cooperating states. This is an objective limitation."(143)

CONCLUSION

The foregoing constraints on East-West cooperation notwithstanding, leading Soviet officials and international affairs specialists affirm that the USSR can deepen economic ties with the industrialized capitalist states without fear of excessive interference in socialist development - that is, without making the USSR unduly vulnerable to harmful political, economic, social, or cultural influences. The conservative and especially the reformist reasoning in support of this conclusion goes well beyond the mutual dependencies argument of Maksimova discussed above.

First, and most important, Soviet analysts maintain that the USSR has developed an industrial base strong enough to provide for its basic economic and military needs. Tomashevskii declares: "The Soviet Union's powerful economic, scientific, and technological potentials [and] the successes of other socialist countries . . . make it possible for them to cooperate with the capitalist countries on an equal footing and successfully withstand any hostile moves."(144)

Second, the Soviet leadership can allegedly manage the problem of controlling excessive vulnerabilities through planned intervention in its own economy and those of other Soviet bloc nations. Maksimova contends: "The development of the Soviet Union's external economic ties, the formation of their volume, structure, forms, and methods is not a spontaneous, arbitrary process, but a regulated and carefully balanced process, because it has gone forward in a socialist economy with a state monopoly of foreign trade."(145)

Third, the existence of serious "interimperialist contradictions" is thought to provide the USSR with a margin of protection against direct or coordinated Western exploitation of dependencies and vulnerabilities in the Soviet economy. Despite a common class interest, Western Europe and the United States have developed different orientations toward detente. As Davydov observed even before the Soviet occupation of Afghanistan, "The ruling circles in Western Europe understand the Soviet approach to detente much better than those in the United States."(146)   A key difference in this "understanding" concerns the nature and functions of East-West economic relations. Davydov concludes: "While the United States wishes to use its economic relationship with socialist states for the purpose of exercising influence on the political situation, Western Europe wishes to use the political relationship with socialist states to strengthen trade and economic relationships between East and West in order to deepen the detente relationship."(147)

Hence, the Brezhnev adminstration's efforts to "combine" the STR with the advantages of Soviet-type economies is a strategy that seeks to stimulate increased scientific, technological, and production initiatives at home through greater involvement in the global economy. Although Soviet analysts routinely assert that the USSR independently can provide for its basic needs, they argue even more often, as has A. Karenin, that "in conditions of the ongoing STR, the CPSU and the Soviet state are orienting our economy to take the fullest advantage of the opportunities to participate in the international division of labor."(148)

The pursuit of economic advantage, however, is only one component of Soviet foreign policy. Other prominent elements include East-West military relations, and in particular the strategic arms competition between the United States and the USSR. In Chapter 4, we turn to a detailed examination of Soviet perspectives and policies regarding the dramatic scientific and technological advances in the military sphere.

4 "The Scientific-Technological Revolution," Soviet Military Preparedness, and East-West Military Relations

"THE SCIENTIFIC-TECHNOLOGICAL REVOLUTION IN MILITARY AFFAIRS"

Throughout the post-Stalin period, Soviet leaders have emphasized the significance of the worldwide "STR in military affairs" or, more simply, "the revolution in military affairs." Soviet analysts maintain that science-based technology is essential to the development of strategic and conventional weapons systems, and that scientific and technological competition is the most dynamic factor in the accelerating military competition between the United States and Soviet Union in the 1970s and 1980s.

Soviet officials affirm that science-based technology has had many decisive effects on the nature and course of the Soviet-American political and military rivalry.

First, Soviet writers contend that the development and deployment of nuclear weapons has had an extraordinary impact on military affairs. The integration of nuclear weapons with rocket-launched carriers is viewed as a watershed in the history of warfare.(1) That is, dramatic scientific and technological advances have made strategic rocket forces crucial to Soviet and American military power, and these strategic weapons in turn have produced a revolutionary shift in the nature of military and political competition. Marshal Sokolovskii declares:

> The achievements of modern science, technology, and industry in the creation and production of nuclear charges, rockets of various types and classes, and military radio-electronics constitute the base upon which the entire system of armament of a modern

117

army is constructed. It must be assumed that in the
near future radical corrections will be able to be
introduced into this system as a result of the
incorporation of various cosmic means. All of this in
turn conditions the nature of a future war, the
methods of waging it, and the principles of organization of the armed forces.(2)

Second, scientific and technological breakthroughs have
prompted both the United States and the USSR to rethink
fundamental strategic issues, as well as to develop new weaponry. Fresh thinking about the centrality of science and
technology to military competition and practical steps to
implement these ideas have become ongoing challenges. Major
General Cherednichenko asserts: "The development of military
art during the postwar period has taken place at ever-
increasing rates. . . . It should be noted that substantial
changes in military art have taken place . . . on the average
every six to eight years. At their root is the replacement of
the basic types of weapons by new, more powerful, ones."(3)
Marshal Ogarkov recently underscored the impact of science
and technology upon military theory in these words:

Military art has no right to lag behind the combat
potential of the means of armed struggle, particularly at the present stage, when on the basis of scientific and technological progress the main arms
systems change practically every 10-12 years. In
these conditions, sluggishness, failure to revise
outlooks, and stagnation in the development and
particularly in the practical assimilation of new
methods of utilizing the armed forces in war are
fraught with serious consequences.(4)

Third, the development of strategic rocket forces has
altered the space and time dimensions of conducting and preparing for war. Spatially, the distinction between the front
and the rear is considerably blurred, both in terms of the
nature of strategic operations and of the mounting significance
of the nation's scientific, technological, and economic capabilities as a source of military power.(5) Similarly, the time
factor has been altered substantially by strategic rocket
technology. D.D. Gorbatenko comments: "Time has always
played an important role in military affairs. But today its
importance is by far greater than it ever was in the past.
Nor are we wrong in stating that, in addition to becoming more
vital, time has acquired a new meaning."(6) Specifically,
Soviet analysts consider the temporal dimension to be critical
because the USSR must keep pace with the ongoing process of
strategic modernization, protect its strategic forces against

surprise attack, and maintain its capacity to launch a nuclear blitzkrieg to maximize strategic advantage in the event a war occurs.(7)

Fourth, the accelerating impact of the STR upon industrialized economies and societies in general, and on military institutions, practices, and weapons in particular, means that the superpowers are locked into a scientific and technological rivalry that has become increasingly militarized. Soviet strategists fully recognize that, even with arms control agreements, East-West competition to produce new weapons technology and to refine existing technologies will continue indefinitely and will probably intensify. As Colonel Bondarenko notes,

> Absolute limits for the development of combat technology and weaponry can never be established on the basis of research simply into the capabilities of science and technology. In so far as there are no limits to the knowledge of natural laws, so there are not, nor can there be, limitations to the application of these laws in technological designs. From this point of view, no ultimate, formidable weapon can be called absolute, since the next one can be more powerful, based on the latest achievements of science and technology.(8)

Fifth, the STR poses a formidable challenge to the Soviet military, especially to its strategic forces, because the United States places great emphasis upon developing the military applications of its scientific and technical knowledge. V.V. Borisov asserts that postwar "American leaders have counted on the broad use of the latest achievements of science and technology for military goals . . . ," specifically to maintain American global "hegemony."(9)

The striving by the United States for military-technological superiority has continued throughout the 1970s and is likely to continue throughout the 1980s. Borisov states: "Even in conditions of strategic parity, the U.S. has sought to expand its power on the basis of the growth and development of technologically sophisticated weapons."(10) Similarly, Ogarkov argues that the United States has continued to improve existing strategic systems and to develop new systems for future deployment, even or especially in the conditions of detente.(11) With the downturn of detente in the early 1980s, the United States is expected to place even greater emphasis upon innovative weapons technology, as we will discuss shortly.

Sixth, the USSR has been able to achieve strategic parity in large part because of its technological accomplishments. Arms control agreements could not substitute for decisive inferiority in strategic force technology. Cherednichenko declares:

Possessing powerful strategic nuclear weapons which were kept at a high state of combat readiness, the Soviet Armed Forces acquired the capability of delivering a devastating nuclear response to an aggressor under any and all circumstances, even under conditions of a surprise nuclear attack, and of inflicting on the aggressor a critical level of damage. An unusual situation developed: an aggressor who would initiate a nuclear war would irrevocably be subjected to a devastating retaliatory strike by the other side. It would prove unrealistic for an aggressor to count on victory in such a war, in view of the enormous risk for the aggressor's own continued existence.(12)

Hence, deterrence is thought to depend on Soviet achievements in the development of strategic arms.

Seventh, the high levels of scientific, technological, and economic development in the West, and especially in the United States, are perceived to pose a continuing threat to the Soviet Union. The strategic balance is tenuous and can be upset by major scientific and technological developments. For example, V.M. Kulish maintains that a stand-off between the strategic forces of the USSR and the United States can be characterized only as "an approximate parity," because the balance of power and technological levels are not constant. "They are in continuing motion and are subject to periodic fluctuations and changes in favor of one side or the other. There is every reason to view this balance as a correlation between the strategic nuclear missile might of the two great powers at the present time, and also as a continuing process in the further development of this might."(13)

Significantly, Kulish adds: "The appearance of new types of weapons could seriously affect the balance of military forces between the two world systems. . . . Far-reaching international consequences could arise in the event that one side possessed qualitatively new strategic weapons."(14) To dispel any possible doubt about which side he expected to try to produce such weapons, Kulish concludes: "Even a relatively marginal and brief superiority by the United States over the Soviet Union in the development of certain 'old' or 'new' types and systems of weapons could significantly increase the strategic effectiveness of American military force, exert a destabilizing influence on the international political situation throughout the entire world, and create very unfavorable consequences for the cause of peace and socialism."(15)

Eighth, the use of strategic rocket forces in a future war would severely harm the global environment and human existence. Having extensively examined Soviet sources, Robert Arnett, a Western observer, concludes: "Most Soviet military spokesmen who discuss the consequences of a nuclear war appear to have little doubt that the United States has the capability to inflict unacceptable damage upon the Soviet Union."(16) Furthermore, Sokolovskii, in his authoritative Soviet Military Strategy, declares:

> The losses in a world nuclear war will not only be suffered by the US and its NATO allies, but also by the socialist countries. The logic of a world nuclear war is such that its effects would fall on an over-whelming majority of the world's states. As a result of a war many hundreds of millions of people would perish, and most of those who would remain alive, in one respect or another, would be subject to radioactive contamination. That is why we are talking of the unacceptability of a world nuclear war, of the necessity for its prevention.(17)

Ninth, Soviet analysts maintain that the USSR has entered into strategic arms limitation talks and agreements with the United States for several reasons, at least two of which are directly related to the effects of "the revolution in military affairs." The USSR's first objective is to reduce the risk of nuclear war, which most Soviet commentators consider to be extremely undesirable and avoidable if the USSR can sustain or augment its deterrent capabilities. The USSR's second aim is to introduce a greater predictability into the strategic arms race, and, if possible, to forestall American technological breakthroughs that would prove threatening to Soviet strategic interests.

An arms race fueled by scientific-technological competition is difficult to control by the arms control process alone. V. Karpov, a long-time member and eventually head of the Soviet delegation to the SALT negotiations, and D. Asatiani contend:

> In assessing the basic provisions worked out in the course of the strategic arms limitation talks, we should note the importance of combining quantitative and qualitative limitations. The role of qualitative limitations grows significantly when equal maximum levels of strategic arms are established for both sides, and especially when these levels are reduced. The need to combine quantitative and qualitative limitations is dictated by the principle of equality and mutual security. . . . Qualitative limitations eliminate the possibility that either side might gain a decisive advantage through improvements in arma-ments, even if quantitative limitations remain the same. In other words, there is a constant possibil-ity of a so-called "technological breakthrough" - creation of new forms of weapons which, when placed

in the hands of one of the states participating in the
strategic arms limitation talks, could provide it with
a unilateral advantage.(18)

Soviet officials throughout the Brezhnev period have been
concerned with the possibility of a "technological breakthrough" by the United States in the strategic arms field.
Cherednichenko, writing in 1973, notes: "It is essential to
increase vigilance, to prevent the military superiority of
aggressive forces, to eliminate the possibility of unexpected
major technological achievements on their part."(19) Similarly,
Major General Simonian stated in 1980: "The programs and
practical measures carried out by Washington in its development of strategic nuclear forces show that the development of
qualitatively new weapons is concealed behind the term 'modernization.'"(20) Simonian focuses upon the mobile based MX
missile, the Trident submarine, and the cruise missile as key
threats in this regard.
    In short, Soviet spokesmen affirm that new science-based
technology and its introduction into the military sphere have
produced portentous changes in the substance and style of the
military competition between the United States and the USSR
and in the nature of modern warfare itself. Soviet interpretations are not based upon a simplistic technological determinism, in which victory in war is ensured by scientific and
technological superiority. Instead, Soviet analysts have
developed some distinctive ideas about the reciprocal relationships between technology and politics in socialist and capitalist
states, and they frequently cite the American defeat in Vietnam to support their views.
    First, Soviet officials explicitly deny that their perspec-
tives and policies are based upon the kind of technological
determinism they discern in the thinking of many Western
analysts. The Soviet dialectical approach focuses on the
interaction between scientific, technological, and economic
developments, on the one hand, and political and administrative aims and decisions, on the other.(21) In other words,
Soviet analysts maintain that recent scientific discoveries and
technological innovations are not produced in a sociopolitical
vacuum by random or uncontrollable forces, but that the generation and use of science-based technology are goal directed.
    Second, as the authors of Marxism-Leninism on War and
Army declare, "Nuclear missile weapons are not simply the
result of scientific and technological progress in the United
States. They are the embodiment in 'hardware' of the aggressive antisocialist policies of U.S. imperialism."(22) Human
values and purposes shape the production and utilization of
new technologies in developed socialist societies, too. But
Soviet writers argue that, in contrast to the destructive and
self-serving goals of Western leaders, the CPSU promotes the

interests of all of the people of the USSR, of the Soviet bloc, and of the "progressive" forces throughout the world.

Third, wars are caused by competing social systems that prepare for and resort to armed struggle to further their respective interests. Military-technological competitiveness is a manifestation of the irreconcilable conflict between states with different production relations and superstructures.

Fourth, Soviet analysts contend that advanced technology considerably enhances the importance of the human factor in war. The authors of Marxism-Leninism on War and Army affirm: "The colossal increase in technical possibilities has vastly increased the role of man's ideological, moral-psychological readiness to act in conditions in which nuclear weapons are invoked. The psychological effect of these weapons raises the role of the moral element of the armed forces' combat power. The enormous possibilities of the new equipment have put higher demands on the soldier's military technical standards."(23)

Fifth, Soviet analysts emphasize that the political attitude of the masses toward a nuclear war is absolutely essential to victory, especially in an age of advanced military technological competition which carries with it the threat of nuclear war.(24) M.P. Skirdo asserts: "Successful completion of the truly enormous amount of work involved in the timely preparation of a country for a nuclear missile war is possible only with the active support of the general populace. Only the efforts of the general populace in the course of a war can ensure the fullest realization of the country's economic, moral-political, and military potential."(25)

Sixth, although the strategic arms race is clearly fueled by a science-based technological competition, the political consequences of this competition are of primary importance, according to Soviet spokesmen. On the one hand, an arms race focused on advanced technology ensures that only the United States and the USSR will achieve superpower status. As S.A. Tiushkevich puts it: "Only those industrially developed states with a high degree of concentration of production and broad production relations among specialized sectors, with large reserves of natural and energy resources and a large population, can take part in the revolutionary transformation in military affairs. The United States and the USSR are such states, and to a significantly greater extent than any other states."(26)

On the other hand, Soviet analysts view strategic parity as the sine qua non for successful political competition and cooperation with the West. William Husband, a Western student of Soviet interpretations of American diplomacy in the 1970s, notes: "No single factor dominates the Soviet explanation of the improved climate for cooperation which began to develop at the outset of the present decade. Foremost, of course, is the claim that the Soviets achieved strategic parity by 1970. The importance of this factor is paramount; without it, the possibilities for cooperation would have been even more severely limited than they have been."(27)

In short, Soviet officials, military analysts, and foreign relations specialists recognize the crucial impact of the STR on military affairs, while emphasizing the political context and the political implications of competitive coexistence or detente. Colin Gray, a Western military analyst, reiterates that the East-West strategic arms race is political in character.(28) But the technological competition in general, and especially its effects on the strategic weapons competition, are central elements of Soviet perspectives about the changing international system, the causes and consequences of the STR, and the need for innovative political and military policies. Hence, Gray underestimates the significance of advanced technology in the thinking and policy recommendations of military analysts in the USSR.(29)

Soviet spokesmen view science-based technology as the most dynamic force in the strategic arms race. To be sure, an ever-changing geostrategic balance is thought to be a critical component of the ongoing political competition between the United States and the USSR. But Soviet officials are very sensitive to the political and military consequences of destabilizing technologies, and to the political and military implications of technological lags in the strategic weapons competition.

Briefly stated, Soviet leaders and commentators emphasize that a reciprocal relationship exists between scientific and technological development, on the one hand, and Soviet and American political and military capabilities, on the other hand. It is to a further analysis of this relationship which we now turn.

THE IMPACT OF THE STR UPON THE NATURE OF
MILITARY CAPABILITIES

Soviet military theorists underscore that the STR has produced fundamental transformations in military competition in the post-World War II period. Writing in the authoritative Soviet Military Encyclopedia, M.M. Kir'ian asserts: "Basic qualitative changes are occurring under the influence of scientific and technological progress and by the further development of the productive forces. These changes are affecting the instruments of combat, the organization and preparation of military personnel, and the means of conducting war and military activity."(30) The revolution in military affairs is "a consequence of the STR and the transformation of science into a direct productive force. Science is increasingly linked to the

production process, which creates fundamental changes in the
material-technological basis of production."(31)

Soviet analysts assess the significance of "the STR in
military affairs" on two levels.

On the broader or infrastructural level, the STR is
viewed as a process that is altering the political and military
capabilities of the USSR and other advanced industrial states.
As Bondarenko puts it, "The USSR's defense capability can be
increased only in the context of the ongoing STR in our country."(32)   Similarly, Defense Minister Ustinov argues: "On the
basis of the achievements of the STR, together with the advantages of developed socialism, the party has developed
economic strategies and a program of social transformation in
the interests of building communism.   Their implementation also
reliably promotes the strengthening of the country's defense
capability."(33)   General Pavlovskii adds: "Successes in the
development of the Soviet economy, science, and technology
are steadily moving our society forward along the path of
creating the material and technical bases of communism.   At
the same time, they are helping to strengthen the material
basis of the country's defense capability."(34)

On the narrower or sectoral level, the STR is thought to
have introduced a multitude of important changes in military
weapons, command and control systems, the scope and nature
of military management, and military organization.   Ogarkov
affirms: "In modern conditions the rapid development of science, technology, and the economy makes it possible to create
relatively quickly new models of armaments and combat hardware, which, upon reaching the troops, bring about an objective need for changes and developments in the existing forms
and methods of armed struggle, and which, in turn, require
the further improvement of the organizational structure of the
army and navy and of methods of controlling troops."(35)   Or,
as Marshal Moskalenko succinctly declares: "Successes in the
development of the socialist economy and achievements in the
sphere of science and technology have made possible substantial qualitative transformations in all spheres of military
affairs."(36)

In the present section we will examine Soviet perspectives
on the general effects of the STR upon the modern state and
its capacity to conduct and avert wars.   In the next section
we will focus upon more specific aspects of "the revolution in
military affairs."

Soviet officials maintain that the STR has decisively
influenced the components of national security in both developed socialist and advanced capitalist societies.   Scientific,
technological, economic, organizational, and social levels of
development are now having a much greater effect on military
capabilities.   Ustinov asserts: "The party strictly follows
Lenin's teaching about the dialectical unity of economic,

scientific, technical, and moral-political potentials as the basic components of the defense might of the state. And in the present organic combination of these components, this unity has become even more close and multifaceted."(37)

Soviet analysts contend that in order to enhance the military capabilities of industrialized communist and capitalist societies, several factors are critical.

The first element of growth is the dynamic economic potential of a nation. G.S. Kravchenko, writing in Soviet Military Encyclopedia, views economic potential as "the state's capabilities to provide for the material needs of life and the development of society, as well as for everything necessary in case of war. . . . In general, economic potential is express-ed in the level and volume of social production and in the tempo and possibilities for its further growth."(38)

Soviet theorists affirm that the STR is dramatically altering the preconditions, nature, and consequences of eco-nomic development in the East and West. New factors of eco-nomic development - science, technology, and organizational rationalization - have become essential to further economic growth and productivity in the USSR. That is, the key chal-lenges to which the Soviet economy must respond are the ad-vances in science and technology, the need for managerial and organizational adaptation, and the generation and utilization of more and better information of numerous kinds.

Several Soviet military analysts have stressed the impor-tance of shifting from "extensive" to "intensive" economic growth to meet Soviet security needs. For example, Colonel Bartenev affirms: "An extremely important feature of the party's economic policy . . . is the augmentation of the role played by intensive economic growth factors. This means altering national proportions and improving the advanced sectors. This economic policy is also consistent with the need to develop defense production."(39)   Bartenev concludes: "Highly dynamic economic development and a national economy capable of reacting flexibly and efficiently to changing circumstances are becoming increasingly important today."(40) Similarly, Pavlovskii notes: "The CPSU's economic strategy, which takes real account of the internal and external con-ditions and opportunities for strengthening the economic foundations of the Soviet state's defense capability, is now exerting considerable influence on the safeguarding of the country's defense. In this important matter, special signifi-cance is attached to the course steered by the party toward improving the quality of output and the efficiency of social production."(41)

The Soviet Minister of Defense has been a vigorous advo-cate of the primacy of "intensive" factors of economic growth to meet existing and anticipated security needs. In a recent collection of Ustinov's speeches and writings, he frequently underscores the importance of the economic preconditions of military preparedness.(42) Ustinov deems the traditional heavy industrial base vital to the Soviet economy, but he does not consider heavy industry to be the most "progressive" sector of a modern economy. He contends that the scientific, high-technology, and educational sectors are even more critical for economic development and national security in advanced industrial societies.

Moreover, Ustinov stresses that improved methods of economic planning and management must be introduced in the USSR in order to sustain economic growth and productivity. He asserts: "In contemporary conditions, when the Soviet economy is entering a new stage of development that is characterized by the rapid advance of the STR and by powerful productive forces, the complex tasks confronting our economy compel it to develop on the basis of fundamental qualitative shifts in all spheres of social production."(43) A Soviet reviewer of Ustinov's work concludes: "In a profound and universal fashion, this book analyzes the dependence of the defense preparedness of our state upon the level of economic development."(44)

The second element of growth is the dynamic scientific potential of a nation. According to Bondarenko, writing in Soviet Military Encyclopedia, scientific potential is "the capacity of science to solve effectively short-term and long-range tasks that confront society."(45) Moreover, "the possibilities of science are characterized by the quantitative and qualitative indicators that express the level of scientific activity in a country."(46)

Scientific capabilities are reflected in such quantitative indicators as the number of scientific workers, the extent of economic resources allocated to basic and applied scientific research, and the economic resources committed to the training and motivation of scientists. But the funds and human energies devoted to scientific progress are not boundless in advanced societies. Social theorist Afanas'ev observes: "The possibilities for extensive development of science are limited. Society cannot indefinitely increase the share of the national income devoted to science and to the expansion of the scientific research force. Hence, there is an urgent need for the intensification of science - that is, for the saving of time spent on scientific investigations and their technological applications, and for more efficient work by individual researchers and scientific collectives."(47)

Soviet analysts contend that a country's scientific potential in the era of the STR is manifested above all in the qualitative dimensions of scientific activity. Effective and efficient use of scientific resources is a critical dimension of the current worldwide shift from the extensive to the intensive phase of scientific progress. Among the dimensions of the

transition from the extensive (quantitative) to the intensive
(qualitative) development of R&D, Afanas'ev underscores:

> Increased effectiveness through improved methods
> and means of research, further specialization and
> cooperation of the work of researchers and research
> teams, improvement of their equipment and experi-
> mental base, gradual mechanization and automation of
> research, improved organization and management of
> scientific work, and the strengthening of communica-
> tion links between science and production and be-
> tween science and all of social life.(48)

In short, Soviet commentators stress the importance of
broadening and deepening scientific capabilities to meet the
ongoing defense needs of the state. The fast-paced and multifaceted advance of science is thought to be decisively affecting
social development in general and military affairs in particular.
Bondarenko notes that one of the key aspects of the contemporary relationship between scientific progress and national
defense is "the expansion of the scientific sectors that impact
upon the development of military affairs. These include
practically the entire sweep of scientific knowledge."(49)
Moreover, scientific research must become increasingly productive in order to meet the USSR's changing and growing sociopolitical and military needs. Bondarenko adds: "The level of
the effectiveness of scientific research and the tempo of its
intensification is a major indicator of the scientific potential of
a country and an element of its military-scientific potential as
well."(50)

The third element of growth is the dynamic technological
potential of a nation. In advanced societies, science-based
production drives the innovative process. Soviet analysts
stress that the transition from a recently industrialized
economy to a developed socialist economy rests upon the growing "scientization" of technological development. Science as "a
direct productive force" is considered to be a factor decisively
affecting economic performance. A. Kuzin asserts: "The essence of the present-day STR is the transformation of science
qua science through its application to the productive process."(51)

R&D is the key to greater growth and productivity in the
mature socialist economy, according to Soviet commentators.
The most important dimensions of the economic development of
socialist society are "the creation of conditions for the further
expansion of the comprehensive mechanization, automation, and
cybernetization of production, the optimal concentration and
specialization of production so that the latest achievements of
science and technology can be used more fully and efficiently,
and the steady growth of the productivity of labor."(52)   All
of these factors are part of the current efforts to shift from

extensive to intensive methods of economic development in the USSR. This shift has been made necessary by the highly complex interdependencies among modern economic planning, production, and management mechanisms, by the growing scarcity of certain manpower and material resources, and by the increasing mutual benefits of scientific-technical and economic cooperation between the Soviet Union and other socialist and nonsocialist nations.

Nurturing technological innovation in the economy and society is crucial to the enhancement of military capabilities and to the conceptualization and implementation of effective defense policies. Because of the multifaceted East-West rivalry, and because of the impending scarcities in material and human resources in the USSR, the Soviet armed forces and defense-related industries are at the forefront of the campaign to shift from extensive to intensive development. As Colonel Kozlov puts it, "Under present-day conditions, in connection with the military-technological revolution, it is no longer sufficient merely to possess great production capacity; it is vitally essential to possess the most modern, unique branches of industry. . . . Products of a totally different quality are demanded of the traditional branches."(53)

Significantly, Soviet analysts recognize that the capacity of societies to innovate is becoming a crucial factor in the competition between socialist and capitalist states. Progress is increasingly defined with reference to creativity and dynamism in the scientific-technological sphere, and to the capacity to integrate indigenous and imported discoveries and inventions into a society, economy, or polity with a minimum of short- or long-term "negative" effects. These negative consequences are usually broadly defined to include ecological, as well as cultural, social, economic, and political, repercussions. Furthermore, Soviet theorists and officials clearly perceive that the task of coping with the harmful and unpredictable side-effects of the STR is an ongoing responsibility. Decisions cannot be made once and for all, because "problem situations" are rarely resolved fully or permanently. Hence, Khrushchev's exuberant optimism and emotional exhortations to the public have given way to Brezhnev's sober confidence, lowering of targets and expectations, and emphasis on durable cooperative relationships among policy groups and institutions. The collective leadership has persistently looked for more empirically grounded approaches and technically competent personnel to help manage complex, interrelated, and recurring public policy choices.

Current Soviet leaders recognize that a decisive change has taken place in man's role in production - notably, in the increasing need for applied scientific knowledge, rather than increments of physical labor, to spur economic growth and productivity. This change, in turn, necessitates different forms of management, or, at the very least, considerably improved functioning of existing planning and management mechanisms. New approaches must be capable of combining innovations in the scientific-technical sphere with feasible social goals and with the evolving social structure of society. Soviet analysts declare: "The progress of science, technology, and production continuously places people, directly or indirectly, in situations that require a ramified but at the same time efficient managerial apparatus and constant flexible intervention in the affairs of society."(54)

The fourth element of growth is the dynamic moral-political potential of a nation. V.A. Karnoukhov, writing in Soviet Military Encyclopedia, defines this potential as "the spiritual possibilities of a country's populace that reflect, in turn, the definite stage of development of the political and moral consciousness of the people, and that can be understood as a factor in achieving social, economic, political, and military goals."(55) The moral-political potential refers, on the one hand, to the citizens' attitudes toward their government, and, on the other hand, to the citizens' social relationships, skills, and level of educational and cultural development.

The commitment of a population to its way of life and to its government as the articulator and defender of that way of life are critical factors in determining victory in war. As N.A. Lomov comments, "The moral-political potential of a country . . . is expressed in the response of a people to a war and in the degree of their unity with the ruling party and its government."(56) Although economic, scientific, and technological developments do not determine the nature of the bond between the populace and government, such developments are important contributors to the legitimacy of a modern state. Furthermore, economic or technological shortcomings may have decisive effects on the "spiritual" factor in the case of war. As I.E. Shavrov and M.I. Galkin affirm, "Technological superiority that is expressed in terms of new weapons, the quality of armaments, and the level of their deployment can increase or decrease the moral factor."(57)

The moral-political factor refers as well to the level of professional skill and educational development. Christopher Jones, an American who has studied Soviet views on the moral factor in war, observes: "Contrary to some Western theorists, the Soviets argue that technology does not reduce the importance of man in war but actually heightens the importance of the human factor, because advanced technology demands greater skills."(58) This theme is frequently interspersed Major General Il'in's authoritative work, The Moral Factor in Contemporary War. Il'in declares: "One of the fundamental conditions for the successful realization of the profound revolutionary transformation in the military sphere, which is based on new arms and weapons technology, is the growth of

the ideological-political maturity and technological culture of
the Soviet soldier."(59)

No greater testimony to the impact of technology upon
military competition is the emphasis that Soviet commentators
on the moral-political factor in military affairs have given to
technological innovation. Il'in notes in an important article in
Voennaia mysl':

> Radical transformations in military affairs take place
> not only as a result of social revolutions, but also
> owing to the sharp jump in the development of
> equipment which is transforming the technical base
> of the army. Specifically, this is characteristic of
> the revolution now taking place in military affairs.
> Its origins are the further development of the
> productive forces of society and the unprecedented
> acceleration of scientific-technical progress. . . .
> The fact that this revolution is related to the rapid
> development of technology and not to social revo-
> lution to a considerable extent overshadows its
> political essence and class nature. Owing to this,
> the present revolution can only be understood as a
> natural result of the development of technology and
> the achieving of new heights in the field of science,
> all the more so since it has essentially taken place at
> the same time both in our country and in leading
> imperialist countries.(60)

Thus, innovative approaches to scientific, technological,
economic, and moral-political challenges are increasingly central
to Soviet perceptions of security in the broadest sense. The
development of the military capability of a state depends upon
the growth of its scientific, technological, economic, and
moral-political potentials. Bondarenko notes:

> The contemporary stage of scientific-technical
> progress is changing the qualitative level of produc-
> tion. Its structure is being improved, new branches
> are appearing, and the list of products and qualita-
> tive indices of production of the traditional branches
> of industry are changing. Today the situation is
> such that the lagging of any separate branch of
> production, even with a small but important volume
> of output, may influence in the most serious manner
> the overall capabilities of industry in the production
> of defense-related goods.(61)

Similarly, a Pravda editorial observes: "The strengthening of
our country's defense is carried out on the basis of further
increasing the Soviet state's economic might, developing
science and technology, and the continued flourishing of the
people's spiritual potential."(62)

Greater military capability is an expression of organizational and managerial effectiveness as well. Much of Soviet
thinking about the STR has revolved around the question of
improving organizational and managerial effectiveness, especially in the scientific, technological, and economic sectors.

Soviet analysts have developed various approaches to the
general problem of managerial innovation in the context of the
STR. Managerial effectiveness can be increased through the
introduction of new technologies, such as computers. Also,
managerial effectiveness can be enhanced by new techniques of
formulating and executing administrative tasks, such as the
use of systems analysis and goal-oriented methods of management. In addition, the development of a science of management to guide the education, retraining, and practical activity
of executives is deemed necessary to increase administrative
effectiveness and efficiency.

Furthermore, Soviet officials have begun to "rethink the
organizational weapon." Paul Cocks elaborates: "The STR has
posed the issue of governmental effectiveness in new terms.
In the 1970s, the USSR has placed increasing emphasis on the
urgency of administrative improvement for national development, and on the need to enhance managerial capabilities in
coping with problems of advancing technology and complexity."(63)

A critical dimension of increased governmental effectiveness is the management of information. The generation and
use of information are means of augmenting power and are
thought to be absolutely essential if the party-state is to lead
and to administer successfully in the era of the STR. Power
is gained by expanding and utilizing all the sources and types
of information about current policies, political-administrative
procedures, and the domestic and international environments.
Power is increased by obtaining the data needed to formulate
feasible short-range plans and long-range options concerning
substantive policies and priorities. And power rests upon an
ability to translate information flows into decisions, and to
reassess outcomes continuously, adjusting decisions and decisionmaking processes, if necessary, in light of changing
sociopolitical, economic, and scientific-technical conditions.

To master the STR, the information-processing capabilities
of a developed socialist society must grow tremendously,
according to Soviet analysts. They consider the generation
and use of information to be vital means of enhancing the
leaders' capability to control and coordinate complex subsys-
tems and to review periodically strategic policy and its
implementation. The managers of information must possess
political acumen, foresight based on the social and physical
sciences, and sophisticated technology. Hence, more flexible
and integrated policymaking and administrative procedures,
differentiated approaches to problem identification and solving,

and a heightened degree of sensitivity or responsiveness to diverse environments are viewed as sources of power, not of vulnerability, in the current advanced stage of socialism.

In short, Soviet leaders and theorists conclude that managerial and organizational capabilities will determine how effectively a developed socialist society can fulfill its growing political, economic, social, and military potentials and needs. Soviet commentators frequently stress the military importance of administrative and economic development. Kozlov, for example, comments:

> An important area for securing national defense capacity is continuous improvement in the system of economic management, ensuring an efficient system of production specialization and cooperative manufacture, as well as coordinated functioning of all elements in the economic system. Lenin noted that only a strengthening of the foundations of the socialist society, a balanced coordination of the nation's productive resources and production management constitute "the way to create military strength and socialist power."(64)

Similarly, Colonels Trushin and Gladkov observed shortly after the Kosygin economic reforms of 1965: "The economic reforms implemented in the USSR are aimed at strengthening the economic, and, it follows, the defensive power of the country, based upon scientifically founded plans. [National defense] calls for an increase in the efficiency of all social production, based upon economic stimulation and the scientific organization of national-economic administration."(65)

We will now examine more fully Soviet thinking about the impact of science and technology on the nature of and preparation for war.

THE IMPACT OF THE STR ON WARFARE AND THE PREPARATION FOR WAR

In the official Soviet view, the pursuit and attainment of strategic goals result in "a radical change in the military, political, and strategic situation during a war as a whole or in a theater of hostilities."(66) Moreover, "the revolution in military affairs" makes it necessary continuously to reassess Soviet war-fighting and deterrent capabilities.

New weapons technologies have introduced a qualitative change in the Soviet concept of strategic power. Indeed, the nuclear weapons and rocket delivery systems associated with the early phases of the STR in the 1950s have become equated with strategic power. For example, Soviet Military Encyclopedia defines strategic arms as those "different types of rocket nuclear arms and the technical means and systems of control and defense that are designed to meet strategic goals in war."(67)

Soviet analysts have repeatedly emphasized the qualitative impact of the STR on the conduct of war, on the preparation for war, and on the deterrence of war. Hence, the authoritative Soviet Armed Forces affirms:

> The essence of the revolution in military affairs is a
> sharp and profound transformation in the use of
> nuclear rockets as a means of struggle and of other
> corresponding means to achieve strategic goals in
> war. Combining nuclear weapons with rockets and
> automated control systems has led to the creation of
> new types of weapons - nuclear rocket weapons in
> which nuclear warheads are launched by interconti-
> nental ballistic missiles. These weapons have
> changed previous ideas about the processes of pre-
> paring for the conduct of war, the roles and signifi-
> cance of time and space in these processes, the
> theaters of military activity, the correlation between
> types of weapons and types of wars, and the char-
> acter of the interrelationships necessary to prepare
> for war.(68)

Impact of the STR on the Nature of a General War

The revolution in military affairs has decisively affected the nature of a general war. According to former Defense Minister Grechko, "The appearance of nuclear missiles radically changed the old concepts of the speed and processes of war and fundamentally changed the traditional role and significance of time and space."(69) In other words, the STR is thought to have significantly altered the strategies, tactics, and material components of modern warfare.

Soviet analysts affirm that the temporal dimension of warfare has changed in five crucial ways.

First, strategic weapons can have profound effects in a very brief time span. Indeed, Sokolovskii argues that the essence of military strategy in the contemporary period is critically influenced by the temporal dimension: "Military strategy under conditions of modern war becomes the strategy of deep nuclear rocket strikes in conjunction with the operations of all services of the armed forces, in order to effect a simultaneous defeat of the armed forces and the destruction of the economic potential throughout the enemy territory, thus accomplishing the war aims within a short time period."(70)

Second, a strategic exchange would create a highly dynamic situation. Nuclear war makes necessary the speedy and ongoing reassessment of goals and tactics. According to Major General Begunov, "The chief content of a strategic maneuver is the redirection of nuclear strikes and nuclear groupings for the fast and complete destruction of large enemy groupings and the achievement of strategic results."(71)

Third, the coordination of a wide range of activities by diverse elements of the armed forces is crucial to the successful execution of military strategy during a nuclear war. V. Mernov and A. Bogomolov assert: "There will be an especially fast change in the situation in the course of a battle or operation in a nuclear war, when the development of combat operations are combined with the broadest use of various methods of armed struggle and types of maneuvers."(72) Under such conditions, command and control capability becomes a vital dimension of military power. As Joseph Douglass, a Western analyst, underscores: "In the Soviet Union, command and control receive as much attention as any major weapon system. Following the nuclear warhead, long-range means of delivery, and the troops themselves, it is viewed as the single most important element of the Soviet military forces."(73)

Fourth, the extraordinary changes that would quickly occur in the event of nuclear war require the development and refinement of a highly effective military force structure or mix of forces. In the context of the revolution in military affairs, this means that the strategic rocket forces must play a critical role. Pavlovskii declares: "The strategic rocket forces that have most fully absorbed the achievements of contemporary scientific-technological progress form the basis of the defensive might of the Soviet armed forces."(74) Moreover, Soviet analysts stress the importance of integrating the strategic rocket forces within the overall force structure. Party and military leaders do not rely only upon strategic forces and the assurance of mutual vulnerability. Instead, Soviet spokesmen have repeatedly emphasized the need to prepare for massive ground-based theater operations to achieve victory if war occurs.(75) Skirdo, for one, affirms: "The course and outcome of an armed struggle will be strongly affected not only by such factors as the suddenness of the attack and the force of the first nuclear strike, but also by the shift of the economy to a wartime footing, by the preparation of the theaters of military operations, and by the degree of readiness of the armed forces and the populace for war under the new conditions."(76) Or, as Steve Kime, a Western commentator, observes: "Mass, not sophistication, is the Soviet 'style' of superiority. Nevertheless, the Soviets never surrender in the technological race, particularly insofar as nuclear missiles are concerned."(77)

Fifth, Soviet strategists underscore that the element of surprise is increasingly important in modern warfare. Marshal Moskalenko asserts: "In view of the immense destructive force of nuclear weapons and the extremely limited time available to take effective countermeasures after an enemy launches its missiles, the launching of the first massed nuclear attack acquires decisive importance for achieving the objectives of war."(78)   Similarly, Colonel Larionov notes: "The first surprise nuclear missile strikes can cause unprecedented destruction, exterminate tremendous numbers of troops in places of their usual quartering, and destroy a significant part of the populations of large cities."(79)

Nonetheless, Soviet sensitivity to the importance of surprise in a nuclear war does not constitute advocacy of preemption as a desirable goal or tactic to ensure the victory of socialism in its historical contest with capitalism. Formidable problems are thought to impede the successful implementation of a preemptive strategy. As Marshal Krylov, writing in Voennaia mysl', declares:

> It must be stressed that in present conditions, when the Soviet Armed Forces are in constant combat readiness, any aggressor who begins a nuclear war will not remain unpunished; a severe and inevitable punishment awaits him. With the presence in the armament of troops of launchers and missiles which are completely ready for operation, as well as systems for detecting enemy missile launchers and other types of reconnaissance, an aggressor is no longer able suddenly to destroy the missiles before they are launched from the territory of the country against which the aggression is committed. They will have time during the flight of the missile of the aggressor to leave their launchers and inflict a retaliatory strike against the enemy. Even in the most unfavorable circumstances, if a portion of missiles is unable to be launched before the strike of missiles of the aggressor, as a result of the high degree of protection of the launchers from the nuclear explosion, these missiles will be retained and will carry out the combat missions entrusted to them.
>
> Thus, in modern conditions, with the presence of a system for detecting missile launches, an attempt by the aggressor to inflict a sudden preemptory strike cannot give him a decisive advantage for the achievement of victory in war and, in any case, will not save him from great destruction and human losses. Moreover, in a number of cases the aggressor will have to pay with even a greater amount of destruction and victims.(80)

Protection against the possibility of a surprise attack is crucial to successful deterrence. Lieutenant General Gareev observes that "the most important task of the Soviet Army and Navy [since the 1960s] was to prevent a surprise nuclear attack and to ensure annihilation of the aggressor if he dared initiate a war against our country."(81)

Hence, prevention of a surprise nuclear attack and maximization of the capability of the USSR to strike first if a war appears unavoidable and inevitable are deemed to be legitimate goals for Soviet military policy. Major General Vasendin and Colonel Kuznetsov affirm:

Any aggressor risks unleasing a nuclear war only with confidence of achieving victory. And confidence in the success of a nuclear attack can occur in conditions whereby there is a sufficiently high guarantee that nuclear strikes will be delivered to the objectives of destruction, that a mass launch of ballistic missiles and takeoff of aircraft will occur for a relatively long time undetected by the country against which the attack is being carried out, and that the armed, forces, and above all the strategic nuclear means of the enemy, will suffer such destruction that they will be incapable of carrying out a powerful retaliatory nuclear strike. In order to eliminate the possibility of such a favorable situation for the aggressor and deprive him of the temptation to risk the unleashing of a nuclear war, it is necessary to maintain strategic nuclear means in constant high combat readiness, dispersed and well concealed, and to have a reliable system of early warning of a mass launch of strategic missiles and takeoff of strategic aircraft, as well as effective means of combating the nose cones of ballistic missiles and the aircraft of the enemy.(82)

In short, Soviet analysts stress that numerous temporal factors decisively influence the nature of modern warfare.

Furthermore, Soviet writers contend that the spatial dimension of warfare has changed in five crucial ways.

First, the distinction between front and rear has become blurred. Strategic weapons can strike key targets deep in the rear. In nuclear wars, according to Sokolovskii, "The annihilation of the enemy's armed forces, the destruction of capabilities in the rear areas, and disorganization of the interior will be a single continuous process."(83)

Second, the revolution in military affairs has redefined the nature of the targets that are considered to be strategic in nature. Soviet analysts maintain that strategic objectives include political, administrative, economic, and scientific centers, not just military forces per se. Especially significant targets are the command and control centers of the adversary or adversaries. Colonel Shirokov states: "Under conditions of a nuclear war, the system for controlling forces and weapons, especially strategic weapons, acquires exceptionally great significance. A disruption of the control over a country and its troops in a theater of military operations can seriously affect the course of events, and in difficult circumstances can even lead to defeat in a war."(84)

Third, the need to protect command centers and key industrial sectors underscores the importance of civilian and strategic defense systems to ensure continued war-fighting capability after the initial nuclear exchange.(85)

Fourth, submarine launched ballistic missiles also expand the spatial scope of strategic conflict. Admiral Gorshkov, for example, asserts:

> Scientific and technical progress has produced submarines as the most perfect carrier of modern weapons, the launching site of which is in effect the whole World Ocean. The fleet concentrates in itself numerous mobile carriers of strategic weapons, each of which may carry a very large number of long-range missiles and is capable of maneuvering with launching sites over an area exceeding many times the area which land-based missile troops can use. Sea carriers of strategic means also possess the ability to maneuver in depth, sheltering themselves by width of water and using it not only for protection but also for masking, which greatly adds to the viability of naval strategic weapons systems. Thus, objective conditions of armed conflict in a nuclear war produce as a strike nuclear missile force the missile-carrying fleet, rationally combining the latest achievements of science and technology, enormous strike power and mobility, viable strategic means and high readiness for their immediate use.(86)

Gorshkov concludes: "In the course of the scientific-technical revolution, naval forces have assumed the significance of one of the most important strategic factors, capable by direct action on enemy groupings of troops and vitally important objectives on his territory, of exerting a very considerable and sometimes decisive influence on the course of war."(87)

Fifth, outer space has become an increasingly important domain of military activity, both in terms of potential weapons deployments (e.g., lasers) and of communication and control capabilities. Sokolovskii stresses that "the concept of the 'geographic expanse' of war will have to be substantially broadened in the future, inasmuch as military operations may embrace outer space."(88)

In short, Soviet analysts emphasize that both the temporal and spatial dimensions of war are changing and are, in turn, increasing the significance of military leadership and management in preparing for and conducting modern warfare. Effective command and control are essential to the successful outcome of a future nuclear war, and the quality of military leadership and management is in itself a strategic factor of profound significance.

Military leadership is perceived to be more and more challenging and multifaceted in the era of the STR. Ogarkov observes: "The management of military forces in contemporary conditions is increasingly complex due to the unending growth in the volume of work confronting the organs of strategic decisionmaking, and the time for meeting these tasks is shortened."(89)

Although the development and deployment of new weapons systems have placed greater demands upon military officials, new technologies and methods of management have emerged to ease the burdens of leadership.(90)

Cybernetic technology has become a critical means of expanding managerial capabilities.(91) Computers greatly facilitate the processing of diverse information. Without such technology it would be impossible to compete in modern warfare, because the informational demands on decisionmakers far exceed the capacity of leaders unaided by computers.

Also, automated systems of management are an important "higher" stage of cybernetic development that is crucial for command and control decisions in a future nuclear war.(92) The automated management of war couples cybernetic technology with rationalized methods of management. New management methods are deemed critical to the effective fulfillment of managerial tasks in wartime. War modeling and operations research, for example, are attempts to improve military command performance. Operations research helps to obtain a more accurate picture of the dynamic changes in battlefield conditions, so as to determine the most effective uses for the remaining military forces.

Hence, Soviet strategists maintain that the revolution in military affairs has introduced significant qualitative changes in the nature of war. These changes, in turn, create ongoing pressures for military modernization and for higher levels of defense preparedness to deter, survive, or win a modern war. It is the impact of new technologies upon the continuous preparation for war to which we now turn.

Impact of the STR on the Nature of Military Preparedness

The dynamic revolution in military affairs has decisively shaped the nature, scope, and significance of the tasks of military preparedness. According to Soviet analysts, national defense has changed in three major ways.

First, dramatic qualitative advances in science and technology are continuously taking place in both the United States and the USSR. The high probabilities of breakthroughs on the scientific front and their application in new weapons or managerial systems have created a sense of uncertainty and urgency in both nations. As Major General Parkhomenko notes:

> It can be stated with certainty that during the life span of a weapons system inventions and discoveries will occur that make obsolete certain principles underlying existing weapons systems. This creates the necessary prerequisites for continuous improvement in weapons and rapid obsolescence of systems already developed or in a state of development. Moreover, there is the possibility of unanticipated or sudden use by the enemy of improved weapons, embodying the latest advances in science and technology. The element of technical surprise has always existed and will always exist in military science, and is one of the reasons for secrecy in the development of new weapons, even though major scientific-technical discoveries, representing a basic improvement in weaponry, rapidly become joint property in the scientific community. The essence of the matter is how rapidly and completely the enemy succeeds in incorporating these discoveries in the design of his weapons.(93)

In a word, qualitative competition and challenges are ongoing and open-ended. There is no final plateau for East-West technological rivalry in the military sphere.

Second, continuous improvement of military management is required to cope with change and to promote strategic and technical innovation. Altukhov states: "In connection with the new [scientific and technological] conditions, great significance is attached to developing indicators and criteria for evaluating the effectiveness of military management, and to developing methods of analyzing the problems of management that conform to contemporary demands."(94)

Third, the changes associated with the development of science-based weapons and with the improvement of managerial capabilities are part of the ongoing process of strategic rethinking. These changes have made necessary the constant reconceptualization of national security and the means of achieving it. Moreover, new strategic ideas must be implemented in an exceedingly fluid and competitive international environment. Hence, technological advances do not necessarily enhance, let alone ensure, national security - in fact and/or in the eyes of leading policymakers. Because military strength must always be measured in relation to that of one's enemies, and because the qualitative dimension of military competition is much more difficult to interpret and predict than the quantitative, the linkages between technological breakthroughs and defense capabilities are often uncertain and short-lived.

The development of more and more sophisticated weapon systems and management methods creates the need continuously to redefine existing missions and to reshape existing force structures. Sokolovskii and Cherednichenko declare:

> The theory of strategy must always take into account the progress of technology, or else it will fall behind. Military strategy must generalize and analyze the laws and tendencies of the development of technology, develop a single line of technical improvement, and actively influence its realization on the basis of strictly economic calculations. The selection and substantiation of variants of development of systems of armament and military equipment and the determination of their effectiveness is a new and important component part of the theory of strategy. It determines the most technically progressive and economically effective directions and provides proportionality and completeness to the development of equipment. It is well known that improvement of the means of armed struggle leads to changes in strategy; at the same time strategy plays an active role in the development of technical policies.(95)

That is, strategic thinking must promote, as well as react to, changes in technology and technique. Batitskii comments: "Continuing scientific and technical progress demands that we conceive clearly the trends in military matters and correctly determine the ways and means further to improve the troops' combat readiness. The importance of military science, which has become one of the most important factors in strengthening the country's defense capability, is now greater than ever before."(96)

In short, leading Soviet officials maintain that the nature of military preparedness is inextricably intertwined with the optimal development and deployment of modern weapons systems, the maximization of managerial effectiveness, and the development and refinement of an effective military strategy.

Moreover, Soviet strategists contend that military power in the age of the STR is increasingly dependent upon scientific discoveries and technological innovations, on the one hand, and their application to the theory and practice of warfare, on the other. To link the development of science and technology with the development of military capabilities entails the resolution of eight key challenges.

First, the scientific component of military-technology policy must be continuously nurtured. For example, Bondarenko emphasizes the need for a broad research effort to enhance defense capabilities. Bondarenko argues that the "military-scientific potential" of an advanced state is affected by developments in all fields of scientific knowledge. He affirms that this capability must be used "in the interests of increasing the military power of the state."(97) According to Bondarenko, the R&D organizations directly involved in the defense effort will be influenced by the overall scientific performance of both civilian and military institutions. "There are a whole range of possibilities for strengthening the level of the country's defense through the creation of optimal relationships between the country's system of scientific institutions and its system of military R&D and design organizations."(98) The improvement of these linkages has been a major goal of the Brezhnev administration.(99) But some Soviet analysts, such as Bondarenko, recognize that there is room for considerably better integration of civilian and military R&D efforts.

Second, the science-technology-production cycle in the military sphere is considered crucial to defense preparedness.(100) In fact, Pavlovskii contends that the improvement of military R&D is a central challenge confronting Soviet leaders in present-day conditions. Pavlovskii states:

> The interests of the USSR armed forces' combat readiness and the reliable defense of the Soviet state require that there should be no easing-up on the scientific research front, that scientific research and experimental design work should continue to create promising models of arms and combat equipment, and that the time taken for the introduction of the results of scientific research into production should be reduced.
>
> This is particularly important now that the material base of the army and navy is fundamentally changing as a result of the intensifying scientific and technological revolution, that weapons are becoming increasingly expensive, and that military equipment is becoming obsolete more rapidly. Therefore, the planning organs at all levels should stipulate and do everything possible to ensure that the leading industrial sectors constantly and rapidly

modernize technology and create fundamentally new
weapons, while the scientific research institutes and
design bureaus, in developing promising military
forms of technology, should investigate more profoundly the secrets of the future, carefully assess
the trends and natural laws of the development of
arms, correctly analyze their consequences, and take
into account the technical achievements of related
sectors of the economy. As a whole, we must presently consider the fact that questions of scientific
forecasting, comprehensive long-term planning, and
the determination of the optimum correlation between
different types of arms and military equipment
acquire paramount significance and are a most important factor in our armed forces' combat might.(101)

Soviet officials divide military technology policy into two
broad categories - the ongoing modernization of existing
weapons and the creation of fundamentally new weapons.(102)
Soviet strategists often maintain that decisive breakthroughs in
weapons systems will promote the development of existing
technologies necessary for security.(103) Western analysts
have noted, however, that Soviet military R&D institutions are
far more effective in modernizing existing weapons than in
developing fundamentally new kinds of weapons.(104)
Third, more effective and efficient military technology
policies must be formulated and carried out. Decisions must
be "optimal" - that is, they must have the greatest impact for
the least cost. As Lieutenant General Semenov and Major
General Prokhorov assert:

Determining the best ways to use scientific-technical
achievements in the interests of the armed forces has
now been transformed into an object of strategic
studies, and this aspect of military strategy is
developing rapidly in all the main countries of the
world. It more and more encompasses not only the
qualitative side of the weapons arsenal, but is
beginning to be applied also for the analysis of
combat means, especially those designated to fulfill
one and the same or two similar strategic tasks.
With the high cost of modern weapons it is extremely
important to determine the optimal number of models
of each complex system so as to prevent wasteful
expenditures.(105)

A sound economic policy is crucial to the implementation
of an effective military policy, especially in the selection of
weapons. Major General Kornienko and Captain Korolev observe:

Since the burden upon the economy is becoming greater, even the nations which are highly developed economically are unable to establish all the armament systems which are being developed by scientific and design organizations. The striving to attain military-technical superiority over a potential enemy and the limited nature of the material resources to accomplish this task make it necessary to select the most economical solutions and to seek maximum combat efficiency at minimum expense. This requires military-economic analysis, which must result in a clarification of two questions: a determination of the efficiency of replacing one armament system with another which performs similar combat missions, and a determination of the efficiency of each combat arm and branch of the armed forces.(106)

In the growing field of military economics, Soviet analysts are developing new managerial techniques and methods to aid in making cost-effective choices in military technology policy. As David Holloway, a Western analyst, notes, "Military planners have turned to new management, planning, and forecasting methods to help raise the efficiency of resource utilization and increase the 'correctness' of their procurement decisions."(107)

The goal of military economics has been clearly articulated by Colonel Gorshechnikov:

Since the resources of a society have definite limits and the implementing of the established goals is possible with various combinations of forces and means, the task of all levels involved in decision-making is in each case to find the optimum variants of action, that is, the best under the given conditions, which will provide for the achievement of the desired results with minimum expenditures. The choice of such decisions presupposes their obligatory subjection to military-economic analysis, and in this analysis the possible variants of the accepted criteria are worked out and compared from the standpoint of effectiveness and economy.(108)

Fourth, military management must become more "scientific." The use of operations research, systems analysis, and various war modeling techniques and forecasting methods are crucial to raising managerial effectiveness. For example, forecasting has been used to shape strategic policies and to make decisions about the development and deployment of weapons systems. Cherednichenko writes: "In our times, a distinguishing feature of which is the unusual acceleration in the rate of social progress and a rapid scientific and technical

revolution, the need has arisen to raise sharply the soundness, accuracy, duration, and objectiveness of prediction.
And this is possible on the basis of more advanced and accurate methods of scientific research. Such prediction has come
to be called forecasting."(109)

Fifth, the technological base for military management must
be continuously improved.(110) Modern telecommunications and
information processing technology are especially important,
because of the increasing impact of the temporal dimension of
warfare.

Sixth, military skill levels, as well as organizational
effectiveness in using these skills, must be continuously
enhanced. As Kozlov notes, "the need for skilled personnel
and for the development, manufacture, and utilization of
modern weapons increases abruptly with the mounting complexity of modern hardware."(111)

Seventh, it is crucial to develop a systems-thinking
capability at key stages and levels of decisionmaking, in order
to ensure the more effective development and deployment of
weapons. For example, V.A. Bokarev notes that due to the
greater complexity and cost of military equipment, the effectiveness of a given weapon can be determined only in terms of
its impact on deployed weapons systems. The optimality of a
weapons choice can be ascertained only in relationship to the
characteristics, structure, and assigned purpose of the system
of armaments.(112) David Holloway observes: "Systems analysis refers in particular to the direction of research and
development and the evaluation of alternative choices in
weapons selection. The concern, of course, is not with the
maximization of effectiveness in itself, but with the maximization of effectiveness within given resources."(113)

Eighth, the high economic costs of the qualitative competition in weaponry underscore the need to develop indicators
and methods to determine optimal choice. Mathematical methods, cybernetic technology, and systems approaches are useful
in developing the kind of forecasting capability necessary to
make cost-effective choices. Such a forecasting capability is
particularly important, because expensive weapons and military
equipment are now becoming obsolete quite rapidly. Colonel
Kulikov affirms:

> The process of weapon obsolescence . . . is oc-
> curring today much faster than in the past. Total
> replacement of the operational arsenal of weapons
> today, for example, takes place in a period of 10
> years, while obsolescence is even faster for such
> types of military hardware as aircraft and missiles.
> The present level of material production and the
> rapid pace of development of science, the rapid
> acceleration of weapons obsolescence, the rapid rise

in the cost of weapons design, manufacture, and utilization, and the limited resources which can be devoted to military purposes - all these factors have forced the economically developed nations to step up the search for ways to achieve efficient utilization of military appropriations.(114)

In short, Soviet analysts recognize that the elements of defense preparedness have become much more numerous and the challenge of effectively coordinating them has become much more complex. The key to resolving these problems is thought to be the improvement of macro-military managerial capabilities and the further development of their scientific and technological base. The greater need for military preparedness and managerial capabilities has enhanced even more the temporal dimensions of modern war, and has accelerated to a dynamic pace the development of weapons systems essential to fighting that war.

A high degree of combat readiness is necessary at all times. Moskalenko affirms: "In the nuclear age, armed forces' constant combat readiness acquires national importance and essentially becomes a strategic category. . . . Constant combat readiness on the strategic level has foreign policy importance in addition to purely military importance. The constant combat readiness of the Soviet Armed Forces acts as an inhibiting factor in the unleashing of a new world war by an aggressor."(115)

Also, the long lead-time associated with the development of basic scientific discoveries requires a high level of governmental support for the ongoing scientific research effort and for the effective and efficient use of that effort. Only through planning and incentives for the practical application of the latest scientific findings, in the shortest time and at the lowest possible cost, can weapons technology and management systems be transformed. Furthermore, the long lead-time in developing new weapons systems requires a high level of domestic political support for military-technological policy and for its successful implementation.

In a word, Soviet strategists contend that military preparedness is essential both to win and to avert wars. Commentators have extensively analyzed military competition with the major Western powers. It is the perceived American challenge in the age of "the STR in military affairs" to which we now turn.

"THE STR IN MILITARY AFFAIRS" AND THE AMERICAN
CHALLENGE

According to Soviet analysts, the United States poses a series
of economic and military challenges to the USSR in the era of
the STR for four major reasons.

First, American scientific, technological, and economic,
capabilities have vastly increased in the post-World War II
period.(116) These capabilities provide a formidable infrastructure for meeting broadly conceived strategic needs effectively and efficiently. The high degree of success the United
States has had in developing its scientific, technological, and
economic potentials has produced revolutionary advances in
American military power. In turn, American strategic goals
have spurred the STR at home and abroad.

Second, the United States has built a "permanent" wartime economy in the peacetime postwar years.(117) The American economy mobilizes many civilian industries for military
purposes and nurtures the ongoing process of preparing for
war. That is, the unfolding of the STR in the United States
is focused upon the conduct and/or deterrence of nuclear and
conventional warfare.

Third, the United States has demonstrated considerable
innovativeness in adapting American foreign policy to changing
global conditions.(118) This ingenuity, combined with the
political, economic, and scientific-technological resources
sustaining it, pose a never-ending challenge to the makers and
executors of Soviet foreign policy.

Fourth, U.S. foreign policy continues to give vent to the
"aggressive" nature of American capitalism.(119) The United
States tries to use all of the spheres in which it excels to
advance its interests and to undermine those of the Soviet
Union and other "progressive" forces. The period of detente
in the 1970s served only to channel American aggressive in-
stincts in less dangerous directions, but detente did not
eliminate the fundamental sources of American aggression
itself. Colonel Rut'kov states: "One of American imperialism's
reasons for intensifying the arms race and utilizing its own
temporary superiority in the area of labor productivity, which
has been sustained by historical conditions, was to force the
Soviet Union to spend a greater portion of its national income
on weapons."(120) All four of these challenges will be discussed in the present section and elaborated upon in the
following section.

U.S. Scientific, Technological, and Economic Capabilities

The chief factor in the Soviet assessment of the American
military and foreign policy challenge to the USSR is the
strength of the American economy and especially the strength
of its highly developed scientific and technological sectors.
Soviet analysts emphasize the vitality of the American challenge
and of American power in the 1970s and 1980s and for the
foreseeable future. Although U.S. dominance has been eroded
by the persistent but growing competition from Western Europe
and Japan, the American economy is still viewed as preeminent
in the advanced capitalist world. Of the many adaptations the
United States has made to maintain its dominance, M.I. Zakhmatov considers these to be critical: "The utilization of the
scientific-technological gap between the USA and other capitalist states to strengthen American foreign economic expansion,
the further export of capital as a basic means of accelerating
the foreign economic expansion of American monopolies, and
the speeding up of the export of scientific-technological and
managerial knowledge."(121)
     Soviet analysts have underscored a number of major
strengths of the American economy in the era of the STR.(122)
The United States has been relatively successful in adjusting
to the new demands of the global economy. The United States
has developed a number of key interdependencies, especially in
the manufacturing and marketing spheres. These links have
sustained the American economic growth rate and helped to
prevent further erosion of American productivity.
     The United States is the most independent economy among
the highly developed capitalist economies. The United States
has a relatively strong domestic raw material base, including
its impressive agricultural sector, which buffers the American
economy against the fluctuations and disturbances of the world
market.
     The United States has developed a highly skilled work
force and a broad-based educational infrastructure to meet
diverse labor needs.
     The United States has developed the most advanced mana-
gerial techniques and methods in the capitalist world.
     The United States has created a strong basic scientific
research community, which is rooted firmly in the university
system.
     The United States has sustained an effective civilian R&D
effort. "Spin-offs" from military to civilian sectors, as well as
sophisticated civilian R&D, have ensured a formidable American
infrastructure for the STR.
     The United States has established the most extensive
communication and information networks in the Western world.
These networks rely heavily on automated mechanisms, which
in turn encourage the further development of cybernetic technology.

The United States has by far the greatest number of large-scale science-based industries in the capitalist world. This quantitative lead provides an important stimulus for a qualitative lead in world-class technology.

An advanced chemical industry provides synthetic materials that can be substituted for natural raw materials, giving the United States flexibility in dealing with persistent or periodic commodity shortages.

America's advanced technology industries tend to dominate global markets. The twin stimuli of foreign trade and a large domestic market nurture creativity in American high technology industries. For example, the aerospace industry, heavily supported by governmental contracts and serving a large domestic market, effectively dominates the international aviation trade. And, because U.S. aerospace companies innovate constantly, they are likely to dominate international markets for the indefinite future.

To enhance or maintain these American strengths, U.S. capitalism has made two major structural adjustments, according to Soviet analysts.

First, the large-scale national and multinational corporations (MNCs) have become the dominant innovative component in American capitalism. Progress is achieved through improved centralized control over social and production processes, and this control is enhanced by the judicious use of new organizational technology and management methods. With the growing power of technologies to mediate man's relationships to his social and natural environments, the universalizing elements of production are strengthened. Such universalizing factors objectively require higher levels of centralization in both socialist and capitalist societies. American capitalism has met this historical requirement by creating huge and powerful corporations, especially the MNCs.

From the Soviet perspective, an MNC provides the centralization necessary to gain control over the entire process of technological development. By managing the complete product cycle, international corporations (individually or collectively) are able to regulate both supply and demand and to stabilize markets. As a result, market control enables technological development to proceed at a rapid or leisurely pace, usually without a significant impact on profitability or on the stability of this highly advantageous arrangement for the major producers and suppliers. By guaranteeing markets and by providing the large amounts of capital necessary to develop sophisticated technology, international corporations are in a position to dominate a technological sector. The risks and costs of experimentation are thereby substantially reduced.

In addition, an American science of management has been developed to increase the control of the monopolistic corporation over its economic sector. "From being an art which in the past was based on experience and intuition, management is today becoming transformed into a science without which it would be impossible to guide industrial development."(123)

Managerial science, in the view of Soviet analysts, has several basic components.

First, through the use of psychological and sociological sciences, laws of human behavior are being discovered. Management can then employ these laws to take actions that will increase the effectiveness and efficiency of the production process.(124)

Contemporary managerial science is associated with the systems concept. The elements of production are cognized in an interrelated manner. Managerial initiative can be centralized and intervention can be exercised dynamically in a comprehensive or selective way.(125)

The corporations use economic science to provide the tools for managerial choice. Economic science produces insight into the opportunity cost of various economic decisions (e.g., the determination of various capital costs and returns on investment).

Management consultant firms, such as Arthur Little, Inc., proffer outside expertise. With such organizational, technical, and marketing counsel, corporate managers can acquire a diverse range of accurate information. This information is then used to make and implement decisions more effectively and to improve the quality of the decisionmaking process itself. Finally, the managerial revolution in the American corporation has produced executives who are trained in administrative science and who run their firms accordingly.(126) These managers are not viewed as a new class, but as a distinct stratum serving the interests of finance capital.

The concentration of American capital provides a strong economic base for the organization and financing of R&D.(127) The development of managerial science has encouraged executives to concern themselves with the administration of R&D. A special subfield of management has been created, namely the management of science, which is designed to maximize the effectiveness of primary scientific research for the corporation, and to establish new organizational linkages between science and production. Flexible forms of bureaucratic organization have been needed, in order to exploit the potential of science for production. New economic modes of analysis (e.g., econometrics) have been created to improve the R&D process. And new marketing strategies and techniques, especially those associated with consumerism, have been formulated to sell the new products spawned by the R&D efforts.

Briefly stated, corporate capitalism has resourcefully generated modern techniques and technologies to deal with and to profit from the STR. At the same time, the essential elements of capitalist production relations remain unchanged.

The means of production are still privately owned, and the managerial revolution has not replaced capitalist entrepreneurs. But capitalist values, endeavors, and organizations have been skillfully adapted to the new conditions of the STR.

A second major structural adjustment of U.S. capitalism concerns the greatly enhanced role and functions of the American national government. The United States has had to develop new forms of state-monopoly capitalism to cope with and to meet the challenges associated with advanced modernization.

Soviet theorists argue that the STR has put pressure upon the capitalist state to play a more assertive role vis-a-vis the corporation in the further development of the productive forces. For example, the relationship of the national government to organized science increases the power of the former as well as the latter. Corporate activities are oriented toward short-run profit, whereas the advanced capitalist state must preserve the broader and longer-range interests of capitalism. The growth of science becomes inextricably intertwined with the emergence of the state as the central lever for strategic development in contemporary capitalism. As Gromeka asserts, "The STR creates a situation in which the capitalist state takes on the function of leading and organizing scientific, industrial, and technical construction work."(128)

Also, economic science has become an important instrument of state management. The Keynesian revolution justified ideologically an expanded role for the state in directing the economic process.(129) And modern economic science has provided the state with a wide range of tools for intervening in the economy. New linkages have been created between the U.S. government and corporate, scientific, and educational institutions. These linkages produce a flow of expertise that the state needs to participate more effectively (directly and indirectly) in the management of the economy.

Soviet analysts consider the nurturing and management of innovation to be major achievements of American state-monopoly capitalism. The motivational and organizational capabilities of American capitalism are viewed as the keystones of the ongoing and multifaceted U.S. challenge to the USSR. Significantly, the adaptability of the U.S. political and economic systems to the STR is thought to provide a firm basis for "the revolution in American military affairs." The impact of this "revolution" or the U.S. capability to prepare for modern warfare is the subject of our next section.

The STR and American Preparedness for War

Soviet spokesmen affirm that, prior to World War II, American geographical isolation allowed the United States to depend upon long lead times to mobilize its civilian economic capabilities for

military purposes.   But the introduction of nuclear weapons,
and especially of intercontinental ballistic missiles (ICBMs),
ended American geographic invulnerability and changed the
American conception of the time needed to ready the country
for war.   Continuous preparation for war became a preoccupation of U.S. military planners, and a "permanent" U.S. military economy was created.   G. Evgenev contends:

> The American lag in the field of development of
> intercontinental ballistic missiles at the end of the
> 1950s radically changed the strategic position of the
> United States [and] put an end to its former invul-
> nerability. . . . Main attention was turned to
> preparing the United States for conducting a general
> war with the use of nuclear missiles and, in this
> connection, to the accelerated creation of offensive
> weapons. . . . During the campaign launched in
> the country for a reevaluation of war strategy and
> the role of new combat equipment in modern war,
> former conceptions of using the military-industrial
> potential under conditions of peace and war were
> comprehensively reassessed.   Such factors as the
> necessity of carrying out an unprecedented volume
> of scientific research work, sharply growing techni-
> cal complexity, prolonged periods for working out
> and producing missiles and space equipment, and the
> fabulous cost of their manufacture greatly complicate
> the creation of a missile and space system during the
> course of war and shift the emphasis of military
> preparations to peacetime.   The new approach to the
> utilization of military-industrial potential requires
> maintenance of the defense industry under conditions
> of peace in a state of incomparably high mobilized
> readiness and, consequently, entails very large
> military expenditures. (130)

The central manifestation of these developments has been
the emergence of the American "military-industrial complex" or,
as some Soviet analysts put it, the "military-scientific-
industrial complex."   On the one hand, the concept is used for
propagandistic purposes. (131)   The American "military-
industrial complex" is the cause of virtually all of the major
foreign policy problems confronting the USSR.   It produces
the arms race.   It undermines detente.   It blocks disarmament.
And so on.   Hence, Soviet "rebuffs" to the "aggressive actions" of the American "military-industrial complex" are always
justifiable.

On the other hand, the concept of "the military-industrial
complex" is used for analytical purposes. (132)   A large U.S.
military establishment is viewed as a manifestation of the
permanent need for an advanced capitalist economy to prepare

for nuclear and conventional war. This analytical usage is the one that we will now examine.

There are three key components of the Soviet conception of the American military-industrial complex: the American national government, the military managers at the Pentagon, and the national and multinational corporations engaged in various aspects of weapons production.

First, the executive and legislative branches of the American national government are thought to be the patrons and protectors of the military-industrial complex, and the power of the federal government has expanded correspondingly. The importance of the U.S. government has increased largely because of the efforts of American political and business leaders to develop a scientific, technological, and economic infrastructure adequate for perceived national security needs. Soviet analysts have underscored the importance of several elements of this infrastructure, all of which have augmented the influence of the American national government in the business community.

1. The U.S. government, especially under the Reagan administration, has maintained a high level of political commitment to military needs. The state has used various means, especially propaganda and information control, to constrain social expectations and to mold public opinion about the legitimacy and primacy of military aims and programs.

2. The U.S. government has amply funded basic scientific research, especially projects with obvious or likely military applications. R. A. Faramazian asserts: "In the postwar years the role of the capitalist state has significantly increased not only in terms of financing R&D efforts, but in defining the basic directions and shaping the basic character of the nation's scientific efforts."(133) The national government has become more and more powerful, because complex scientific and technological projects require large amounts of fiscal, managerial, and intellectual resources. Also, the state's influence has increased because of the militarization of the economy and of science. Political leaders play a major role in defining the strategic security interests toward which scientific and technological efforts are directed.

3. The U.S. government has developed a substantial budgetary commitment to the promotion of civilian, as well as military, R&D. The state provides corporations with the "risk capital" for long-range R&D activities. A well-funded R&D base is essential to protect the dominant position of American firms in global markets, and the maintenance of such dominance is vital to American national security interests.

4. The U.S. government has actively intervened in the selection of R&D projects. Scientific and technological priorities are established through "management by objectives" and coordinated through "program control." The state's role is to

construct the elements of a managerial system through which such new approaches and techniques can be introduced. This is especially the case in the military and military-related sectors, where the U.S. National Aeronautics and Space Agency (NASA) is the archetypal case cited by Soviet analysis.(134)

For these reasons especially, the functions of the American national government, and its impact upon scientific and technological development, have expanded considerably since World War II.

Second, the growing scope and complexity of American military activities have led to the development of a large-scale and multifaceted national security bureaucracy. A continuous military effort in peacetime, coupled with the expansion of the scientific, technological and economic dimensions of national security affairs, has placed a premium on greater organizational capabilities.

The United States has met this managerial challenge effectively, according to Soviet analysts. Indeed, the improved administrative capabilities of the American national security system are perceived to be central to the success of American foreign policy. V. F. Petrovskii observes that the U.S. "doctrine of 'national security' places great emphasis upon the organizational dimensions of the managerial problems which are embodied in the decisionmaking mechanisms."(135)

Soviet commentators emphasize several major developments in the postwar American national security bureaucracy.

1. The National Security Council (NSC), the staff of the NSC, and the office of the special assistant to the President for national security affairs have all helped to improve policy coordination.(136)

2. Several reforms in the management of the Pentagon have promoted greater effectiveness and efficiency in weapons development and deployment. For example, the introduction of planning, programming, and budgeting systems (PPBS) are frequently cited as a promising attempt by the capitalist state to augment its power by technical means.

Moreover, managerial reforms in the Pentagon have been at the forefront of administrative rationalization throughout the U.S. political and economic systems. B.D. Piadyshev affirms:

> Having started its military research drive, the MIC [military-industrial complex] has made the utmost use of the resources of cybernetics, electronics, mathematics, physics, and other sciences to solve the scientific and technical problems of preparing for war.
> During the 1960s, the MIC started a veritable boom in planning, in intensive development of new methods of forecasting social processes, and in

scientific, technical, and economic development. The study of scientific and technical methods of forecasting was begun within the Department of Defense and then spread to other departments, assuming extensive proportions in government and industry. From the formulation of short-term military-strategic, budget, and economic programs, such efforts have been extended to long-term and complex research. (137)

3. Linkages have been established between the Pentagon and major scientific institutions, in order to improve the development of primary research with direct military applications. For example, Piadyshev maintains that the Department of Defense has underwritten approximately one-half of all research conducted at American universities in the natural sciences. He cryptically adds: "Under Pentagon contracts, the universities have dealt with the most diverse problems." (138)

4. Close ties have been created between the Pentagon and civilian industry, in order to ensure more effective weapons development. Piadyshev declares: "An intricate and ramified system of business relations, personal ties, joint operations in allocating contracts and profits, and mutual assistance in risky ventures undertaken by the MIC has developed between the military and private enterprise, and has been operating for the benefit of both sides. One of the principal forms of their cooperation is the massive and mutually agreeable exchange of personnel between the private business sector and the Pentagon." (139)

5. A research contact system has been established to provide for greater flexibility and innovation in linking "civilian" scientific, technological, and economic institutions with the national government and especially the Pentagon. V.A. Fedorovich, in his major study of the American contract system, concludes that federal contracts have increasingly replaced direct governmental investment in R&D activities. By the 1970s federal contracts had become "the most important instrument for . . . military-economic regulation and the management of production." (140)

The contract system has become a crucial mechanism for mobilizing American "civilian" industries for military purposes. The militarization of the American economy has stimulated the science-technology-production cycle in the form of state contracts. Gromeka, in his notable work on American scientific and technological capabilities, observes: "The extensive militarization of the U.S. economy and of scientific-technological development have led to a situation in which 'spin-offs' have become the most important form of the transmission of technology, that is, the utilization in the civilian

economy of the achievements that have been made in the
course of military research, development, and production."(141)

In short, the U.S. government has developed contractual
arrangements that are a key instrument in meeting military
R&D needs. Since the vast majority of R&D funding is in the
military sector, a military-science-industrial complex has been
firmly established in the United States. The state provides
the overall supervision and funding. The corporation contributes the organizational base for constructing military
technology. And scientists work in governmental, industrial,
educational, and research organizations. Moreover, private
"think tanks" have emerged as an important source of expertise that provide decisionmakers with alternative channels of
information. Think tanks, like management consultant firms,
often nurture innovation, but both may be used merely to
legitimize the preferences of certain competing groups within
the government.

The net effect of the developments discussed above has
been to strengthen the infrastructure of the American national
security bureaucracy and to generate greater creativity in
American military and civilian management. Hence, the militarization of science is an integral element of contemporary
capitalism.

Third, Soviet analysts have stressed the significance of
the corporate components of the American MIC. To develop
advanced technologies and to sustain a science-technology-
production cycle, it is necessary to provide reliable and stable
markets for private enterprise. Long lead times are needed
for product design and marketing, which require ample financial resources and informed corporate planning. Government
contracts for weapons development are an important means
whereby the American system meets these objective needs of
the science-technology-production cycle.

The U.S. firms most closely tied to the military contract
system are among the most technologically advanced industries,
the fastest growing, and the most involved in foreign economic
relations. As Gromeka notes, the contract system is an "important instrument for financing corporate activity in new
areas of scientific and technological progress. The contract
system stimulates such progress by generating a demand for
the expansion of production and the improvement of the quality
of new technological products."(142) He adds that the
contract system provides a "guaranteed market" for these
products and thus stimulates their development.(143)

Governmental contracts spur the development of advanced
technologies that are of military significance and are commercially marketable. That is, the government provides a sizable
and secure market for sophisticated weaponry, which the
large-scale American firms then profit from in other ways as

well. Not only do firms sell new kinds of armaments to the
government, but they also benefit from commercial applications
of advanced military technology. Gromeka observes: "The aviation companies use the large expenditures in building military
aircraft in order to reduce the cost of constructing civilian
aircraft. Similar tactics are used by other companies involved
in production for both military and civilian markets, such as in
the electronics and laser technology industries, etc."(144)
    The majority of industrial firms involved in the American
"military-industrial complex" are MNCs. By providing the
MNCs with lucrative contracts, the national government
strengthens itself and the capitalist system in several ways.
A continuous supply of advanced military technology is
assured, sophisticated arms for foreign sales are produced,
and the commercial position of the MNCs is strengthened within
global markets. The MNCs are interested in developing
technologically sophisticated weapons for profit, and
governmental contracts provide the crucial means to dominate
advanced technology markets at home and abroad.
    According to Soviet analysts, U.S. firms that seek and
receive military contracts emphasize corporate planning, heavy
investment in advanced technologies, aggressive recruitment of
highly trained scientists and technical specialists, innovations
in managerial techniques and styles, sophisticated information
processing and communications, and considerable lateral mobili-
ty for upper- and middle-level executives whose work alter-
nates between the public and private sectors. Moreover, the
close ties between technological innovation and high growth
rates create shared interests between the U.S. executive and
legislative institutions and private corporations. Contractual
support for modern weaponry sustains the growth of the economy, which is vital to the power, effectiveness, and popularity
of both Democratic and Republican administrations and con-
gressmen of both parties.
    In short, the operations of the American MIC are such
that the development of advanced technology is a vital means
of pursuing overall U.S. "superiority" in the military competition with the USSR. Borisov affirms:

> The maintenance of technological superiority over
> adversaries has become the basic principle of Ameri-
> can military-technology policy in the postwar period.
> The U.S. has placed a great deal of hope on techno-
> logical superiority. The creation and production of
> ever newer and more complex and technologically
> advanced systems of arms have become a basic trend
> in the development of American military power. The
> pursuit of technological superiority strengthens a
> tendency to develop the military applications of each
> new technological achievement in the shortest time

possible. The tendency is actively encouraged by
the military-industrial firms that develop and
produce military technology.(145)

For various reasons, then, the U.S. government is
thought to have shifted its primary emphasis from ground
forces to technologically intensive weaponry.   According to a
notable Soviet study of American military policy, the U.S.
tendency to "absolutize the role of armaments" is due in large
part to "the attempt of the bourgeoisie to lessen to the
greatest extent possible its dependence upon mass armies, the
existence of which is fraught with serious political consequences for them."(146)
    Hence, the development of advanced weaponry has become
the cornerstone of American military policy, and the leadership
of the Pentagon has become increasingly technocratic.   Piadyshev asserts: "Pentagon leaders have been making ever more
frequent attempts to link the highly intricate problems arising
from scientific and technical progress with political and military-political doctrines and with the country's economic potentialities, in the hope of laying a theoretical basis for a rational
military-technical policy.   They attach so much importance to
technical superiority that it has even come to be regarded as
an inalienable element of U.S. military strength."(147)
    Nonetheless, Soviet analysts argue that technology has a
contradictory impact on the arms race.   On the one hand,
technological virtuosity is a vitally important factor spurring
the development of new weaponry.   A major impact of the STR
upon American military affairs has been to encourage the
United States to strive for technological superiority over the
Soviet Union.   R. Faramazian and V. Borisov contend: "American imperialism emphasizes the creation of new and even more
devastating weapons systems and also the constant refinement
of existing systems.   This course, dictated by the desire to
achieve, through some kind of scientific and technical breakthrough, military-technical and military superiority over the
Soviet Union, leads to rapid growth in the technical complexity
of means of armed struggle."(148)
    On the other hand, the American drive for technological
superiority and the "rapid growth in the technical complexity
of means of armed struggle" carry with them pressures for the
limitation of the arms race.   The cost of weapon systems is
dramatically increasing with each new "generation" of weapons
that is designed and deployed.   Colonel Vlas'evich maintains
that there is a

direct connection between the continuous changes in
generations of armaments and the tremendous increase in spending for their production.   The inter-

national competition for military power is constantly
making new demands on the tactical and technical
capabilities of various types of weapons. This leads
to the creation of better, but at the same time, more
expensive, combat systems. Is this according to
principle? Basically, yes. The fact is that qualitative changes in products are always accompanied by
cost increases unless labor productivity increases as
rapidly as the changes in the quality of the manufactured article. . . . However, significant rises
in the level of labor productivity take time, and in
the present arms race, as a rule, there is insufficient time. (149)

Recognition of the economic limits of the technological
arms race is considered to be a critical dimension of the
"realism" of certain Western politicians who have sought to
negotiate strategic arms limitation agreements with the Soviet
Union. Kornienko declares:

According to the estimate of authoritative experts, a
quantitative increase in strategic forces no longer
makes any real sense. It would be much more mean-
ingful to achieve qualitative improvement within the
limits of economic capability. U.S. ruling circles
refuse to roll back on their world political ambitions.
But it is becoming increasingly difficult for them to
support these ambitions in a military and economic
respect. Within certain circles there has developed
a comprehension of the political fruitlessness of
further growth in strategic arms. . . . For this
reason there is a good possibility that compromises
will be sought in important political decisions. The
crux of the matter lies in this duality. With a
certain turn of events, the reactionaries may impel
the United States to broaden the front of aggression
and to push the world to the brink of nuclear war.
But another situation is also possible: the sober-
minded segment of the bourgeoisie will seek ways to
achieve political settlement of problems. (150)

It is Soviet assessments of the contradictory impact of
modern weaponry upon the basic nature of the U.S.-Soviet
strategic competition to which we now turn.

THE STR AND THE U.S.-SOVIET
STRATEGIC ARMS COMPETITION

Soviet analysts view the STR as a crucial component of the
strategic arms race.   Advanced technology is thought to affect
all of the dimensions of East-West competition.   The introduction of nuclear weapons and the technological revolution
associated with those weapons have decisively influenced the
nature and conduct of a general war.   The centrality of the
advanced technological competition has increased the number of
factors involved in the military competition.   Because of the
STR, the "civilian" scientific, technological, and economic
sectors have become critical elements in the military arena, and
the concept of military preparedness has been substantially
altered.   The ongoing challenge perceived in the USSR is to
continue to link scientific and technological progress with the
development of diverse military capabilities.   The relative
success of the United States in meeting this challenge has
made it a formidable adversary.   The USSR's success in meeting this challenge in the 1960s and 1970s was crucial in
deterring American assertiveness.   Hence, "the STR in military
affairs" has become an integral part of the U.S.-Soviet strategic competition.
     But has the technological competition associated with the
strategic arms race made strategic parity a practical and
desirable goal?   Has the technological competition made parity
substantially less valuable than superiority in serving the
goals of Soviet foreign policy?
     There are different Soviet responses to these especially
critical questions.   For Soviet strategic conservatives, the STR
is a crucial element of military power.   The scope and dynamism of the STR significantly affect the possibilities of victory
in a nuclear war.   Such a war may well be instigated by the
"imperialists" in an adventuristic reaction to their declining
position in the global arena.   Hence, the USSR can and must
achieve strategic superiority.   Superior force is necessary to
win a general nuclear war that may be unavoidable given the
nature of the class enemy.
     For Soviet strategic modernizers, the STR has decisively
influenced the character of political and military competition
and has made the avoidance of a general nuclear war a necessary goal for the U.S.-Soviet diplomacy.   Strategic parity is
thought to be useful for both military and diplomatic reasons.
Militarily, strategic parity allows greater operational flexibility
below the nuclear threshold.   Diplomatically, strategic parity
makes possible arms regulation talks that have produced controls (SALT I) and could lead to substantially more controls
(SALT II and III) of the ongoing U.S.-Soviet strategic competition.   Hence, strategic parity, by reducing the likelihood of

a general nuclear war and by helping to curb the East-West strategic arms race, enables the Soviet leadership to pursue more successfully its diverse foreign and domestic policies.

In short, Soviet strategic conservatives maintain that the STR affects the means of fighting a general war. But Soviet strategic modernizers contend that the STR alters the nature of military competition by necessitating diplomatic efforts to control this competition, on the one hand, and by increasing the importance of competition below the nuclear threshold, on the other hand. These contrasting perspectives of Soviet conservatives and modernizers will now be analyzed.

Strategic Conservatives

To summarize the position of Soviet strategic conservatives, warfare is the continuation of the politics of classes and states by violent means (following Lenin's adaptation of the famous Clausewitzian dictum), even to the level of a general nuclear war. Advanced technology has merely changed the means of fighting and winning a general war. When such a war occurs, it will necessarily become nuclear in character. Hence, the deterrence of a general war requires the development of a nuclear war-winning strategy and the nuclear superiority to support such a strategy. The U.S.-Soviet technological competition is a key component affecting victory in a general nuclear war. But any Soviet technological inferiority can and must be compensated for by the superior mobilizational capabilities of the Soviet Union. "American imperialism" has responded to the effective Soviet mobilizational programs by attempting to use its technological superiority to achieve strategic superiority. Strategic arms talks, then, cannot reduce the American striving for scientific, technological, and economic superiority, or the need for the Soviet Union to deter or to ensure victory in a nuclear exchange.

Strategic conservatives view nuclear war as the ultimate expression of political conflict. Colonel Sidelnikov affirms that "the appearance of any weapon, including a nuclear weapon, exerts tremendous influence on the methods and forms of warfare. But no weapon can change the political essence of war. It has been and remains a continuation by violent means of the policy of the state and classes."(151)

Surprisingly, the strategic conservatives' contention that nuclear rocket weapons have not essentially changed the nature of war as an instrument of policy is in sharp disagreement with the publicly stated positions of Brezhnev and some of his closest political colleagues. A Foreign Broadcast Information Service Report concludes:

By far the most consistent spokesmen for the more
militant, hardline position on [nuclear warfare] have
been a group of military ideologists associated with
the Lenin Military-Political Academy. Apparently
regarding themselves as guardians of the traditional
ideology, they have repeatedly criticized those who
have suggested that nuclear weapons introduce a
new degree of destructiveness into warfare which
calls into question the possibility of surviving or
winning such a war. They have consistently been
out of sympathy with the main thrust of Brezhnev's
detente   policies   and   on   occasion   have   directly
challenged publicists who have been known support-
ers of Brezhnev's policies.(152)

A future nuclear war, like all other wars in the past, will
be won by one side or the other, according to strategic conservatives. V. F. Khalipov maintains: "There is a profound
error and harm in the disorienting claims of bourgeois ideo-
logues that there will be no victor in a thermonuclear world
war. The peoples of the world will put an end to imperialism,
which is causing mankind incalculable suffering."(153)

Soviet conservatives do not welcome a general nuclear
war, but they underscore that such a war remains a distinct
possibility. These analysts insist that the innate aggressiveness of the "imperialist enemy" makes nuclear war an increasingly serious threat for the foreseeable future. For example,
Colonel Ponomarev comments: "Today, militarism permeates the
entire sociopolitical life of imperialist countries; the higher the
level of economic development of the imperialist nation, the
further   the   extent   of   its   militarization."(154)   In   a   word,
Soviet   conservatives   take   an   undifferentiated   view   of   "the
American imperialist."

Also, strategic conservatives argue that the threat from
American imperialism mounts as "the general crisis of capitalism" deepens. The imperialists will become more adventuristic
and irrational as the problems confronting them accumulate.
As the authors of Marxism-Leninsim on War and Army underscore, "The imperialists intend to save capitalism through war,
the danger of which is great at present and is threatening all
the peoples of our planet. It is precisely because capitalism at
its highest stage has entered the period of its decline and ruin
and is going through a new, third stage of its general crisis,
that its aggressive strivings are not decreasing but are inces-
santly growing."(155)   Briefly put, American aggressiveness is
thought   to   intensify   as   the   scientific,   technological,   and
military capabilities of the United States, on the one hand, and
the social, economic, and political problems of the United
States, on the other hand, simultaneously increase.

The only way to meet the growing "American threat" is through deterrence by means of military superiority. Sidelnikov maintains:

> Soviet soldiers are profoundly aware that the greater the combat might and combat readiness of the armed forces of the USSR and all armies of the fraternal socialist countries and the greater their cohesion and cooperation, the more durable will be peace on earth, the more genuine the security of our peoples, and the broader the opportunities for consolidation and development of the successes of the policy of peaceful coexistence and for making irreversible the positive changes in the international arena.(156)

At the core of this view of superior force is the ability of the USSR to win a nuclear war if it occurs. A nuclear war-winning strategy is central to the strategic conservatives' position. This strategy heavily relies upon Soviet mobilizational superiority, coupled with a continuous drive for technological modernization, to compensate for Western technological superiority.

The STR affects the military power of the Soviet Union primarily by making necessary the upgrading of its equipment and technology for conducting a war. Skirdo asserts: "The appearance of new means of waging war would be unthinkable without the STR. . . . Indeed, it is precisely this revolution that has served as a basis for improvements and changes in the means of armed struggle."(157)

The mobilizational superiority of the USSR is a crucial element of the country's military capability, according to Soviet strategic conservatives. There are five elements of this mobilizational superiority that are considered to be essential to achieve victory in a nuclear war.

First, the Soviet Union has developed a well-integrated military structure that can prevail in any nuclear exchange. The USSR's conventional superiority in Europe is linked to a strategic force structure that can win an all-out or a limited nuclear war. Marshal Rotmistrov comments: "Giving new types of weapons and especially nuclear weapons their due, our military doctrine proceeds from the fact that victory in war, if the imperialists unleash it, will be won by the efforts of all types and categories of troops."(158)

Second, the Soviet Union has developed a more effective technological policy than the imperialists, due primarily to the planning capability of the USSR. Even if Soviet equipment is less sophisticated or even inferior to the United States', the USSR can and does produce weaponry that may be more successful in the conduct of an actual war. For one thing, Soviet equipment is simpler and more standardized than U.S. equipment. For another thing, the USSR produces a greater amount of weaponry, and the abundance of equipment can compensate in part for qualitative inferiority.

Third, the Soviet capability to mobilize its economy is greater than that of the United States. The USSR's economy could meet military needs much more quickly and effectively in the early days and months of a nuclear war, the period most crucial to victory. As Skirdo notes, "The socialist nations possess indisputable advantages over capitalist countries with respect to the economic organization of society and the necessity of planned development of all sectors of the economy."(159) These advantages will guarantee that there is

> timely provision for maintaining a high level of production when needed so that the necessary supplies can be stockpiled, but will also ensure that the economy is at its maximum stability. To ensure the viability of a nation's economy during a nuclear missle war, the political leaders must implement a number of special measures in advance. They include duplication, dispersal, and concealment of important economic installations, as well as the establishment of an effective antiaircraft and antimissle defense system.(160)

Such preparation is considerably less difficult in a planned economy. Military aspects of economic activity can be coordinated and controlled by the political leaders and existing planning institutions.

Fourth, the USSR is far more advanced in meeting its civil defense needs than is the United States. In other words, the survivability of the USSR in the event of a nuclear war is greatly increased by its extensive civil defense programs.(161) Soviet conservatives are major proponents of civil defense activities as a means of guaranteeing the survival of the present Soviet system and the victory of the USSR in a future nuclear war.

Fifth, the mobilizational superiority of the USSR would be especially important if the international situation made a nuclear war appear to be unavoidable, and if the Soviet leadership deemed a preemptive launch essential for the defense or very survival of the nation. Moskalenko argues: "In view of the immense destructive force of nuclear weapons and the extremely limited time available to take effective countermeasures after an enemy launches its missles, the launching of the first massed nuclear attack acquires decisive importance for achieving the objectives of war."(162) Moskalenko makes it clear that seizing the strategic initiative will be crucial to

winning a nuclear war, if such a war appears to be imminent.
Soviet conservatives believe that the USSR has the mobilizational superiority to take such an initiative, if necessary.

In short, Soviet strategic conservatives hope that the
military superiority of the USSR will deter the "American
imperialists" from unleashing a nuclear war. Major General
Nikitin and Colonel Baranov assert: "No lags will be allowed in
the military field; maintaining reliable military technical superiority is a task conditioned by the international duties of
the Soviet Union."(163)

The USSR's reliance on military power to deter the aggressor is a position consonant with the traditional Soviet view
of war. Steve Kime, a Western analyst, notes: "War is a
country-wide preoccupation in the Soviet Union. Historical
experience, a domestic political system heavily dependent upon
the perception of external threat, and nuclear age geopolitics
combine to make the threat of war and the need for massive
military forces persistent realities for the ordinary citizen.
World war, even in the nuclear age, is thinkable."(164)

Nonetheless, the Soviet conservatives' war-winning strategy undercuts the process of mutual deterrence critical to even
a modicum of stability in the East-West arms race. Also, the
Soviet strategic conservative orientation undermines the
American doctrine of "mutual assured destruction," which has
contributed to that stability. Samuel Payne, a Western commentator, affirms that a war-winning strategy "makes it difficult for the Soviet Union to accept strategic parity with the
United States, and it is difficult for the United States to
conclude strategic arms limitation agreements on any other
basis."(165)

The Soviet conservatives' desire to win a nuclear war if it
occurs does not blind them to the opportunities and challenges
inherent in parity. The more effective use of military power
and the more efficient organization of military forces are
considered especially important in deterring an adversary
under conditions of parity. These very same factors, together
with scientific and technological breakthroughs, are deemed
essential to move beyond parity to superiority. Superiority is
the maximal goal and parity the minimal goal, but the means of
achieving both objectives are basically the same. The perceived problem, however, is that the United States is attempting to regain in the 1980s the superiority it lost in the 1970s.
And to do so, the United States is placing renewed emphasis
on its forte - technologically sophisticated weaponry that is
based on the best and latest scientific research. Colonel
Fedorov asserts:

The "modernization" of U.S. nuclear strategy is
aimed at seeking out new methods of achieving the
aggressive objectives of international, and above all

American, imperialism. Like all the previous strategies, it is based upon the bankrupt policy of "from
a position of strength," and on the hopeless search
within the existing balance of forces for "radical"
methods for resolving the disputed problems of
modern times unilaterally - that is, in a direction
advantageous for itself.(166)

Whereas Soviet conservatives have underscored the military
and diplomatic advantages of strategic superiority, Soviet
modernizers have underscored the advantages of strategic
parity. It is to the orientation and arguments of the strategic
modernizers to which we now turn.

Strategic Modernizers

To summarize the position of Soviet strategic modernizers,
nuclear war is not the continuation of the politics of classes
and states by violent means. An all-out nuclear war between
the NATO and Warsaw Pact nations would represent a radical
departure from normal politics and would have catastrophic
results for both the capitalist and socialist adversaries. One
side would emerge victorious in a nuclear war, but only in the
sense that it would survive with a little less devastation than
the other. Neither set of combatants would gain a clear
advantage vis-a-vis one another and both would lose power
vis-a-vis the other major nations in an increasingly multipolar
world, especially those nations less involved in or less
damaged by the nuclear exchange.
    Hence, Soviet modernizers consider strategic parity to be
both desirable and possible, primarily because of the growth of
Soviet military power and because of the increasing "realism"
among the capitalist ruling circles, which are rather accurately
calculating the dangers that a nuclear war poses to their
political and socioeconomic systems. For strategic modernizers,
diplomatic efforts to regulate the strategic competition through
the SALT process and efforts to develop effective military
power to support Soviet foreign policy goals are mutually
reinforcing. Strategic parity, in this view, expands Soviet
military and foreign policy options.
    A general nuclear war, strategic modernizers argue,
would not be in the Soviet national interest. As long ago as
1965, the late Major General Talenskii contended: "In our days
there is no more dangerous illusion than the idea that nuclear
war can still serve as an instrument of politics, that it is
possible to attain political objectives by using nuclear weapons
and still survive."(167) Moreover, Soviet modernizers affirm
that "objective changes" in the global arena have made it pos-

sible to avoid nuclear war by means of strategic arms diplomacy. Modernizers offer three basic reasons to support this
conclusion.(168)

First, both the United States and the USSR have developed assured retaliatory or second-strike capabilities. G. A.
Trofimenko, in a notable work on American military policy,
emphasizes this point:

> When McNamara advanced his theory of "deterrence"
> or "mutual deterrence" by means of a second strike
> that would produce "unacceptable losses," he con-
> ceptualized parity in terms of "mutual assured
> destruction." The Pentagon leaders, however, cal-
> culated privately that the United States had greater
> capabilities in the sense that only the United States
> had a "full-valued capability" for a second strike.
> . . . [This capability] gave the United States an
> opportunity to continue a policy of pressure "from
> positions of strength" against the USSR. But
> regardless of the illusions that American strategists
> based on this calculation in the 1960s, and regard-
> less of the political capital that they attempted to
> extract from it, the 1970s completely destroyed such
> hopes: no one in the United States now doubts that
> the USSR can deal "unacceptable losses" in a second
> strike, even under circumstances of a massive Amer-
> ican nuclear attack on the Soviet Union.(169)

Second, "realist" forces in the American "ruling classes"
are increasingly aware of the futility of using general nuclear
war to further their political goals. Colonel Kondratkov notes:

> Nuclear missiles have made substantial changes in
> the relationship between politics and war, and they
> have turned war into an exceptionally dangerous and
> lethal means of politics. . . . Nuclear war cannot
> help the militant imperialist circles and their
> supporters achieve their cannibalistic plans. This
> truth is more and more being understood by realis-
> tically thinking political, state, and military leaders
> in the capitalist West who are coming out in favor of
> deepening detente and peaceful coexistence.(170)

The existence of such "realist" forces, even within the U.S.
military-industrial complex, is affirmed by various Soviet
analysts - for example, General Mil'shtein, a leading Soviet
expert on the strategic arms race.(171)

Third, the processes associated with the STR in general, and "the revolution in military affairs" in particular, have made the avoidance of a general nuclear war both desirable and possible. N. M. Nikol'skii and A. V. Grishin stress that the objective changes associated with the STR are forcing the "imperialists" to realize that a global nuclear war is not a feasible political instrument. "The STR in military affairs creates new types and systems of weapons of massive destruction . . . which sharply increase the significance of the question of war and peace for human society, and the potential consequences of a worldwide nuclear rocket conflict. [But] the contemporary correlation of forces in the international arena . . . creates real possibilities for confronting and solving the problems of war and peace."(172)

These three processes - the growing strategic capability of the USSR, the growing significance of "realist" forces in Western societies, and the growing recognition of the catastrophic consequences of an all-out nuclear war - have contributed greatly to the perceived importance of strategic arms limitation negotiations. V. F. Petrovskii noted in 1981:

> During the first half of the seventies the U.S. political leadership did not limit itself merely to stating the fact of strategic parity. It reached the rather more long-term conclusion that any attempts to upset this parity cannot be crowned with any substantial, and, more to the point, long-term effect. If parity is upset it will inevitably be reestablished, but at a higher level of weapon systems development. The withdrawal of the capitalist states from their earlier foreign policy doctrines and lines was necessitated by the appearance of realistic thinking on the part of a number of the leaders of the Western powers. . . . [It was also] the result of the bold, creative policy of the CPSU, its Central Committee, and the Central Committee Politburo.(173)

The SALT process, in the opinion of Soviet strategic modernizers, is an integral part of the creation and maintenence of nuclear parity. Ogarkov comments: "The agreements between the USSR and the U.S. on limiting strategic arms, which were concluded on the basis of full equality and equal security, are a just balance of Soviet and American interests."(174)

The linkage between strategic arms diplomacy and strategic arms development constitutes the core of the position articulated by Soviet modernizers. They present three major reasons why strategic diplomacy is an essential component of strategic modernization.

First, the SALT process provides a more stable environment for strategic planning than would be the case without arms limitation agreements. A more predictable environment helps policymakers to design and deploy the weapons necessary to maintain strategic parity. Raymond Garthoff, an American analyst, affirms: "There is good evidence that the [Soviet] national leadership, including at least some senior professional military men, have increasingly come to accept negotiated strategic arms limitations as a contributing element in providing more stable and less costly deterrent military forces."(175)

Second, Soviet security is increased by strategic predictability and is decreased by an unbridled strategic arms race. Aleksei Arbatov comments: "By itself even a large arsenal of [strategic] weapons cannot guarantee national security."(176) Petrovskii elaborates: "Whereas in the past it was considered that security was ensured first by the maximum disposition of force, detente has demonstrated that political wisdom lies not in the uncontrolled buildup of arms but in agreement to mutual restraint."(177)

Third, the SALT process is helpful in constraining American technological innovation. The strategic arms competition is driven by scientific and technical competition. To reduce American technological superiority is to reduce the American potential for strategic arms superiority.

Soviet modernizers, however, recognize the "dialectical" nature of the relationship between strategic arms development and strategic arms control. For modernizers, the twin processes of technological innovation and diplomacy lie at the heart of the modernization process. Soviet modernizers perceive the American approach to strategic modernization to encompass weapons development and arms limitation talks. The American military strategy of the 1970s has been characterized as an attempt "to combine conceptually two contradictory processes: the development of armaments and their limitation. In this strategy the first tendency clearly predominates."(178)

At the same time, Soviet modernizers acknowledge that the USSR also has combined these "two contradictory processes." Fritz Ermarth, a Western commentator, notes that Soviet analysts "have tended to accept the destabilizing dynamism of technology as an intrinsic aspect of the strategic dialectic, the underlying engine of which is a political competition not susceptible to stabilization. For the Soviets, arms control negotiations are part of this competitive process. Such negotiation can help keep risks within bounds and also, by working on the U.S. political process, restrain U.S. competitiveness."(179)

Soviet modernizers, such as V. M. Kulish, maintain that the balance between the strategic forces of the USSR and the United States can be characterized only as an "approximate parity," because the balance of power and technological levels are dynamic. "There is every reason to view this balance as a correlation between the strategic nuclear missile might of the two great powers at the present time, and also as a continuing process in the further development of this might."(180)

Nonetheless, Soviet strategic modernizers expect that this dynamism can be maintained within an essential condition of parity. Karpov and Asatiani contend:

> The principle of equality and mutual security is essentially an expression of the recognition by both sides that parity is needed to limit strategic arms, and that a balance in strategic missile power must be maintained, be it precarious or, at times, dynamic. The principle of equality and mutual security, the sole possible foundation for an agreement on strategic arms limitation, is organically associated with the very nature of modern weapons and with the objective balance of strategic forces between the USSR and the USA.(181)

According to Soviet modernizers, there are three basic pressures upon the strategic balance that make the forging of strategic parity an ongoing challenge of great difficulty.

First, there is the continuous technological challenge. The United States has an "aggressive" and "vigorous" R&D program to support its strategic arms buildup. Also, the United States has adopted a "bargaining chip" approach to arms control. This approach emphasizes the need to develop new technological options as a means of challenging Soviet strategic power. Soviet commentators on the STR and American foreign policy observe that "the dramatic advances in weapons technology continuously outstrip the progress of arms limitation talks."(182)   Hence, the worldwide STR in military affairs, coupled with the persistent U.S. pursuit of technological superiority, means that "scientific-technological achievements that are applied in the military sphere frequently exercise a destabilizing influence on the limitation and reduction of arms."(183)   Throughout the authoritative Soviet collective work from which this quote is taken, the authors clearly imply that both American and Soviet technological innovations often disrupt the East-West strategic equilibrium. Nonetheless, Soviet strategic modernizers call for the intensification of R&D programs. Modernizers view the ongoing process of technological innovation as a key component in the strategic balance, and they stress both development and deployment capabilities in their assessments of strategic equivalence.

Second, the United States accepted in the SALT I accords the principle of numerical or quantitative equivalence. But the

United States did not accept strategic equivalence in the
dynamic sense. Rather, the United States shifted the competition to the qualitative sphere - that is, to the improvement of
warhead accuracy, the capacity to carry multiple warheads,
the development of cruise missles, the neutron bomb, the
space shuttle, and so on.(184)   Soviet modernizers perceive
that the shift in American strategic policy from the quantitative to the qualitative dimensions of the East-West competition
plays to American strengths, thus complicating the problem of
ensuring a strategic balance.   Dennis Ross, a Western analyst,
notes: "Because they have always been concerned about superior American scientific prowess, the Soviets tend to be fearful
that technological breakthroughs will yield the United States
strategic advantages."(185)   This concern apparently spurs
the strategic modernizers' efforts to reduce American qualitative advantages through the development of Soviet weaponry
and through major diplomatic efforts, such as the Protocol to
the SALT II accord.
     Third, continued political conflict between "realist" and
"anti-Soviet" forces in the United States is thought to create
the possibility that the "bargaining chips" produced by the
"realist" forces as a hedge against Soviet strategic power will
become the weapons used by the "anti-Soviet" forces in the
quest for American strategic superiority.   The hardening of
American viewpoints in the last two years of the Carter administration and the confrontationist rhetoric and policies of
the Reagan administration are perceived to verify Soviet fears
that the United States is striving for strategic superiority
rather than parity.
     But for modernizers there are "objective" pressures on
any American administration, making strategic superiority
difficult to achieve, and providing a substantial basis for
"realism" in American foreign policy.   Aleksei Arbatov argues:

> Washington's policy in the strategic arms sphere and
> its approach to the SALT negotiations remain a
> subject of acute political struggle within the United
> States.   This is not accidental, because the sources
> of today's difficulties in stabilizing the military
> equilibrium and reducing its levels lie in the major
> problems that confront American foreign and military
> strategic policies, which must adapt to the objective-
> ly developed nuclear parity between the USSR and
> the United States.   These circumstances, which do
> not accord with Washington's wishes, promote the
> objective and long-term concurrence of the United
> States' true national interests with mutual strategic
> arms limitation by means of Soviet-American agree-
> ments.(186)

Furthermore, the quest of the United States for strategic superiority will not increase its national security. Such an effort by the United States will be matched by the USSR. O. Bykov notes that any attempt by the West to destabilize the strategic balance will not go unchallenged.

> If one side disrupts the balance, the other is capable, using its economic and scientific-technical potential, of nullifying the adversary's temporary and partial advantages by building up its own power. The balance is consequently restored at a higher level, at an enormous material cost and with an ultimate reduction in mutual security. In light of these realities, the only reasonable solution that reflects the objective coincidence of interests of the parties is to maintain, not to disturb, the global strategic balance.(187)

For Soviet conservatives, the U.S. drive for superiority seriously limits the possibility of strategic diplomacy. For Soviet modernizers, however, the USSR's production and installation of strategic weapons cannot by themselves ensure national security. Modernizers acknowledge the difficulties in dealing with the United States, but they insist that strategic parity is a desirable and feasible goal that is more in the national interests of the USSR than is the chimerical pursuit of superiority vis-a-vis a technologically formidable rival.

Soviet modernizers stress that strategic parity furthers the USSR's military and foreign policy goals in ways other than the modernization of ICBMs. Strategic parity enables the USSR to strengthen dimensions of its military power that could prove even more valuable in serving Soviet diplomacy than an all-out arms race and the risk of nuclear war.

In particular, the modernization of conventional military forces can be used for the projection or expansion of power. Roman Kolkowicz, an American writer, observes: "A stabilization of U.S.-Soviet strategic capabilities at parity levels would still give the Soviet Union a wide range of options for the pursuit of policy objectives by means of conventional forces."(188) This has been the position of the Soviet strategic modernizers who have embraced "the two spheres" argument of Georgii Arbatov discussed in Chapter 2. Strategic stability is possible in East-West relations, but intense political, economic, and military competition will continue in the Third World. Soviet modernizers believe that central strategic systems do not help to project power into the Third World, but that the USSR can and should improve its power projection capabilities to support a forward strategy in selected Third World countries.

Hence, Soviet strategic modernizers contend that the most politically useful military capabilities are those below the nuclear threshold. That is, modernizers view general nuclear deterrence through arms control as a means of allowing greater operational flexibility short of nuclear war. Dimitri Simes of Johns Hopkins University notes: "When Moscow talks about strategic stability, it does not mean stability on all levels of military competition; it seeks stability that deters action only on the highest (holocaust) level of superpower confrontation to create more favorable conditions to exploit its conventional military advantages."(189)

In conclusion, Soviet strategic conservatives stress that "the STR in military affairs" has introduced a number of decisive changes in the nature and conduct of war, but that the basic character of military competition remains mutually antagonistic on all levels. The strategic competition is perceived to be a zero-sum game that involves the use of advanced Soviet technology and Soviet mobilizational superiority to win a general nuclear war if such a war becomes unavoidable. In contrast, Soviet strategic modernizers emphasize that the spiraling East-West strategic arms race is highly interactive and that the national security of the USSR is enhanced by certain forms of interdependence between the USSR and its adversaries.

Soviet modernizers are strongly inclined to regulate the strategic competition and to keep conflict below the threshold of a general nuclear war. Modernizers seek to decouple power projection forces from the threat of a nuclear war. They consider it necessary to develop the military technology and strategy for a global interventionist capability, because they think that this form of military power can best serve the political and economic interests of the USSR. Hence, modernizers view military might as an effective means of furthering the USSR's international goals, but only if East-West competition is regularized and if confrontation is not permitted to escalate to or even near the level of a general nuclear war.

The different orientations of Soviet strategic conservatives and strategic modernizers reflect a broader conflict among party and state officials regarding the impact of the STR on world politics, East-West relations, and the development of the USSR. We will summarize and assess these competing perspectives and policy preferences of Soviet conservatives and modernizers in our concluding chapter.

5 Conclusion

Present-day Soviet policymakers and theorists are keenly sensitive to the reciprocal relationships between scientific and technological change and international politics. We have documented this contention extensively in the preceding chapters. We conclude our book by identifying the chief parameters of consensus among Soviet leaders and commentators on these themes. We then discuss the major differences between Soviet conservative and modernizing orientations. We proceed to argue that the competition between conservative and modernizing tendencies has been and will continue to be a central component of Soviet politics in the Brezhnev years. Finally, we assess the impact of these competing Soviet views on East-West relations in the 1980s, especially on the USSR's foreign policy during and after the portentous developments in Afghanistan and Poland.

CONSENSUS IN SOVIET THINKING

Soviet analysts underscore at least eleven major changes that the STR has introduced into contemporary international relations. Here, briefly stated, are these generally agreed upon and influential Soviet assessments of the STR as an "objective" force in world politics.

First, the STR has launched a "revolution in military affairs." Scientific discoveries and technological innovations have dramatically increased the destructiveness of warfare, endangering the very existence of the human species. Modern weaponry cannot be manufactured or deployed without advanced scientific research and technological virtuosity, especially in the fields of nuclear energy and guided missile systems. Because both strategic and conventional weapons are becoming more automated, the capacity of a nation to win or deter wars increasingly rests upon its scientific and technical potential. N. A. Lomov asserts: "The ever growing role of science in strengthening the military might of a state is now a clearly expressed pattern. Without considering this pattern, it is impossible to examine with sufficient profundity and completeness the present military capability and prospects for strengthening the military might of a state."(1)   Hence, the STR makes necessary the rapid modernization of armaments and of the strategies and tactics for waging and preventing war. International competition in this sphere is intense and ongoing.

Second, the STR generates a number of "global problems" whose resolution would benefit socialist, capitalist, and Third World countries.   The reduction of environmental pollution and ecological imbalances, for example, increasingly necessitates international cooperation.   R. A. Novikov declares: "In this epoch, the further progress of human civilization requires more than ever before the direction of social energy to deal with the preservation of nature, the utilization of natural resources, the rational and comprehensive management of the entire system of 'man-society-nature' from the standpoint not only of the present but of the long run, not only from a national but from a global ecological perspective."(2)   Some Soviet analysts acknowledge the emergence of an environmental crisis in advanced capitalist and developed socialist societies, implicitly calling into question the advantages of socialist planning and management.   But Soviet commentators maintain that, by encouraging "self-criticism" on environmental issues and by initiating international efforts to resolve environmental problems, the leaders of developed socialist states can help to reduce the abuse of nature and can demonstrate to their own citizens and to other peoples the superiority of socialist problem-solving capabilities.

Third, the STR creates opportunities to cope with dilemmas that result from powerful demographic forces, such as the more than doubling of the world's population in the second half of the twentieth century and the concomitant shortages of food, energy, and raw materials.   Soviet spokesmen emphasize the importance of international collaboration, especially between the most industrialized socialist and capitalist states, to develop the resources of the world's oceans.   N.I. Lebedev adds: "The current scientific-technical revolution makes it objectively necessary and possible to arrange for long-term economic, scientific, and technical ties in many other fields requiring collective effort: exploration and development of outer space, transport (especially air-borne), peaceful uses of atomic energy, and the battle against the most widespread and dangerous diseases."(3)

Fourth, the STR promotes "the internationalization of economic life." Soviet theorists maintain that the specialization and concentration of production are "objective laws" governing industrial development throughout the world. The pursuit of economic self-sufficiency can lead to wasteful duplication of efforts by competing nations. Soviet conservatives stress the importance of integrating the Comecon economies and of selectively expanding links with advanced capitalist and Third World economies. Soviet modernizers call for greater emphasis on East-West commercial ties. But most conservatives and all modernizers would agree with M. M. Maksimova that, "In the conditions of the current STR, all countries are equally interested in making use of its achievements and in implementing the advantages of the international division of labor, which is providing ever new opportunities for the enhancement of social production, the acceleration of technological progress, and the establishment of higher living standards for the population."(4) Or, as V.L. Mal'kevich states: "Foreign economic ties in the age of the STR stimulate the development of the productive forces, the deepening of international specialization, the emergence of new types of productive activity, scientific research, and satisfaction of rising social requirements."(5)

Soviet officials and researchers recognize that present-day international economic relations are generating problems as well as opportunities. The USSR's economy has become increasingly open or permeable to economic disturbances from the external environment. The centralized planning and management systems of Soviet-type economies do not respond promptly or flexibly to fluctuations in world prices and to the supply of and demand for imports and exports. To be sure, the USSR benefited considerably from the inflated prices of oil and gold in the late 1970s. But the rising prices of grain, the stagnating prices of oil, and the declining prices of gold in the early 1980s have made it much more difficult for the USSR to plan its foreign trade and to manage its hard-currency debt. These difficulties have been compounded by Eastern Europe's mounting dependency on subsidized energy imports from the Soviet Union and by the chaos in the Polish economy in the early 1980s, especially Poland's huge debt to Western banks and governments. With the creditworthiness of the entire Soviet bloc undermined, and with production and distribution bottlenecks disrupting the economies of numerous Comecon countries, some of the liabilities of socialist economic integration became more apparent and troublesome to the Brezhnev administration. In short, the Soviet optimism about international economic ties in the early 1970s was tempered by a more cautious assessment of the costs and risks of extensive participation in and exposure to the increasingly unstable and unpredictable global economy of the 1980s.

Fifth, the STR spurs the internationalization of scientific and technological activity.(6)   Previously, the exchange of manufactured goods and natural resources had been the basic type of economic interaction among states.   But, in the era of the STR, fundamental scientific research and technical know-how transcend national borders.   A Soviet scientist or an engineer may well have more professional skills and interests in common with a Western specialist in the same field than with Soviet colleagues in his own institution.   Collaboration among the scientists and technical experts of different countries and the dissemination of existing knowledge promote mutually advantageous economic growth and productivity, and reduce the duplication of primary research and its practical applications. International team studies and the sale of licenses, for example, are particularly important in fields where the costs and risks of talent- and time-consuming R&D are extremely high.   Moreover, certain scientific and technological projects (for example, space and energy R&D) are so costly and complex that long-term international financing is often required.

Soviet conservatives and modernizers think that the coordination of East-West scientific, technological, and economic policies is unfeasible, given the basic differences between socialist and capitalist systems and the multifaceted competition between them.   But Soviet analysts emphasize the importance of integrating the economies of the USSR and its Comecon partners, and of expanding some economic ties between socialist and capitalist nations.   Hence, most conservatives and all modernizers would agree with Lebedev and Mal'kevich that

> Scientific-technical autarky is an impermissible luxury. In the final analysis it holds back scientific and technical progress, and consequently the growth of each country's productive forces. . . . No country, even the most highly developed, can secure maximum results in all areas of science, technology, and material production. For as the volume of knowledge grows in breadth and depth, the STR penetrates every sphere of economic activity. The multiformity and complexity of scientific and technological progress require much greater expenditure of manpower and finance for research and development and the material embodiment of their results. The scale of the integrated problems confronting science and technology at the present time makes it obligatory for individual countries to join their efforts for common goals.(7)

Sixth, the STR enhances the importance of a nation's ability to compete in an increasingly internationalized science-technology-production cycle or division of labor.   In order to become more competitive in the world economy, the USSR must use scarce resources more effectively and efficiently, produce more and better industrial and agricultural goods, market its wares abroad (especially manufactured items) more successfully generate more hard currency, and more skillfully select and thoroughly assimilate the products, services, and information that can be purchased or obtained from other nations. Both conservatives and modernizers perceive international scientific-technical and economic competition to be integrally connected with domestic economic challenges and pressures, and they recognize the importance of coordinating domestic and international objectives. Modernizers emphasize that in order to improve the quality and quantity of Soviet industrial and agricultural products and to meet the growing demands and needs of Soviet consumers, the closer linking of domestic production with foreign trade is becoming more and more significant. A major Soviet study concludes: "Foreign economic ties give us great additional opportunities for successfully fulfilling [our] economic plans, for saving time, for increasing the efficiency of production, for accelerating scientific and technological progress, and for attaining the primary objective - the further upgrading of the standard of living of the Soviet people."(8)

Seventh, the STR fosters scientific, technological, and economic cooperation between East and West, which, in turn, increases the likelihood and longevity of political accords. Georgii Skorov argues that "tension between countries always forces each of them to harden its position. At the same time, extension of commercial and economic relations on an equal and mutually profitable basis always provides the conditions for closer attention to the partner's opinion, induces pursuit of a more flexible policy, and justifies a tendency to compromise."(9) A. P. Aleksandrov, president of the USSR Academy of Sciences, affirms that the importation of foreign experience and technical capability on a reciprocal and regularized basis promotes "the strengthening of trust and the growth of economic incentive for the preservation of peace. Long-term agreements would give these changes a stable instead of a chance character."(10) In a word, the selective expansion of international scientific, technological, and economic ties is an integral part of the Soviet concept of detente.

Eighth, the STR heightens the significance of nonmilitary forms of power in the international arena. As Oleg Bykov puts it: "Neither strategic nor technical innovations can help imperialism to regain the capability of resolving the question of war and peace at its own discretion. For with the present correlation of forces, including the strategic equilibrium, military might becomes less and less suitable a means of resolving the differences between the two social systems [socialism and capitalism]."(11) The mounting international influence of Japan derives almost entirely from its economic successes, and the rising assertiveness of Western Europe vis-a-vis the United States is similarly grounded on its commercial accomplishments and interests. Such factors must be given more and more weight when assessing a nation's overall capabilities and when predicting the future of "inter-imperialist contradictions."(12)

However, Soviet commentators stress that the relative scientific, technological, and economic capabilities of industri-alized states are a major source of political influence. This argument has some important implications for East-West re-lations that Soviet spokesmen rarely address (for example, the continuing "technology gap"). As for relations among the Western powers, a comprehensive Soviet-East German study affirms: "The growth of the role of Western Europe does not automatically entail the weakening of the positions of the USA. The USA continues to command a massive economic potential, and far [outpaces] its West European rivals in the areas of science and technology. In the military sphere Western Europe keeps [oriented toward] the USA as the power which commands the greatest stockpile of nuclear weapons in the capitalist world. In the political sphere the USA has kept hold of certain means of influencing the course followed by some West European states."(13)

Ninth, the STR establishes new forms of international dependency, especially in scientific and technological fields. G. A. Arbatov declares that "states which cannot create a sufficiently powerful scientific and technical potential of their own are faced with a difficult dilemma. They have to choose between falling seriously behind . . . or tying themselves firmly to a country which possesses such a potential."(14) At the same time, Soviet leaders and analysts emphasize that the STR introduces new forms of interdependence as well. Highly industrialized nations must secure diverse and stable natural resource bases. Hence, some Third World countries with tech-nological dependencies possess commodities that establish reverse dependencies.(15) Oil is a particularly important example of the capitalist world's need to maintain businesslike relations with a cartel of developing nations (OPEC). Also, the STR creates a demand for certain previously unusable raw materials. For instance, the aluminum industry is the only consumer of bauxite.

Tenth, the STR has sparked a worldwide "information explosion." As Y. Kashlev observes, "The objective social, political, scientific, and technological processes of the modern world are enhancing the role of information and propaganda in society and international relations."(16) This is due in part to a "dramatic and unparalleled expansion of communication tech-nology," and to an "expansion of international economic, commercial, financial, scientific, technical, cultural, and other links."(17) Indeed, many regions of industrialized nations are becoming increasingly permeable to ideas and information from other regions and from abroad. Also, the political leaders of industrialized nations are striving to improve the transmission and processing of information, because effective decisions in virtually all issue areas depend upon a continuous flow of accurate and timely data from domestic and international environments. Y. Zakharov affirms: "This is an objective process which stems from the general laws of development of the productive forces and the requirements of the international division of labor. The STR is speeding up this process."(18)

Eleventh, the STR produces increasingly complex and shifting international relationships, which, in turn, necessitate adjustments in the foreign-policymaking and domestic policies and processes of modern industrialized states. Traditional diplomacy must be supplemented by the contributions of greater numbers of civilian and military politician-administrators, technical specialists, and production executives. These officials often work in ostensibly "domestic" functional areas, but they have a growing stake in defining the international interests of the state. Diplomatic, commercial, military, and intelligence activities are being transformed by experts who analyze segments of the international environment and, less frequently, internal/external linkages. For example, many Soviet analysts are publicly and privately acknowledging the need to modify some of the institutions and operations of the USSR's highly centralized economic system, in order to improve the growth and productivity of the economy and to compete more successfully in world markets. Top political officials retain the power to ignore this specialized knowledge. But most socialist and capitalist leaders are thought to be using such information and counsel to identify and assess the problems and opportunities spawned by the STR, and to formulate and implement differentiated national policies that seek to preserve their currently held values in a rapidly changing international system.(19)

Thus, leading Soviet officials and theorists understand that the STR is profoundly influencing international politics in the contemporary era. As Lebedev succinctly concludes: "Scientific and technical progress has made our world smaller and more crowded. The masses react to problems of war and peace much more sensitively than before. Wars, particularly world wars, have always been a calamity for the masses. However, formerly wars had never jeopardized the physical existence of entire countries and peoples. In view of the huge stockpiles of thermonuclear weapons, the life of every person in the world now depends on the intelligent solution of problems of foreign policy."(20)

SOVIET CONSERVATIVE AND MODERNIZING
PERSPECTIVES(21)

Soviet leaders and international affairs specialists differ, however, in their assessments of "intelligent" foreign policy initiatives and responses. Soviet conservatives and modernizers disagree about foreign policy priorities, the most effective means of implementing them, and the risks and costs of alternative programs. Officials also debate the nature and significance of important processes of change, such as the STR and "the general crisis of capitalism," and their political implications, such as the merits of pursuing relatively autarkic or interdependent strategies of development. The military and civilian sectors of the Soviet economy continuously compete for scarce resources, which is another fundamental source of bureaucratic conflict over power and policy.

Official Soviet spokesmen view East-West relations as a dynamic mix of conflict and cooperation and of centrifugal and centripetal tendencies. But conservatives emphasize East-West conflict and West-West cooperation; modernizers emphasize East-West cooperation and West-West conflict; and both conservatives and modernizers emphasize the competitive aspects of cooperation as well as of conflict.

Conservatives stress that Soviet foreign policy should actively support the "objective" and "subjective" forces that will eventually make the polities and societies of capitalist and Third World nations similar to those of the USSR; modernizers stress that socialist, capitalist, and Third World countries have more and more mutual interests in contemporary international relations and should adjust their foreign policies (but not necessarily their sociopolitical systems) accordingly. Most conservatives and all modernizers share Mal'kevich's belief that the "STR has appreciably accelerated the [economic merging] of nations, has intertwined their economic contacts and interests, notably in scientific research and industry."(22) Modernizers view this process with confidence and as a potential benefit, whereas conservatives view it with caution and as a potential liability.

Assessing the effects of the STR on West-West relations and East-West detente (see especially pages 68-73), Soviet modernizers emphasize that major cleavages are developing between Western Europe and the United States. These cleavages are widening primarily because of the capitalist powers' different economic and security interests. West European countries, modernizers argue, are seeking to increase scientific, technological, and economic cooperation with the Soviet bloc, in order to enhance their economic competitiveness vis-a-vis the United States and Japan and to reduce their

political dependence upon the United States. East-West diplomatic and commercial relations, as well as the limitation of
strategic arms and the reduction of conventional military
forces, can and must be "mutually advantageous" to socialist
and capitalist states in the coming decades. Political and
economic ties with Western countries will spur the development
of the Soviet economy, modernizers contend, and will eventually induce all Western nations to accept the Soviet interpretation of detente or will increasingly split the Western alliance.

Soviet conservatives, in contrast, underscore that the
West's approach to East-West relations "is dominated by a unity
of class interests, displaying a tendency toward coordinating
their political courses."(23) The military-industrial complexes
of Western Europe and the United States have compelling mutual interests, conservatives maintain. Most West European
countries and Japan, notwithstanding their growing economic
power, lack the motivation and capabilities to transform that
power into political leverage vis-a-vis the United States. The
policies of America's allies are greatly influenced, conservatives argue, by the continued U.S. superiority in many key
areas of scientific research and technological innovation in
military and nonmilitary spheres.

Evaluating the impact of the STR on the global economy
and the USSR's economy (see especially pages 93-110), Soviet
modernizers emphasize that foreign economic ties have beneficial effects on domestic growth and productivity. The
quality, mix, pricing, cost-efficiency, and profitability of
Soviet products can be enhanced or "rationalized" by the
challenge of competing in world markets. Two Western analysts contend that "subject to certain conditions - above all a
satisfactory degree of openness to foreign technology and
preparedness for its infusion - the transfer of technology from
a developed country to a medium developed country becomes
the dominant source of growth in the medium developed country."(24) This premise, and the feasibility and desirability of
applying it in the USSR, are central to the thinking of Soviet
modernizers.

Soviet conservatives, however, favor less extensive and
more selective importation of advanced technology. Most
conservatives believe that Western computers, telecommunications, and automated production systems can improve the performance of the Soviet economy, thereby preserving its highly
centralized features and forestalling systemic reforms. Conservatives tend to view the importation of Western technology
as a "one-shot" or "quick-fix"(25) approach to pressing problems. Whereas modernizers argue that Western imports are a
means of continuously stimulating indigenous technological
innovation, conservatives stress that overreliance on Western
technology perpetuates "sluggishness" in the Soviet science-
technology-production cycle. Brezhnev, having shifted from

the modernizing position he shared with Kosygin in the early and mid-1970s, articulated a conservative position on East-West technology exchange at the Twenty-sixth Party Congress in 1981. "We must look into the reasons that we sometimes lose our [competitive advantage in certain fields of science, technology, and production] and spend large sums of money to purchase from foreign countries equipment and technologies that we are fully capable of producing ourselves, and often of a higher quality too."(26)

In short, Soviet conservatives and modernizers have different perspectives on the economic effects of importing sophisticated Western technology, whereas their perspectives on the appropriate nature and volume of high technology imports are much more similar. For instance, photocopying machines are anathema to conservatives and most modernizers, and both are eager to import sizable quantities of oil drilling equipment and of piping and turbines for the compressor stations needed to transport natural gas long distances.

Analyzing the consequences of "the STR in military affairs" on the Soviet-American strategic rivalry (see especially pp. 160-173), Soviet modernizers emphasize the importance of balancing military and general political and economic capabilities. Modernizers argue that civilian sectors should derive more benefits ("spin-offs") from science-based technological advances in the military sphere. Strategic modernizers affirm that the STR dramatically alters the nature of contemporary warfare every decade or so, and that Soviet goals and methods should be reconceptualized and adjusted accordingly. For example, conventional military forces and economic competitiveness are viewed as increasingly significant modes of advancing Soviet global interests. Moreover, modernizers think that strategic arms limitation agreements are an important means of reducing the likelihood of nuclear war between the superpowers. Because of the emergence of "realistic" Western leaders and public opinion, effective arms control treaties can be negotiated. Lebedev, for one, affirms that national security cannot be guaranteed by the continuous modernization of strategic arms, and he concludes that "in international relations a nuclear war can no longer be a means of attaining political objectives."(27) Hence, modernizers underscore the benefits of maintaining strategic parity and the pitfalls of either the Soviet or American pursuit of strategic superiority.

Soviet conservatives stress the primacy of both the strategic and conventional military components of national security, Conservatives reiterate that survival in a hostile international environment takes precedence over all other claims on human and material resources. Strategic conservatives anticipate that new weapons technologies, together with much better military training of the traditional armed forces and of the general population (e.g., civil defense), will ensure victory in any kind of war that aggressive capitalist leaders might initiate. Conservatives are less sanguine than modernizers about reducing the chances of a military confrontation with the West through arms control, economic ties, or diplomatic negotiations, and about limiting a war, once started, to conventional combat or intermediate-range ("theater") nuclear exchanges. Conservatives view the overall military superiority of the Soviet bloc as the major means of furthering the global interests of the USSR and as the most effective deterrent to the expansion of Western, especially American, political, economic, and military influence throughout the world. Modernizers, in contrast, imply that the actual or perceived Soviet quest for strategic superiority might spur U.S. leaders to use their formidable military capabilities to advance American interests more aggressively, and might broaden the U.S. interpretation of these interests to include new substantive and geographical areas and new "linkages" between areas.

Briefly stated, Soviet conservatives and modernizers disagree about the merits of pursuing strategic superiority. Conservatives stress the risks and costs of failing to confront the global military and sociopolitical challenges posed by the common interests of bellicose capitalist states. Modernizers emphasize the economic challenges presented by contemporary capitalism and the diverging interests of Western nations, whose policies are shaped by both "belligerent" and "realistic" elements. Conservatives do not belittle the benefits of nuclear parity, but, unlike modernizers, they perceive strategic superiority to be a feasible and desirable means of enhancing national security. In order to achieve strategic superiority, conservatives affirm, the Soviet military and heavy industrial sectors must continue to receive a disproportionate share of scarce resources. Hence, conservatives have a strong vested interest in the argument that military power (not economic power) is the primary component of political influence in the generally hostile (not highly differentiated) present-day international environment.

CONSERVATIVES VERSUS MODERNIZERS IN
THE BREZHNEV YEARS

Whereas Stalin's conception of "socialism in one country" combined a domestic strategy of rapid industrialization with highly selective importation of Western technology, Khrushchev's view of "socialism" and "communist construction" and Brezhnev's view of "developed socialism" link internal goals with a different international orientation. Stalin's successors have pursued a strategy of economic development that is predicated upon the broadening and deepening of interdependent relationships with a dynamic global economy and a more and

more fragmented international political system. The USSR's
policy of active peaceful coexistence and detente with the most
industrialized powers of the West, particularly in the late 1950s
and early 1970s, and the USSR's persistent efforts to expand
long-term trade and industrial cooperation with diverse West
European and Third World countries, demonstrate that many
contemporary Soviet leaders have viewed economic interdependence as a key policy objective.

The increasingly multipolar world of the 1970s and 1980s
(especially the relative decline of American influence) and the
growing impact of science and technology on world politics
(especially the balance of strategic power between the United
States and the USSR, the proliferation of nuclear weapons
among other nations, and the burgeoning of international
economic ties) have significantly altered the external environment in which Soviet foreign policy must operate. Brezhnev's
"collective leadership" portrays the world outside of the Soviet
bloc as a veritable sea of change. Soviet spokesmen, particularly modernizers, acknowledge that international trends and
events are having a mounting effect on conditions within the
USSR, and that the USSR's exposure to foreign economic influences is increasing because of the "objective" characteristics of
the STR (especially the expanding international division of
labor).

At the same time, the current Soviet leadership seeks to
preserve traditional goals and institutional relationships. The
Brezhnev administration underscores the soundness of conservative Soviet values and of the basic features of the existing
Soviet political system. But top party and state officials
recognize that changes of some kind are needed to sustain
minimal rates of socioeconomic progress and to adjust
long-standing priorities and authority patterns in a new and
uncertain historical context. For example, top Soviet leaders
clearly understand the political, as well as the economic,
importance of preventing further slippage in the rates of
growth of industrial and agricultural output and productivity
in the USSR, and of meeting the public's rising dissatisfaction
with inadequate food, housing, consumer goods, health care,
and social services.

Which changes in the Soviet polity and economy constitute
"reform"? Which changes constitute "adaptation" of the traditional policies and political-administrative procedures to new
domestic and international circumstances? These questions
have been continuously debated in the Khrushchev and Brezhnev administrations. Indeed, even the technical criteria and
standards for making such judgments have been disputed in
most issue areas.

Soviet leaders and analysts have fueled this debate by
repeatedly proclaiming that the STR is bringing portentous
changes at home and abroad. Brezhnev asserted at the

Twenty-fifth Party Congress in 1976: "The revolution in science and technology requires a cardinal change in the style and methods of economic activity, a determined struggle against stagnation and the rigidities of routine, genuine respect for science, and the ability and desire to seek advice and to take it into consideration."(28) Because of the global nature of the STR, and because of the closer integration of the Soviet economy into the world economy, Brezhnev's statement has major implications for domestic and foreign policy and for the strategies that link them. These implications are not at all self-evident, however, and Soviet bureaucratic coalitions have competing interests in different interpretations of official policy and strategy and of internal and external conditions.

Hence, the Brezhnev leadership, by legitimizing politicized but circumspect debate about the causes, content, and consequences of the STR, has cautiously encouraged the ongoing reassessment of political and socioeconomic changes throughout the world and of their ramifications for Soviet domestic and foreign policy. Soviet analysts, in making such evaluations, often implicitly raise questions of fundamental importance about the institutional, as well as the policy, aspects of Soviet political and economic development. For example, if "cardinal" change is needed in the economy (see Brezhnev's statement just quoted), what corresponding changes are necessary in the role of the Communist Party, especially in its relations with state and production organizations?

Succinctly put, officials in the Khrushchev and Brezhnev administrations have formulated and expressed competing views about domestic and international politics. Also, Soviet leaders have become increasingly aware of the interconnections between - even the inseparability of - domestic and foreign policies in the era of the STR. Consequently, different Soviet perspectives on international relations often advocate or imply different internal policies and institutional relationships. Soviet conceptualizations of "developed socialism," for instance, have been considerably influenced by favorable judgments about economic progress in highly industrialized capitalist countries.(29) Jerry Hough notes that the Soviet authors of an exceptionally authoritative book emphasize the universal or "objective" features of the STR, and he observes that "many of the structural differences between the Western and Soviet economies are attributed to the process of industrialization; hence, the authors . . . are implicitly saying that [these structural innovations in capitalist countries] not only should, but must be adopted in the Soviet Union."(30)

We have seen that contemporary Soviet leaders and theorists hold many similar views about the STR and international politics. We have also observed that, within these parameters of consensus, leading Soviet officials and analysts debate the nature of international change and particularly its implications for diplomatic, economic, and military policy. Both conservative and modernizing premises were incorporated into the important Twenty-fourth Party Congress program in 1971, and the two orientations were given about equal weight. The competition between conservative and modernizing tendencies continued throughout the 1970s and early 1980s, in response to the successes, failures, and unanticipated consequences of Brezhnev's "grand design." Generally speaking, the conservative tendency gained ground in this period - due in part to the mounting inertia and frustrations of the aging Soviet leadership (especially in coping with the increasingly serious economic problems of the Comecon countries) and to the Soviet leaders' perceptions of a more threatening international environment (for example, U.S.-Chinese political, economic, and military collaboration).

Present-day Soviet commentators emphasize that detente must be grounded upon the armed strength of the USSR. The significant build-up of the USSR's military power since the 1960s enables the Soviet bloc to interact with capitalist states from a position of strength, rather than vulnerability, and to establish mutual rather than unilateral dependencies.(31) Hence, "the shift in the correlation of forces in favor of socialism" stems largely from the growth of Soviet military power throughout the world.

However, Soviet efforts to cooperate with the West in certain fields are based on confidence in the USSR's economic and scientific potential as well as in its military capabilities.(32) Soviet spokesmen argue that the most efficient development and utilization of scientific, technical, and economic resources require an international division of labor. Autarky is wasteful and short-sighted, modernizers emphasize. Scientific and technological progress, together with economic growth and productivity, can be accelerated by closer integration of the Comecon economies and by carefully selected commercial ties with highly industrialized capitalist nations, conservatives agree. Conservatives and modernizers recognize deficiencies in the USSR's science-technology-production cycle, and both strongly support the policy of detente, which is striving to improve the performance of the Soviet economy under difficult and changing circumstances. Conservatives and modernizers acknowledge the mushrooming of international economic interdependencies and the increasing openness of the Soviet economy to external disturbances, and both policy groups are responding to these "objective" forces in their own ways.

Soviet modernizers affirm that it is commercially advantageous to socialist and capitalist countries for the latter provide the know-how and credits to help the USSR extract, transport, and market its energy, mineral, and other natural resources. If some Western nations choose not to do so, ade-

quate assistance will almost certainly be forthcoming from other
capitalist governments, corporations, and banks in the short
or long run. And, as conservatives stress, Soviet scientists
and engineers possess the skills and can be given greater
resources and incentives to produce new technologies - more
slowly and expensively, perhaps, but at less political risk and
cost.

Most contemporary Soviet leaders do not prefer an autarkic strategy, but it is perceived to be a possible alternative, especially in light of the mixed political and economic
results of the Soviet detente policy of the 1970s. Conservatives argue that the USSR's capacity to pursue interdependent
or independent courses of development gives Soviet officials a
broader range of choice in international diplomatic and commercial activities than that of their counterparts in the
industrialized West. Conservatives stress that the USSR,
primarily because of its vast untapped raw material resources
in Siberia and the Far East, is much less dependent upon the
Third World than is the industrialized West, and hence has
greater freedom to maneuver in the international arena.
Western dependence on foreign sources of energy, conservatives imply, is a vulnerability that is undermining the entire
capitalist way of life. Modernizers insist that greater Soviet
participation in the world economy contributes significantly to
the growth and productivity of the Comecon economies.

In fact, different strategies of economic development have
competed or have been implemented simultaneously in the Soviet Union for a long time. Thane Gustafson observed in
1981:

> Throughout the Soviet period there has been an
> uneasy coexistence between foreign imports and
> home-grown enterprise (the latter usually entailing
> some degree of reform) as the two principal strate-
> gies for technological innovation, the former predom-
> inating in some periods (such as the First Five-Year
> Plan, 1928-1932) and the latter in others (such as
> the Second Five-Year Plan, 1933-1937). Logically,
> the two strategies should complement one another;
> but in practice they have tended to compete, and
> the balance between them swings with the state of
> mind of the Politburo. The last fifteen years have
> been somewhat exceptional, for both strategies have
> been pursued simultaneously, and more vigorously
> than ever before.(34)

Two Westerners, V. Sobeslavsky and P. Beazley, elaborate:

The import of large quantities of foreign technology is accompanied by piecemeal reform of the existing organizational structure of Soviet industry. Both alternatives are thus by no means mutually exclusive, but, on the contrary, one complements the other. Nevertheless, it is the relative importance of one over the other that counts, and in this respect it must be concluded that at least in the USSR import of technology clearly receives an immeasurably higher priority than the promotion of indigenous technological innovation.(33)

Neither the conservative nor the modernizing tendency is likely to predominate in the near future. Some of the chief reasons behind the considerable support for conservative and modernizing orientations under the Brezhnev administration are: the legitimation of circumscribed debate about policy alternatives and administrative effectiveness; the perceived complexity and fluidity of the domestic and international environments and their interconnections; the perceived need for diverse inputs into policymaking and implementation; and the perceived importance of making differentiated and flexible initiatives and responses to ongoing and interrelated problems and opportunities in a period characterized by increasing scarcities and difficult choices.

Moreover, the criteria and standards for evaluating conservative and modernizing perspectives and policies are not at all clear-cut. Philip Hanson, for one, concludes: "The commercial transfer of Western technology to the USSR has economic consequences for the recipient nation that are somewhere between 'massive assistance' and zero effect. To be slightly less imprecise, the consequences appear to fall well short of the former but are nonetheless sufficiently far above the latter to be of importance to Soviet policymakers."(35) The Soviet leadership, we submit, is similarly uncertain or divided about the actual effects of the international transfer of technology, and about the past and future impact of specific scientific and technical developments on the economy and polity of the USSR. With "collective" or group decisionmaking at many stages and levels, with continued disjunctions between administrative powers and responsibilities, with a general reluctance to alter the technological, informational, and incentive systems into which new equipment is implanted, and with questionable technical and statistical measures of effectiveness and efficiency, party and state leaders are likely to resort to highly politicized but often conciliatory (such as "live-and-let-live") judgments when evaluating conservative and modernizing programs or combinations thereof.

Nonetheless, leading Soviet officials view the STR as a factor critical to the acceleration of domestic economic and sociopolitical progress and to the conduct and deterrence of modern wars. These powerful pressures for and constraints on interdependence have considerably influenced Soviet perspectives on the changing nature of East-West competition. Soviet analysts frequently observe that the STR is a compelling "objective" pressure for detente and that detente consists of the simultaneous development of collaboration and conflict between socialist and capitalist states. While the Soviet modernizers emphasize the cooperative elements of detente, the conservatives emphasize the adversarial. While modernizers stress the importance of establishing ground rules for East-West political, economic, and military competition, conservatives stress the difficulties of creating and maintaining such ground rules. While modernizers underscore the benefits of advancing Soviet global interests by economic and conventional military means, conservatives underscore the primacy of military capabilities and of strategic arms in particular. Hence, the different policy implications of Soviet conservative and modernizing orientations are portentous indeed.

EAST-WEST RELATIONS IN THE 1980s:
AFGHANISTAN AND POLAND

By the mid-1970s, top Soviet officials clearly felt that the USSR could simultaneously support "national liberation movements" and participate more fully in the East-West and North-South division of labor. On the one hand, Angola was the first in a series of Soviet and Soviet-supported adventures in the Third World. On the other hand, strategic arms limitation agreements and substantially expanded U.S.-Soviet economic and scientific-technical cooperation still seemed within reach. The diplomatic and commercial importance of Soviet-West European ties was clearly recognized in the early 1970s, and the benefits of not overly relying on "the American connection" were increasingly recognized from the mid-1970s onward.(36) Indeed, some Soviet leaders and commentators concluded that the active pursuit of the two chief elements of detente-- selected East-West confrontation in the Third World and selected East-West cooperation in bilateral relations--had the added advantage of fragmenting the Atlantic alliance and thereby substantially furthering the USSR's interests in its worldwide political, economic, and military competition with the United States.

Will Brezhnev's detente policy of the 1970s continue to be viable in the 1980s? The "objective" pressures of the STR notwithstanding, the answer to this question depends heavily on the political response of the Soviet Union and the major Western nations to changing international circumstances. Especially important are the momentous recent developments in Afghanistan and Poland. These two crises constitute a watershed in Soviet foreign policy, in East-West relations, and in the relations among the Western powers themselves.

The Soviet occupation of Afghanistan underscored the growing gap between Soviet and American conceptions of detente. The Soviet concept emphasizes collaboration and mutual restraint in East-West relations within Europe, while continuing - even accelerating - the rivalry with the West in the Third World. The American concept stresses East-West cooperation and restraint within Europe as a means of reducing global tensions and of stabilizing the multifaceted competition between the United States and the USSR. The Soviet military action in Afghanistan dramatically demonstrated the will and capacity of the USSR to use its expanding military power to compete with the West, especially with the United States, in the Third World. The Carter and Reagan administrations' responses to the occupation of Afghanistan have made clear the American rejection of the Soviet interpretation of detente. However, U.S. diplomacy and military and economic power have been unable to deter the Soviet leadership from acting upon its own conception of detente, especially vis-a-vis selected African and Asian countries and the major West European democracies during the 1970s and 1980s.

Western and Eastern Europe have been caught between the superpowers. From the outset, the West Europeans refused to define the Afghanistan crisis in East-West terms, perceiving it instead to be a regional crisis requiring regional responses. East-West detente within Europe was dealt a glancing blow, but not a piercing - let alone a fatal - wound. West Europeans have consistently stressed the centrality of detente relationships within Europe. While recognizing the continued existence of East-West competition outside of Europe, West European leaders have assessed that competition largely in terms of its effects on European affairs. This position is congruent with the Soviet Union's emphasis upon political, economic, and scientific-technical cooperation between Western and Eastern Europe and between various West European nations and the USSR. At the same time, the similar West European and Soviet perspectives concerning the priority of collaboration in Europe might lead the USSR's leaders to misunderstand the importance of Atlantic ties for the military security of Western Europe. The Soviet leadership could well be developing unrealistic expectations about the possibility of achieving military detente in Europe on Soviet terms.

No sooner had these tendencies in West-West and East-West relations begun to crystallize after the Soviet invasion of Afghanistan than the East and West were plunged into the Polish crisis. The gains that the Brezhnev administration thought it had realized from the occupation of Afghanistan - in particular, the greater independence of Western Europe from the United States - were immediately jeopardized by the unprecedented confrontation between the state and the workers, as well as the Catholic church, in Poland. Moreover, the Polish developments revived East European assertiveness vis-a-vis the USSR. Greater national consciousness was particularly evident in the desire of the Polish party-government, labor unions, and church to resolve their differences without being dictated to from abroad. In addition, the turmoil in Poland raised the possibility that other East European leaders might be faced with comparable challenges to their power and policies.

Elites and ordinary citizens in Eastern Europe have begun to perceive a choice between overt Soviet intervention and the resolution of domestic crises without such interference. These evolving perspectives are the products, not only of de-Stalinization and desatellization, but of detente itself. Detente has been a gamble in both the East and West. The East has risked unleashing major destabilizing changes within the Soviet bloc by encouraging greater interdependencies and openness to the West. The West has risked long-run political, economic, and military vulnerability vis-a-vis the USSR, as well as additional strains in the Atlantic alliance. For example, Western Europe has invested significantly in the Soviet and East European economies, the United States has substantially reduced its ground forces, and West European public opinion has resisted the installation of U.S. theater nuclear weapons on European soil.

A Soviet decision to have sent Red Army troops into Poland to help crush the independent trade union movement would have vividly demonstrated the determination of the CPSU leadership to reverse the trends in East European countries that have been fostered by East-West detente. Direct Soviet intervention in Poland would also have substantially enhanced West European dependence upon and unity with the United States. However, a Soviet decision to have refrained from extensive involvement in the Polish crisis would have strongly legitimized interdependence between Eastern and Western Europe. Soviet "restraint" in Poland would also have increased West European power vis-a-vis the United States, further emboldening some West European governments to challenge American views of political, economic, and military detente in Europe.

The course actually taken in 1981 - a carefully prepared preemptive strike by the Polish military and police against leading trade union officials and the establishment of martial law - was strongly abetted by the Soviet leadership and covertly aided by the Soviet army and security forces already stationed in Poland. The clandestine but extensive Soviet support for the Polish military regime exacerbated tensions in the Western alliance. The unanticipated and (in the short run at least) ingenious Soviet handling of the Polish situation encouraged some West European leaders to reject the measured U.S. economic sanctions against the USSR, and may have stiffened West European resistance to U.S. preferences regarding the deployment of theater nuclear weapons. Continued or greater Soviet circumspection may well strengthen the already powerful antiwar movements among the citizenry of many West European nations. In a word, the unfolding of the Polish crisis - the key decisions themselves and the processes by which they are reached - has begun markedly to influence East-West and West-West relations in the 1980s.

Soviet conservatives and modernizers have very different views about the impact of events in Poland on the future of East-West relations. For conservatives, "the forces of Atlantic solidarity" are in the ascendency in the West. A Warsaw Pact invasion of Poland would protect "the socialist community" from single-minded and skillful political and economic subversion by the West. Soviet conservatives have emphasized throughout the Brezhnev period that "the class unity" and unmitigated aggressiveness of the Western powers continuously endanger the interests of the socialist bloc countries. No evident disunity in the West seems to dissuade Soviet conservatives from such conclusions, not even the considerable disarray in the Atlantic alliance that followed the Red Army's occupation of Afghanistan and the imposition of martial law in Poland. Instead, conservatives stress the ideological aspects of the Polish situation and the long-term political, military, and economic advantages of an intrabloc or autarkic strategy of development. Conservatives acknowledge that these strategies increase the effort and expense of producing many goods and services, but they insist that the maintenance of one-party rule throughout the Soviet bloc and the collective defense of the USSR and its allies are much more important than economic efficiency.

For Soviet modernizers, "interimperialist contradictions" are so deep and long-lasting that detente with Western Europe can be secured even in the face of strong U.S. opposition. Only a Warsaw Pact invasion of Poland could substantially strengthen the belligerent elements in the West and discredit "the realist forces" that favor detente, modernizers imply. Modernizers are particularly concerned that the overt use of Soviet military power in Poland would undercut the economic benefits of detente to the USSR at precisely the time when the Soviet and East European economies are having considerable difficulties. Soviet modernizers, much more than conservatives, are facing up to some unpleasant realities. Food shortages have become a political, as well as an economic, problem of the utmost importance. The USSR's economy is suffering a steep decline in its overall rate of growth. The

Soviet labor force is expanding at a snail's pace. And sharply diminishing increases in labor and technological productivity in both industry and agriculture, as well as insufficient capital formation, inadequate production returns on R&D expenditures, and inefficient managerial practices and organizational technology, continue to retard Soviet economic development.

Foreign economic ties are an important means of coping with these problems. Especially beneficial to the Soviet economy are product pay-back arrangements, such as the mammoth natural gas deal between the USSR and numerous West European countries. Soviet modernizers are understandably apprehensive that direct Warsaw Pact intervention in Poland would terminate economic cooperation of this kind and would greatly reduce the USSR's participation in the international division of labor. Insularity, modernizers argue, would seriously undermine the process of economic development in the USSR.

Soviet modernizers are fearful that the Red Army's overt participation in any stage of the resolution of the Polish crisis would all but scuttle Brezhnev's Twenty-fourth Party Congress program, which was reaffirmed and refined at the Twenty-fifth Congress in 1976 and at the Twenty-sixth Congress in 1981. Stressing the importance of general economic and sociopolitical capabilities, modernizers conclude that renewed hostilities with the West would decrease the national security of the USSR. For example, Dmitri Ustinov, Soviet Minister of Defense and Politburo member, declared in 1979 that a return to the attitudes and policies of the Cold War would have a very negative impact on the USSR. "The realization of the great plans of communist construction, the achievements of further successes in the economic and social development of our Motherland, depend to a large degree upon how the international arena takes shape."(37) Specifically, Ustinov linked the development of advanced technology in nonmilitary sectors, especially technologies obtained through Western trade and credits, to the furthering of Soviet security interests.

The tremendous potential political and economic costs to the USSR of a Warsaw Pact invasion of Poland - together with the ongoing actual costs of the occupation of Afghanistan - strongly support the Soviet modernizers' interpretation of detente. To be sure, the establishment of military rule in Poland has greatly reduced the likelihood of direct Soviet intervention. The consequences of overt Red Army assistance to the Polish military regime in the event of widespread armed or passive resistance to martial law, especially the spilling of Polish blood by Soviet soldiers, would be far-reaching for Soviet domestic and foreign policy. First, there is the probable loss and certain delay of sorely needed Western technology imports and capital investments in the Soviet economy. Second, there are the formidable political, economic, social, and military problems of managing Poland after a Soviet-led invasion. Third, there is the likely termination of Western financial aid to Poland and of trade and credits to the other East European nations. To date, Western governments have been willing to forestall default on Poland's massive hard currency debt. But many East-West economic ties would be severed for some time, perhaps permanently, by flagrant Soviet military intervention in Poland.

Hence, the outcome of the Polish crisis is critical to the competition between alternative Soviet strategies for domestic development. A Warsaw Pact invasion would strengthen the conservative approach immensely. Nonintervention - even accompanied by considerable intimidation and covert assistance to the Polish military government - supports the aims of Soviet modernizers.

Whatever transpires in Afghanistan and Poland, East-West and West-West relations in the 1980s will be quite different than in the 1970s. Political and economic leaders in the USSR and in Western and Eastern Europe took relatively compatible views of detente in the 1970s, and they established mutually beneficial relationships for themselves, for many of their elites, and for some of their citizens. In contrast, Soviet and American leaders have never agreed upon a similar and workable interpretation of detente. Not surprisingly, relations between the superpowers have deteriorated precipitously since the Nixon-Kissinger era of promising beginnings and unwarranted expectations. Leading U.S. executive and legislative branch officials have been unable or unwilling to understand or to take seriously the Soviet commitment to its own interpretation of detente, in particular the USSR's simultaneous emphasis upon long-term East-West economic cooperation and unfettered East-West competition in the Third World. The Ford, Carter, and Reagan administrations have challenged the Soviet policy of detente. But, because the USSR's policy depends much less on Soviet-American collaboration than does the United States' policy, American leaders have not been able to implement their own conceptions of detente.

Herein lies the significance of Afghanistan and Poland. Unlike the United States, Western Europe has established a detente relationship with the Soviet Union. This relationship is based upon political, economic, and scientific-technical ties that both sides perceive to be mutually advantageous. Should the Soviet-West European bonds developed in the 1970s fail to constrain the USSR from invading Poland, West European leaders and citizens might accept President Reagan's sharply critical assessment of Soviet motivations and behavior. Some West European responses to a Soviet invasion of Poland could be quite hostile, because the policy of Ostpolitik would be further discredited and many of its benefits curtailed or eliminated. For example, West European security interests would be threatened, the liabilities of long-term Soviet-West European economic cooperation (such as the huge natural gas deal) would be underscored, and the multidimensional integration of Western and Eastern Europe would be reversed.

If the USSR does <u>not</u> directly intervene in Poland – regardless of the reasons – the West Europeans' confidence in their interpretation of detente, and in the efficacy of commercial and diplomatic collaboration with the USSR, will be greatly increased. Fissures between Western Europe and the United States will almost surely widen, in part because the Reagan administration interprets Soviet behavior primarily in military terms. That is, U.S. Republican leaders are likely to argue that the Carter administration's strong reaction to the occupation of Afghanistan, and the electoral mandate in 1980 for an even more conservative U.S. foreign policy, played a key role in deterring a comparable Soviet intervention in Poland. In any event, different Western assessments of Soviet intentions and capabilities, and of Soviet responsibility for the Polish military government's repression of the Solidarity movement, are likely to exacerbate West-West disagreements for some time to come. The United States will probably continue to stress the importance of military preparedness to deter future Soviet opportunistic thrusts throughout the world. And Western Europeans will probably emphasize more adamantly than before the political and economic benefits of detente with the USSR and the long-term, rather than the tactical, nature of Soviet restraint in areas of vital interest to the West.

Thus, the Soviet-West European detente, the Soviet-American quasidetente, the intra-Atlantic alliance strains, and the West and East European ties of the 1970s will very likely be superseded by new East-West and West-West relationships in the 1980s. U.S. and West European leaders are working hard to alter one another's conceptualizations of detente, of their partners' interests, and of the collective welfare of the Western alliance. The prospects for detente within Europe will continue to be enhanced if Warsaw Pact troops do not intervene directly in Poland. Soviet-led intervention, however, would significantly intensify the global competition between the United States and the USSR, and would considerably increase tensions between Western and Eastern Europe. East-West negotiations would be limited to the search for ground rules to manage, and perhaps to reduce the danger and expense of, the fierce competition for military advantage and for a modicum of security. In all other geographical and issue areas, the promise of East-West interdependencies and mutual restraint of the early 1970s would be supplanted by confrontationist politics and by a dialogue of the deaf.

Although the unprecedented scientific, technical, and economic developments since World War II have created powerful incentives for international cooperation, we conclude by emphasizing the importance of <u>political</u> perspectives and pursuits. Other nations' intentions, capabilities, and priorities are not easily or objectively ascertainable in the increasingly fragmented international system of the 1980s. Perceptions and interests differ considerably within and among countries. Competing assessments of external and internal environments and competing strategies of political, economic, and social development are becoming more and more salient elements of contemporary intergovernmental and transnational relations. Politicized judgments and choices, not the inexorable "demands" of science and technology, will decisively shape East-West interaction and world politics for the foreseeable future.

Notes

INTRODUCTION

1. See Erik P. Hoffmann and Robbin F. Laird, In Quest of Progress: Soviet Perspectives on Advanced Society (forthcoming).

2. Erik P. Hoffmann and Robbin F. Laird, The Politics of Economic Modernization in the Soviet Union (Ithaca, N.Y.: Cornell University Press, 1982).

3. William Zimmerman, Soviet Perspectives on International Relations, 1956-1967 (Princeton, N.J.: Princeton University Press, 1969).

4. Morton Schwartz, Soviet Perceptions of the United States (Berkeley: University of California Press, 1978).

5. Philip Hanson, Trade and Technology in Soviet-Western Relations (New York: Columbia University Press, 1981).

6. Franklyn Griffiths, in Interest Groups in Soviet Politics, H. Gordon Skilling and Franklyn Griffiths, eds., (Princeton, N.J.: Princeton University Press, 1971), pp. 335-377, especially 342, 372.

7. Skilling, in Interest Groups in Soviet Politics, Skilling and Griffiths, eds. pp. 3-45, 379-416; and Timothy Colton, Commissars, Commanders, and Civilian Authority: The Structure of Soviet Military Politics (Cambridge, Mass.: Harvard University Press, 1979).

8. For example, Edward Morse, Modernization and the Transformation of International Relations (New York: The Free Press, 1976); Robert Keohane and Joseph Nye, Power and

Interdependence: World Politics in Transition (Boston: Little, Brown, 1977); John Granger, Technology and International Relations (San Francisco: Freeman, 1979); Peter Katzenstein, ed., Between Power and Plenty: Foreign Economic Policies of Advanced Industrial States (Madison: University of Wisconsin Press, 1978); and Stephen Krasner, Defending the National Interest: Raw Materials Investment and U.S. Foreign Policy (Princeton, N.J.: Princeton University Press, 1978).

9. For example, G. Kh. Shakhnazarov, "New Factors in Politics at the Present Stage," Social Sciences (Moscow) 1 (1977): 48.

10. W. I. Thomas, quoted in Urie Bronfenbrenner, "Allowing for Soviet Perceptions," in International Conflict and Behavioral Science, Roger Fisher, ed., (New York: Basic Books, 1964), p. 166.

CHAPTER 1

1. "Constitution (Fundamental Law) of the Union of Soviet Socialist Republics," in Robert Sharlet, The New Soviet Constitution of 1977: Analysis and Text (Brunswick, Ohio: King's Court, 1978), p. 85. Translation by The Current Digest of the Soviet Press. All subsequent translations in this book are by the authors, unless otherwise noted. For example, we cite some Soviet works that have already been translated, and we give the titles and publishers of these works in English rather than in Russian.

2. A Study of Soviet Foreign Policy (Moscow: Progress, 1975), p. 18.

3. Ibid., p. 24.

4. Ibid., p. 25.

5. Ibid., pp. 25-26.

6. Ibid., p. 30.

7. P. N. Fedoseev, Dialektika sovremennoi epokhi, 3rd ed., (Moscow: Nauka, 1978), p. 459.

8. Vitalii Korionov, The Policy of Peaceful Coexistence in Action (Moscow: Progress, 1975), p. 28.

9. A Study of Soviet Foreign Policy, p. 29.

10. Korionov, The Policy of Peaceful Coexistence in Action, p. 33.

11. Vladimir Gantman, "Detente and the System of International Relations," Social Sciences 2 (1980): 177, 180-181

(emphasis added). See also G. A. Arbatov, "Vneshniaia politika SShA na poroge 80-kh godov," SShA 4 (1980): especially
51-52.

12. Korionov, The Policy of Peaceful Coexistence in Action,
pp. 28-29.

13. N. N. Inozemtsev, "The Scientific and Technological Revolution and the Modern World," Social Sciences 3 (1980):
9-10.

14. P. N. Fedoseev, "Social Significance of the Scientific and
Technological Revolution," in Scientific-Technological Revolu-
tion: Social Aspects, ed. Ralf Dahrendorf et al. (London:
Sage Publications, 1977), p. 88.

15. Cf. C. Freeman's lucid conceptual distinctions in "Economics of Research and Development," in Science, Technology,
and Society: A Cross-Disciplinary Perspective, ed. I. Spiegel-
Rosing and D. D. De Solla Price (London: Sage Publications,
1977), pp. 225-236.

16. G. N. Volkov, Istoki i gorizonty progress: Sotsiologiches-
kie problemy razvitiia nauki i tekhniki (Moscow: Politizdat,
1976), pp. 22, 41-42 ff.

17. S. V. Shukhardin and V. I. Gukov, eds., Nauchno-
tekhnicheskaia revoliutsiia (Moscow: Nauka, 1976), pp. 59-168.

18. From Brezhnev's address to the 24th Party Congress in
1971, in Materialy XXIV s'ezda KPSS (Moscow: Politizdat,
1971), p. 57 (emphasis in original).

19. Volkov, Istoki i gorizonty progress, pp. 249-250.

20. Julian Cooper, "The Scientific and Technical Revolution in
the USSR" (paper prepared for presentation at the NASEES
Annual Conference, Cambridge, England, 1981) pp. 5-6.

21. Ibid., pp. 14-15.

22. Volkov, Istoki i gorizonty progress, p. 245.

23. Partiia i sovremennaia nauchno-tekhnicheskaia revoliutsiia
v SSSR (Moscow: Politizdat, 1974), p. 34.

24. Nauchno-tekhnicheskaia revoliutsiia i sotsializm (Moscow:
Politizdat, 1973), p. 61 (emphasis in original).

25. V. I. Gromeka, NTR i sovremennyi kapitalizm (Moscow:
Politizdat, 1976), p. 15.

26. Ibid., p. 90.

27. The Political Economy of Capitalism (Moscow: Progress,
1974), p. 212.

202   "THE SCIENTIFIC-TECHNOLOGICAL REVOLUTION"

28. N. N. Inozemtsev, Contemporary Capitalism: New Developments and Contradictions (Moscow: Progress, 1974), p. 61 (emphasis in original).

29. Razvitoe sotsialisticheskoe obshchestvo: Sushchnost', kriterii zrelosti, kritika revizionistskikh kontseptsii, 3rd ed., (Moscow: Mysl', 1979), p. 31.

30. A. S. Akhiezer, "The Scientific and Technological Revolution and the Guidance of Social Development," in The Scientific and Technological Revolution: Social Effects and Prospects (Moscow: Progress, 1972), p. 164.

31. Razvitoe sotsialisticheskoe obshchestvo, p. 103.

32. P. N. Fedoseev, "Developed Socialism: Theoretical Problems," Social Sciences 3 (1977): 15.

33. V. I. Kas'ianenko, Razvitoi sotsializm: Istoriografiia i metodologiia problemy (Moscow: Mysl', 1976), p. 8.

34. See, for example, "Razvitoe sotsialisticheskoe obshchestvo," in Nauchnyi kommunizm: Slovar' A. M. Rumiantsev, ed., (Moscow: Politizdat, 1975), pp. 285-289.

35. Fedoseev, "Developed Socialism," p. 10.

36. Razvitoe sotsialisticheskoe obshchestvo, p. 83.

37. Kas'ianenko, Razvitoi sotsializm, p. 107.

38. Razvitoe sotsialisticheskoe obshchestvo, pp. 83-84.

39. Sotsialisticheskoe obshchestvo: Sotsial'no-filosofskie problemy sovremennogo sovetskogo obshchestva (Moscow: Mysl', 1976), pp. 122-123.

40. Kas'ianenko, Razvitoi sotsializm, p. 129.

41. Inozemtsev, Contemporary Capitalism, p. 55.

42. N. N. Inozemtsev, "Problemy sovremennogo mirovogo razvitiia," in XXV s'ezd KPSS i razvitie marksistsko-leninskoi teorii (Moscow: Politizdat, 1977), p. 93.

43. Inozemtsev, Contemporary Capitalism, p. 55.

44. A. Vakhrameev, "Detente and the World Balance of Forces," International Affairs 1 (1979): 80.

45. A.O. Chubar'ian, Mirnoe sosushchestvovanie: Teoriia i praktika (Moscow: Politizdat, 1976), p. 177.

CHAPTER 2

1. I. A. Sovetov, "Detente and the Modern World," International Affairs 6 (1979): 5, 11.

2. N. P. Shmelev, "Socialism and the World Economy, <u>Social Sciences</u> 2 (1978): 128.

3. G. A. Arbatov, "Detente and the Problem of Conflict," <u>Social Sciences</u> 3 (1979): 51.

4. For a general discussion of the contemporary crisis of capitalism, see N. N. Inozemtsev et al., eds., <u>Uglublenie obshchego krizisa</u> (Moscow: Mysl', 1976); and Inozemtsev, <u>Contemporary Capitalism</u>.

5. I. P. Faminskii, <u>Vliianie NTR na mirogo kapitalisticheskoe khoziaistvo</u> (Moscow: MGU, 1976), p. 415.

6. Vadim Zagladin and Ivan Frolov, "The Global Problems of Our Times," <u>Social Sciences</u> 4 (1977): 67 (emphasis added).

7. Faminskii, <u>Vliianie NTR</u>, p. 117.

8. O. T. Bogomolov, "Internationalization of Economic Life," <u>Social Sciences</u> 2 (1979): 41.

9. See the major statement by Fedoseev quoted in Chapter 1, note 7.

10. P. N. Fedoseev, "Social Science and Social Progress," <u>Social Sciences</u>, 3 (1979): 21.

11. "Obshchii krizis kapitalizma,"in <u>Nauchnyi kommunizm</u>, Rumiantsev,ed., (Moscow: Politizdat, 1975), p. 240.

12. I. Gur'ev, "Obshchii krizis kapitalizma i ego dal'neishee uglublenie," <u>Mirovaia ekonomika i mezhdunarodnye otnosheniia</u> (hereafter cited as <u>Mirovaia ekonomika)</u> 10 (1975): 26.

13. I. Kuzminov, "Aggravation of the General Crisis of Capitalism," <u>International Affairs</u> 8 (1976): 6 (emphasis in original).

14. <u>XXV s'ezd KPSS</u> (Moscow: Politizdat, 1976), p. 48.

15. Iurii Shishkov, "Crisis of the Mechanism of Capitalist Economic Relations," <u>Social Sciences</u> 2 (1979): 101.

16. K. Mikulskii, <u>Lenin's Teaching on the World Economy and its Relevance to Our Times</u> (Moscow: Progress, 1975), pp. 241-243.

17. Georgii Skorov, "Developing Nations in the Struggle for Economic Equality," <u>Social Sciences</u> 3 (1978): 194.

18. The main features of the third stage are the growing influence of socialism on world development, the final collapse of the colonial system of imperialism, and the "exacerbation of the internal contradictions of the capitalist system which are a result of the considerable growth of state-monopoly capitalism." <u>The Political Economy of Capitalism</u>, p. 301.

204   "THE SCIENTIFIC-TECHNOLOGICAL REVOLUTION"

19. I. Kuzminov, "Some Aspects of the General Crisis of Capitalism," International Affairs 6 (1975): 65.

20. Shishkov, "Crisis of the Mechanism," 89.

21. Ibid.

22. Ibid., 90.

23. The Political Economy of Capitalism, p. 198.

24. A. Anikin and V. Kuznetsov, "Gosudarstvenno-monopoliticheskii kapitalizm 70-kh godov," Mirovaia ekonomika 11 (1975): 12-17.

25. Ibid., 17.

26. Iu. In'kov, "Ispol'zovanie EVM v apparate gosudarstvennogo upravleniia SShA," Sorevnovanie dvukh sistem (1975): 371-382.

27. A.I. Pokrovskii, "Gosudarstvennoe programmirovanie kapitalisticheskoi ekonomiki," Sorevnovanie dvukh sistem (1967): 7-17. See also "Gosudarstvenno-monopoliticheskoe programmirovanie ekonomiki," in Politicheskaia ekonomiia sovremennogo monopoliticheskogo kapitalizma, 2nd ed., vol. 2, N.N. Inozemtsev et al., ed., (Moscow: Mysl', 1975), pp. 3-18.

28. See, for example, the discussion of the French planning model in Iu. I. Rubinskii, ed., Frantsiia (Moscow: Mysl', 1973), chapter 1.

29. Inozemtsev et al., Politicheskaia ekonomiia, p. 113.

30. See A. Shapiro's discussion of "the path of capitalist socialization" in "Kapitalizm 70-kh godov," Mirovaia ekonomika, 8 (1976): 61-66.

31. Inozemtsev, Contemporary Capitalism, pp. 89-90.

32. Anikin and Kuznetsov, "Gosudarstvenno-monopoliticheskii kapitalizm," 18.

33. For an extensive discussion of the instability of meta-socialization, see S.P. Novoselov, Osnovnoe protivorechie kapitalizma i sovremennost' (Moscow: Mysl', 1974).

34. S. Menshikov, The Economic Cycle: Postwar Development (Moscow: Progress, 1975), p. 265.

35. Ibid.

36. Ibid., pp. 265-266.

37. Ibid., p. 266.

38. Vadim Zagladin, "The Premises of Socialism and the Socialist Revolution," Social Sciences 2 (1977): 21.

39. Ibid.

40. Ibid., 25.

41. The Political Economy of Capitalism, p. 199.

42. On the linkage mechanisms between the advanced corporation and the state, see S. Peregudov and K. Kholodkovskii, "O sovremennykh tendentsiiakh v sisteme politicheskogo gospodstva monopolii," Mirovaia ekonomika 8 (1975): 56-70.

43. For example, The Political Economy of Capitalism.

44. Shishkov, "Crisis of the Mechanism," 90.

45. Ibid., 90-93.

46. Ibid., 93.

47. "Leninskaia teoriia imperializma sovremennost'," Mirovaia ekonomika 8 (1977): 34.

48. Mikulskii, World Economy, pp. 253-254 (emphasis added).

49. "Leninskaia teoriia imperializma," 35-38.

50. V. Solodovnikov, "Elimination of the Colonial System: An Expression of the General Crisis of Capitalism," International Affairs 8 (1976): 22.

51. S.P. Novoselov, Obostrenie ekonomicheskikh i sotsial'no-politicheskikh protivorechii kapitalizma (Moscow: Mysl', 1977), p. 169.

52. "Neokolonializm," in Nauchnyi kommunizm, Rumiantsev, ed., pp. 229-230.

53. Mikulskii, World Economy, p. 260.

54. K.N. Brutents, "Imperialism and the Liberated Countries," Social Sciences 1 (1979): 169.

55. Novoselov, Obostrenie, pp. 178-198.

56. Ruben Andreasian and Aleksandr Solonitskii, "New Trends in World Economic Relations under Capitalism," Social Sciences 3 (1977): 49-50.

57. S.P. Sanakoev and N.I. Kapchenko, O teorii vneshnei politiki sotsializma (Moscow: Mezhdunarodnye otnosheniia, 1977), p. 171.

58. See e.g., Faminskii, Vliianie NTR.

59. Faminskii, Vliianie NTR, p. 112. See also P.S. Zav'ialov, NTR i mezhdunarodnaia spetsializatsiia proizvodstva pri kapitalizme (Moscow: Mysl', 1974).

60. Faminskii, Vliianie NTR, p. 38.

61. For example, see Shmelov, "Socialism and the World Economy," 136.

206   "THE SCIENTIFIC-TECHNOLOGICAL REVOLUTION"

62. On the nature of the division of labor associated with the STR under capitalist conditions, see V. Markushina, Mezhdunarodnye nauchno-tekhnicheskie sviazi v sisteme sovremennogo kapitalizma (Moscow: Mysl', 1972).

63. Faminskii, Vliianie NTR, p. 103.

64. Ibid., p. 114.

66. On the significance of the foreign market in West Germany, see V.N. Shenaev, ed., Federativnaia Respublika Germanii (Moscow: Mysl', 1973), chapter 8. On the significance of the foreign market in Japan, see Ia. A. Pevzner and D.V. Petrov, eds., Iaponiia (Moscow: Mysl', 1973), chapter 4.

67. Faminskii, Vliianie NTR, p. 115.

70. On the relationship between the MNC and the capitalist international division of labor, see I. Bol'shakova and E. Kochetov, "Strategiia monopolii i protivorechiia kapitalisticheskogo mezhdunarodnogo razdeleniia truda," Mirovaia ekonomika 12 (1977): 28-38.

71. For a major study of the MNC, see R.S. Ovinnikov, Sverkhmonopolii--novoe orudie imperializma (Moscow: Mezhdunarodnye otnosheniia, 1978).

72. Faminskii, Vliianie NTR, p. 122.

73. For example, see P. Khvoinik, "Mezhdunarodnye monopolii i mezhdunarodnaia torgovliia," Mirovaia ekonomika 4 (1975): 99-110; and 5 (1975): 93-105.

74. Faminskii, Vliianie NTR, p. 123.

75. Ibid., p. 132.

76. On the basic forms and tendencies of the development of the MNC, see T. Belous, "Mezhdunarodnye monopolii i nekotorye aspekty ikh deiatel'nosti," Mirovaia ekonomika 7 (1975): 12-24.

77. Faminskii, Vliianie NTR, p. 180.

78. On the contradictions introduced by the MNC in the advanced capitalist system, see the following articles by I. Ivanov: "Mezhdunarodnye korporatsii i burzhuaznoe gosudarstvo: Al'iansy i konflikty," Mirovaia ekonomika 1 (1976): 46-59; "Transnatsional'nye monopolii--ugroza suverenitetu," Mirovaia ekonomika 1 (1978): 26-36; "Evoliutsiia monopolii i ikh roli v obshchestvennom proizvodstve," Mirovaia ekonomika 7 (1978): 24-37.

79. Faminskii, Vliianie NTR, pp. 188-189.

80. Ibid., p. 185.

81. See especially the following: V.I. Gromeka, NTR i sovre-mennyi kapitalizm (Moscow: Politizdat, 1976); P. Khvoinik, "Vneshneekonomicheskaia sfera kapitalizma: Novyi etap razviti-ia," Mirovaia ekonomika 5 (1976): 72-83; M. Maksimova, "Vse-mirnoe khoziaistvo, NTR, i mezhdunarodnye otnosheniia," Mirovaia ekonomika 4 (1979): 12-24; and 5 (1979): 21-33.

82. See S. Medvedkov, "Inostrannyi kapital v kapitalistiche-skoi ekonomike: Puti proniknoveniia i problemy," Mirovaia ekonomika 6 (1976): 64-78; L. Nochevkina and N. Chertko, "70-e gody: Osobennosti investitsionnnogo protsessa v razvi-tykh kapitalisticheskh stranakikh," Mirovaia ekonomika 9 (1978): 47-58; T. Belous, "Novye tendentsii v eksporte kapi-tala: Prichiny i ekonomicheskie stimuly," Mirovaia ekonomika 1 (1979): 55-65.

83. On American foreign economic strategy, see M.I. Zakhmatov, ed., SShA: Vneshniaia ekonomicheskaia strategiia (Moscow: Nauka, 1976).

84. See Iu. Iudanov, "Zapadnoevropeiskii kapital v ekonomike SShA," Mirovaia ekonomika 9 (1976): 78-88; and 10 (1976): 33-42. Also, see Iu. Iudanov, "Eksport kapitala iz Zapadnoi Evropy," Mirovaia ekonomika 12 (1975): 69-83; and 1 (1976): 109-121.

85. For example, see Iu. Iudanov, "Iaponskii kapital v zapad-noi evrope," Mirovaia ekonomika 12 (1977): 39-51; Iu. Stolia-fov, "Ekspansiia iaponskikh mezhdunarodnykh monopolii," Mirovaia ekonomika 1 (1977): 76-87; V. Dybov, "Japanese Multinationals in the Structure of World Capitalism," Interna-tional Affairs 4 (1978): 98-105.

86. Faminskii, Vliianie NTR, pp. 208-209.

87. Ibid., p. 216.

88. Ibid., p. 224.

89. Ibid., pp. 243-244.

90. Ibid., p. 271.

91. Ibid., p. 262.

92. Ibid., p. 287.

93. Ibid., pp. 287-288.

94. Ibid., p. 288.

95. Ibid.

96. Ibid., p. 289.

97. Ibid., p. 320.

98. Ibid., p. 321.

99. Ibid.

100. See the following studies of the major contemporary variants of advanced state monopoly capitalism: S.A. Dalin, SShA: Poslevoennyi gosudarstvenno-monopolisticheskii kapital-izm (Moscow: Nauka, 1972); Ia. A. Pevzner, Gosudarstvo v ekonomike Iaponii (Moscow: Vostochnoi literatury, 1976); Iu. I. Rubinskii, ed., Frantsiia (Moscow: Mysl', 1974); V.N. Shenaev, ed., FRG (Moscow: Mysl', 1973); S.V. Pronin and E.S. Khesin, eds., Velikobritaniia (Moscow: Mysl', 1972); N.P. Vasil'kov, ed., Italiia (Moscow: Mysl', 1973).

101. Faminskii, Vliianie NTR, p. 323.

102. Ibid., p. 325.

103. Ibid., pp. 326-327.

104. For an argument that the current economic crisis in the West is eroding even capitalism's successes in this area, see I. Diumulen, "Trade Battles in the West," International Affairs 3 (1978): 46-54.

105. Faminskii, Vliianie NTR, pp. 326-327.

106. For an analysis of the OECD, see A. Mileikovskii and M. Portnoi, "V poiskakh obshchei ekonomicheskoi strategii," Mirovaia ekonomika 1 (1979): 33-45.

107. For a major study of the Common Market, see Iu. V. Shishkov, Obshchii rynok: Nadezhdy i deistvitel'nost' (Moscow: Mysl', 1972).

108. Faminskii, Vliianie NTR, p. 364.

109. Ibid., p. 366.

110. See L. Afanas'ev and V. Kolovniakov, Contradictions of Agrarian Integration in the Common Market (Moscow: Progress, 1976).

111. See L. Maier, D. Mel'nikov, and V. Shenaev, "Zapadno-evropeiskii tsentr imperialisticheskogo sopernichestva," Mirovaia ekonomika 12 (1978): 22-32.

112. Faminskii, Vliianie NTR, p. 386.

113. See Iu. A. Borko, Zapadnaia Evropa: Sotsial'nye posled-stviia kapitalisticheskoi integratsii (Moscow: Nauka, 1975).

114. See M. Maksimova, "Kapitalisticheskaia integratsiia i mirovoe razvitie," Mirovaia ekonomika 3 (1978): 12-23; and 4 (1978): 14-24.

115. Faminskii, Vliianie NTR, p. 392.

116. A. Utkin, "'Atlantizm' 70-kh godov," Mirovaia ekonomika
5 (1975): 83-92; A. Utkin, "'Atlantizm' i Iaponiia," Mirovaia
ekonomika 6 (1976): 56-63.

117. See A.V. Kirsanov, Ekonomicheskie otnosheniia SShA i
Zapadnoi Evropy na sovremennom etape (Moscow: Nauka,
1975).

118. See. A.M. Sharkov, Iaponiia i SShA: Analiz sovremennykh ekonomicheskikh otnoshenii (Moscow: Mysl', 1971).

119. See A. Shapiro, "Tri tsentra imperializma i mezhimper-
ialisticheskie protivorechiia," Mirovaia ekonomika 12 (1979):
91-95.

120. See V. Matveev, "'Trekhstoronniaia strategiia' i ee
evoliutsiia," Mirovaia ekonomika 3 (1977): 14-24; A. Utkin,
"Kontseptsiia 'trekstoronnosti' v strategii imperializma,"
Mirovaia ekonomika 2 (1978): 13-23.

121. See A.V. Nikiforov, "'Vzaimozavisimost' i global'nye
problemy," SShA 7 (1979): 8-19.

122. Inozemtsev, Contemporary Capitalism, p. 134.

123. See. V.F. Davydov et al., SShA i Zapadno-Evropeiskie
'tsentry sily' (Moscow: Nauka, 1978), pp. 241-259.

124. A. Rusin, "The Rough Edges of the West European Tri-
angle," International Affairs 11 (1977): 110-112.

125. Inozemtsev, Contemporary Capitalism, p. 120.

126. O. Bogdanov, "Competition in the Capitalist World,"
International Affairs, 4 (1977): 43.

127. SShA-Zapadnaia Evropa: Partnerstvo i sopernichestvo
(Moscow: Nauka, 1978), p. 73.

128. Inozemtsev, Contemporary Capitalism, p. 94.

129. Ibid., p. 131 (emphasis in original).

130. See Ia. Pevzner, "Neravnomernost' razvitiia kapitalizma
na sovremennom etape," Mirovaia ekonomika 1 (1975): 23-37.

131. Inozemtsev, Contemporary Capitalism, p. 132.

132. See V. Rymalov, "World Capitalism: Increasingly Uneven
Regional Development," International Affairs 5 (1978): 19-30.

133. See, e.g.: A. Kodachenko, "Neocolonialist Strategy of
the West," Social Sciences 1 (1978): 158-169; N.M. Khriashcheva, Novaia strategiia neokolonializma (Moscow: Mezhduna-
rodnoe otnosheniia, 1976); R.M. Avakov, Razvivaiushchiesiia
strany: NTR i problemy nezavisimosti (Moscow: Mysl', 1976);
Vasilii Vakhrushev, Neocolonialism: Methods and Maneuvers
(New York: Progress, 1973).

134. See, e.g., G. Skorov, "Scientific and Technological Progress and Social Orientation," Social Sciences 1 (1976): 191-204; V.L. Tiagunenko, ed., The Third World and Scientific and Technical Progress (Moscow: Nauka, 1976), chapter 1; I. Andreev, The Noncapitalist Way (Moscow: Progress, 1977), chapter 6.

135. See Skorov, "Developing Nations"; V. Rymalov, "The Agrarian and Raw-Material Basis of Capitalist Economy," Social Sciences 3 (1977): 51-66.

136. On the concept of asymmetric dependency, see E. Primakov, "The Developing Countries: Some Problems," Social Sciences 3 (1979): 72-82.

137. M.M. Koptev and M.S. Ochkov, Tekhnicheskaia 'pomoshch' v strategii imperializma (Moscow: Mysl', 1977), p. 12.

138. Ibid., chapter 1.

139. V. G. Solodovnikov, "Neocolonialism in the 1970s," in Neocolonialism and Africa in the 1970s, E.A. Tarabrin, ed., (Moscow: Progress, 1978), p. 50.

140. Tiagunenko, The Third World, p. 17.

141. Ibid., p. 95.

142. Brutents, "Imperialism and the Liberated Countries," 172.

143. N. Sergeev, "Developing Nations and the Transnational Corporations," Social Sciences 2 (1979): 176.

144. Koptev and Ochkov, Tekhnicheskaia 'pomoshch', chapter 3.

145. Tiagunenko, The Third World, p. 21.

146. Sergeev, "Developing Nations," 175.

147. A. Elianov, "The STR and Socio-Economic Problems of the Developing Countries," Social Sciences 2 (1973): 133.

148. E. Kamenov and E. Malkhasian, "African Countries' Unequal Position in Trade with Capitalist States," in Neocolonialism and Africa, p. 210.

149. G. K. Shirokov, ed., Neftedollary i sotsial'no-ekonomicheskoe razvitie stran blizhnego i srednego vostoka (Moscow: Nauka, 1979).

150. V. S. Baskin, "A New Course in the Policy of 'Aid,'" in ibid., p. 189.

151. Ibid., p. 185.

152. Tiagunenko, The Third World, p. 15.

153. Ibid., p. 22.

154. Ibid., p. 53.

155. Ibid., p. 54.

156. Ibid., p. 66.

157. Ibid.

158. Ibid., p. 137.

159. Kodachenko, "Neocolonialist Strategy," 169.

160. Solodovnikov, in, Neocolonialism and Africa, p. 57.

161. R. N. Andreasian and A. D. Kaziukov, Opek v mire nefti (Moscow: Nauka, 1978).

162. Tiagunenko, The Third World, pp. 72-73.

163. K. N. Brutents, National Liberation Revolutions Today (Moscow: Progress, 1977), p. 42 (emphasis in original).

164. Ibid., p. 301.

165. Ibid., pp. 10-11.

166. Ibid., p. 173.

167. Ibid.

168. Ibid.

169. Skorov, "Scientific and Technological Progress," 198.

170. Major Soviet works on this theme are Khriashcheva, Novaia strategiia neokolonializma; and E. E. Obminskii, Kontseptsii mezhdunarodnogo ekonomicheskogo poriadka (Moscow: Mysl', 1977).

171. O. T. Bogomolov, "CMEA and the Developing World," International Affairs 7 (1979): 25.

172. See "A New International Economic Order," Social Sciences 1 (1978): 170-191.

173. Skorov, "Developing Nations," 191.

174. "Energy Crisis: An Assessment by Soviet Scientists," Problems of the Contemporary World 6 (1974).

175. Brutents, National Liberation Revolutions, pp. 293-294 (emphasis in original).

176. Ibid., p. 292.

177. See The Soviet Union and the World Economy (New York: Council on Foreign Relations, 1979), especially the essays by Toby Gati, Robert Legvold, and Elizabeth Valkenier.

178. G.I. Mirskii and A.S. Solonitskii, "Novyi pod'em natsional'no-osvoboditel'nogo dvizheniia," in Inozemtsev et al., Uglublenie obshchego krizisa kapitalizma, p. 57.

179. Andreasian and Solonitskii, "New Trends," 49-50.

180. Ovinnikov, Sverkhmonopolii, p. 206.

181. Brutents, National Liberation Revolutions, p. 53.

182. European Security and Cooperation: Premises, Problems, Prospects (Moscow: Progress, 1978), p. 39.

183. Ibid., pp. 38-47. See also Schwartz, Soviet Perceptions of the United States, pp. 137-146.

184. European Security and Cooperation, p. 311.

185. See, e.g., N.P. Shmelev, ed., Ekonomicheskie sviazi vostok-zapad: Problemy i vozmozhnosti (Moscow: Mysl', 1976), pp. 12-56.

186. For example, Inozemtsev, Contemporary Capitalism, pp. 134 ff.

187. As cited in Soviet World Outlook 4 (March 15, 1979), 2 (emphasis added).

188. Menshikov, The Economic Cycle, pp. 63-113.

189. Mikulskii, World Economy, p. 58.

190. Zagladin, "Premises of Socialism," 22 (emphasis in original).

191. Of course, the Chinese have hotly disagreed with the contention that detente and Third World liberation progress simultaneously. For an important Soviet response to the critics of Soviet detente policy, see K.I. Zarodov, Tri revoliutsii v Rossii i nashe vremiia (Moscow: Mysl', 1977), pp. 14-111.

192. Faminskii, Vliianie NTR, p. 402.

193. See A.V. Anikin, "Nesostoiatel'nost' kapitalizma pered litsom nasushchnykh problem sovremennosti," in Inozemtsev, Uglublenie obshchego krizisa kapitalizma, pp. 237-254.

194. European Security and Cooperation, p. 133.

195. N.P. Shmelev, "Peaceful Coexistence and Economic Cooperation," Social Sciences 2 (1977): 50.

196. Shmelev, "Socialism and the World Economy," p. 127. Also see the notable argument by Petr Kapitsa in "Vliianie sovremennykh nauchnykh idei na obshchestvo," Voprosy filosofii 1 (1979): 61-71.

197. N.N. Inozemtsev, "Policy of Peaceful Coexistence: Underlying Principles," Social Sciences 3 (1979): 70.

198. Mikulskii, World Economy, p. 61.

199. Ibid., p. 187.

200. Ibid., p. 33 (emphasis added).

201. Ibid., p. 58.

202. M.M. Maksimova, "The Soviet Union and the World Economy," Social Sciences 4 (1978): 140-141.

203. For a representative presentation of the neoisolationist position, see Sovetov, "Detente and the Modern World."

204. For a representative presentation of the interdependence position, see Maksimova, "Vsemirnoe khoziaistvo, NTR, i mezhdunarodnye otnosheniia."

205. Arbatov, "Detente and the Problem of Conflict," 47.

206. Ibid.

207. Ibid. (emphasis added).

208. A. Narochnitskii, "Lenin on International Relations," Social Sciences 1 (1977): 33.

209. Shakhnazarov, "New Factors in Politics," 49.

CHAPTER 3

1. In Materialy XXIV s'ezda KPSS, p. 57 (emphasis in original). See also Chapter I, notes 18 ff.

2. For elaboration of these themes, see Hoffmann and Laird, The Politics of Economic Modernization in the Soviet Union; and Frederic Fleron, ed., Technology and Communist Culture: The Socio-Cultural Impact of Technology Transfer under Socialism (New York: Praeger, 1977).

3. V. Iokhin, in A. M. Voinov et al., Ekonomicheskie otnosheniia mezhdu sotsialisticheskimi i razvitymi kapitalisticheskimi stranami (Moscow: Nauka, 1975), p. 140.

4. Iu. Pekshev, "Vazhnyi faktor mira i sotsial'no-ekonomicheskogo progressa," Planovoe khoziaistvo 12 (1974): 14.

5. L. A. Feonova et al., Organizatsiia i tekhnika vneshnei torgovli SSSR (Moscow: Mezhdunarodnye otnosheniia, 1974), p. 41. Prominent Soviet officials made comparable statements at the 24th, 25th, and 26th Party Congresses (1971, 1976, and 1981).

6. G.L. Rozanov, Politika sotrudnichestva--Velenie vremenii: SSSR i kapitalisticheskie strany, 70-e gody (Moscow: Mezhdunarodnye otnosheniia, 1977), p. 21.

7. Iu. Molchanov, "Peaceful Coexistence and Social Progress," International Affairs 12 (1976): 8 (emphasis added).

214 "THE SCIENTIFIC-TECHNOLOGICAL REVOLUTION"

8. Zapadnaia evropa v sovremennom mire, vol. 2, (Moscow: Mysl', 1979), pp. 289-290.

9. D.I. Kostiukhin, The World Market Today (Moscow: Progress, 1979), p. 155.

10. S. Pomazanov, "Business Cooperation between the USSR and the West," International Affairs 3 (1979): 36.

11. V. N. Sushkov, "Compensatory Long-Term Trade and Industrial Cooperation between the USSR and the Industrial Capitalist Countries," Foreign Trade 5 (1977): 22.

12. Iu. Shiriaev and A. Ivanov, "Detente: Economic Implementation," International Affairs 11 (1975): 29.

13. Ibid.

14. Iu. N. Kapelinskii, Na vzaimo-vygodnoi osnove (Moscow: Mezhdunarodnye otnosheniia, 1975), p. 14.

15. A. Karenin, Sovetskaia vneshniaia politika mira v svete idei XXV s'ezda KPSS (Moscow: Politizdat, 1977), p. 55.

16. V.S. Evgenev, "East-West Economic Cooperation: Realities and Prospects," in Europe and Detente (Moscow: Progress, 1978), p. 111.

17. N. P. Shmelev, "New Horizons of Economic Relations," Mirovaia ekonomika 1 (1973), translated in Soviet and East European Foreign Trade (Summer 1973): 56.

18. V. L. Mal'kevich, "The USSR and International Trade in Licenses," Foreign Trade 11 (1979): 11.

19. Ibid., 11-12 (emphasis added).

20. "Brezhnev: Central Committee Report," Pravda, February 25, 1976, pp. 2-9, translated in Current Soviet Policies VII (Columbus, Ohio: American Association for the Advancement of Slavic Studies, 1976), p. 18 (first emphasis in original; second emphasis added).

21. N. Smeliakov, "Delovye vstrechi," Novyi mir 12 (1973): 223.

22. For development and documentation of this theme, see Hoffmann and Laird, In Quest of Progress: Soviet Perspectives on Advanced Society.

23. Iu. Kapelinskii and A. Kirillov, "The STR and the International Specialization of Production under Capitalism," Foreign Trade 3 (1967): 52.

24. D. I. Kostiukhin, "Organization and Conduct of Foreign Trade on the Capitalist Market," Foreign Trade 6 (1976): 50.

25. D.I. Kostiukhin, "Problems and Contradictions in the Development of the Present-day Capitalist Economy," Foreign Trade 4 (1977): 52.

26. For a broad discussion of combining the STR with the advantages of socialism, see F. M. Volkov and S. S. Il'in, eds., Soedinenie dostizhenii NTR s preimushchestvami sotsializma (Moscow: MGU, 1977); V. G. Marakov, ed., Soedinenie dostizhenii NTR s preimushchestvami sotsializma (Moscow: Mysl', 1977); E. M. Babosov, Sotsial'nye aspekty NTR (Minsk: BGU, 1976).

27. A. Anchishkin, The Theory of Growth of a Socialist Economy (Moscow: Progress, 1977), p. 79.

28. "Brezhnev: Central Committee Report," p. 18.

29. E. I. Khessina, in Volkov and Il'in, Soedinenie, pp. 113-124.

30. For example, M. G. Solnitseva, in ibid., pp. 125-141; and G. I. Sadchikova, in ibid., pp. 142-157.

31. V. N. Kirichenko, in N. A. Tsagolov, ed., NTR i sistema ekonomicheskikh otnoshenii razvitogo sotsializma (Moscow: MGU, 1979), p. 61.

32. B. Z. Mil'ner, "Organization of the Management of Production," Social Sciences 3 (1976): 51-52.

33. Tsagolov, NTR, part one.

34. Mil'ner, "Organization," 55.

35. I. G. Shilin, in Tsagolov, NTR, p. 37.

36. See, e.g., ibid., pp. 83 ff.

37. Il'in, in Volkov and Il'in, Soedinenie, p. 27 (emphasis in original).

38. Ibid., p. 36 (emphasis in original).

39. See the CPSU Central Committee and USSR Council of Ministers resolution "On Improving Planning and Strengthening the Economic Mechanism's Influence in Enhancing Production Efficiency and Work Quality," translated in The Current Digest of The Soviet Press 30 (August 22, 1979): 1-6, 14.

40. Marakov, Soedinenie, p. 115.

41. N. N. Lolosovskii, Problemy territorial'noi organizatsii proizvoditel'nykh sil dal'nego vostoka (Moscow: Mysl', 1974).

42. A. N. Gladyshev et al., Problemy razvitiia i razmeshcheniia proizvoditel'nykh sil dal'nego vostoka (Moscow: Mysl', 1974), p. 153.

43. N. Nekrasov, The Territorial Organization of Soviet Economy (Moscow: Progress, 1974), p. 78.

216   "THE SCIENTIFIC-TECHNOLOGICAL REVOLUTION"

44. See, e.g., V. P. Gukov, Problemy regional'noi ekonomiki Vostochnoi Sibiri (Novosibirsk: IEiOPP, 1976).

45. For example, Organizatsionnye voprosy avtomatizatsii upravleniia (Moscow: Ekonomika, 1972).

46. Il'in, in Volkov and Il'in, Soedinenie, p. 50 (emphasis in original).

47. A. L. Klinskii, Planirovanie ekonomicheskogo i sotsial'nogo razvitiia (Moscow: Mysl', 1974); G. Kotov and I. Proktiakov, "Ob uchastii nauchnykh organizatsii v razrabotke narodno-khoziaistvennykh planov," Planovoe khoziaistvo 12 (1973): 17-25; V. M. Grigorov, Eksperty v sisteme upravleniia obshchestvennym proizvodstvom (Moscow: Mysl', 1976).

48. Il'in, in Volkov and Il'in, Soedinenie, p. 24 (emphasis in original).

49. B. N. Topornin, in B. N. Topornin, ed., Sotsialisticheskoe gosudarstvo, pravo i nauchno-tekhnicheskaia revoliutsiia (Moscow: Iuridicheskaia literatura, 1975), p. 35.

50. M. Rutkevich, in Pravda, September 14, 1973, p. 3.

51. Marakhov, Soedinenie, p. 32.

52. Ibid., p. 71.

53. L. I. Brezhnev, Leninskim kursom: rechi i stat'i, vol. 1, (Moscow: Politizdat, 1970), p. 211.

54. V. G. Afanas'ev, in Pravda, May 21, 1976, p. 2 (emphasis added). Brezhnev and other political leaders have made similar statements.

55. Topornin, Sotsialisticheskoe gosudarstvo, p. 32 (emphasis added).

56. G. M. Prokhorov, Vneshneekonomicheskie sviazi i ekonomicheskii rost sotsialisticheskikh stran (Moscow: Mezhdunarodnye otnosheniia, 1972), p. 72 (emphasis added).

57. Mal'kevich, "The USSR," 14.

58. L. A. Rodina, in Voinov, Ekonomicheskie otnosheniia, p. 160.

59. Ibid., pp. 153-154.

60. V.S. Alkhimov, "Soviet Foreign Economic Relations in the Light of the Decisions of the 25th CPSU Congress," Foreign Trade 7 (1976): 13.

61. Voinov, Ekonomicheskie otnosheniia, p. 45.

62. Rodina, in Voinov, p. 161 (emphasis added).

63. Rozanov, Politika, p. 147.

64. Iu. Shiraev and A. Sokolov, "East-West Business Relations: Possibilities and Realities," International Affairs 2 (1977): 39. See also Osnovnye napravleniia ekonomicheskogo i sotsial'nogo razvitiia SSSR na 1981-1985 gody i na period do 1990 goda (Moscow: Politizdat, 1980).

65. Iokhin, in Voinov, Ekonomicheskie otnosheniia, pp. 113-114.

66. A. K. Kirillov, "Soviet Foreign Trade and its Urgent Tasks," Foreign Trade 8 (1978): 29.

67. V. Salimovskii, "Trade in Licenses is Important and Promising," Foreign Trade 8 (1977): 9 (emphasis added).

68. M. M. Maksimova, USSR and International Economic Cooperation (Moscow: Progress, 1979), p. 67.

69. Mal'kevich, "The USSR," 11-12 (emphasis added).

70. Rozanov, Politika, p. 147.

71. Sushkov, "Compensatory Long-term Trade," 22.

72. "Trading with the U.S.S.R.," Overseas Business Reports (Washington, D.C.: U.S. Department of Commerce, July 1977), pp. 43-44.

73. N. P. Shmelev, ed., Ekonomicheskie sviazi vostok-zapad: Problemy i vozmozhnosti (Moscow: Mysl', 1976), p. 55.

74. Iokhin, in Voinov, Ekonomicheskie otnosheniia, p. 133 (emphasis in original).

75. Maksimova, USSR and International Economic Cooperation, p. 292.

76. V. S. Evgenev, "East-West Economic Cooperation: Realities and Prospects," in Europe and Detente (Moscow: Progress, 1978), p. 119.

77. Rodina, in Voinov, Ekonomicheskie otnosheniia, p. 143 (emphasis added).

78. Feonova, Organizatsiia i tekhnika, p. 43 (emphasis added).

79. Rodina, in Voinov, Ekonomicheskie otnosheniia, pp. 160-161.

80. V. P. Gruzinov, The USSR's Management of Foreign Trade (White Plains, N.Y.: Sharpe, 1979), pp. 56-57 (emphasis added). This book is a translation of Upravlenie vneshnei torgovlei: Tseli, funktsii, metody (Moscow: Mezhdunarodnye otnosheniia, 1975).

81. Ibid., especially pp. 57-64.

82. Ibid., p. 58.

218   "THE SCIENTIFIC-TECHNOLOGICAL REVOLUTION"

83. Ibid., p. 60.

84. See, e.g., Erik P. Hoffmann, "Socialist Perspectives on 'The Scientific and Technical Revolution,' Management, and Law," in The Scientific-Technical Revolution and Soviet and East European Law, Gordon Smith, Peter Maggs, and George Ginsburgs, eds., (Elmsford, N.Y.: Pergamon Press, 1981), pp. 19-46.

85. Gruzinov, USSR's Management, p. 57.

86. Ibid., p. 62.

87. Ibid., p. 63.

88. V. S. Pozdniakov, Sovetskoe gosudarstvo i vneshniaia torgovlia (pravovye voprosy) (Moscow: Mezhdunarodnye otnosheniia, 1976), pp. 61-62.

89. Ibid., pp. 62-63.

90. Ibid., p. 63.

91. Ibid., pp. 63 ff.

92. Ibid., pp. 68-69.

93. Ibid.

94. Ibid., p. 69.

95. Friedrich Levcik and Jan Stankovsky, two Western writers, observe:
"The strict separation between the domestic economy and foreign operations has been modified over time in a number of ways, with considerable differences from country to country [in the Soviet bloc]. The former defensive and protective function they exercised within a predominantly autarkic growth model has been transformed into an offensive function, and the most important task of the foreign trade monopoly has become the expansion of exports to make possible the import of capital goods, technology, and licenses. . . .
This changed function of foreign trade necessitated corresponding changes in the organizational forms and the legal and economic institutions of the state foreign trade monopoly. Under certain circumstances, and after obtaining the required permission, production enterprises in some Eastern countries may now also participate in foreign trade. Producer associations, such as the associations of state-owned enterprises in the GDR, or industrial concerns in Romania, or important enterprises and combines, are also authorized, along with the existing foreign trade enterprises, to export their products themselves. In

NOTES   219

other cases producers can select their own foreign
trade organization, which then engages in foreign
trade transactions on commission and on behalf and
on the account of the producer. Sometimes competition between foreign trade organizations may arise.
In some cases producers are able to join to form
their own foreign trade companies (joint stock or
limited). In all cases the state, as representative of
the foreign trade monopoly, reserves the right to
grant permission for these ventures. . . .
In contrast to most of the other Eastern countries, the USSR has retained the original system of
foreign trade monopoly with exclusive specialized
foreign trade organizations and a strict separation
between domestic and foreign prices. Even the
Soviet Union, however, deals in the currency of the
Western partner country in its foreign trade transactions." Industrial Cooperation between East and
West (White Plains, N.Y.: Sharpe, 1979), pp. 58-59,
61. This book is a translation of Industrielle Ko-
operation zwischen Ost und West (Vienna: Springer-
Verlag, 1977).

96. "The Directives of the 24th CPSU Congress for the Five-
Year Plan for the Development of the USSR National Economy
in 1971-1975," Pravda, April 11, 1971, pp. 1-7, translated in
Current Soviet Policies VI (Columbus, Ohio: American Association for the Advancement of Slavic Studies, 1973), p. 170.

97. Brezhnev's and Kosygin's reports to the 24th CPSU Congress, in ibid., pp. 25, 134.

98. "Basic Guidelines for the Development of the USSR National Economy in 1976-1980," Pravda, March 7, 1976, pp. 2-8,
translated in Current Soviet Policies VII (Columbus, Ohio:
American Association for the Advancement of Slavic Studies,
1976), p. 119.

99. Brezhnev's report to the 25th CPSU Congress, in Current
Soviet Policies VII, p. 25 (emphasis added).

100. Scott Bozek, "The USSR: Intensifying the Development of
its Foreign Trade Structure," in Soviet Economy in a Time of
Change, Vol. 2, (Washington: U.S. Government Printing Office,
1979), p. 516.

101. The additional clause was not included in the published
draft version of the 1977 constitution. The draft and final
versions of the constitution are juxtaposed in Sharlet, The
New Soviet Constitution of 1977. This passage appears on p.
99. Cf. Milada Selucka, "Erosion of the Monopolistic Position
of Eastern European Foreign Trade Enterprises: Legal As-

pects," in Changing Perspectives in East-West Commerce, Carl McMillan, ed., (Lexington, Mass.: Heath, 1974), pp. 91-92.

102. M.M. Boguslavskii, ed., Pravovye formy nauchno-tekhnicheskogo i promyshlenno-ekonomicheskogo sotrudnichestva SSSR s kapitalisticheskimi stranami (Moscow: Nauka, 1980), pp. 4-5. See also Podzniakov's writings cited above.

103. V. Pozdniakov, "The Constitutional Principles of the State Monopoly of Soviet Foreign Trade," Foreign Trade 7 (1978): 15-16.

104. "O poriadke i srokakh reorganizatsii vsesoiuznykh vneshnetorgovykh ob'edinenii vo vsesoiuznykh khozraschetnye vneshnetorgovye ob'edineniia, vkhodiashchie v sistemu Ministerstva vneshnei torgovli," in Sobranie postanovlenii Pravitel'stva SSSR, no. 13, item 91 (1978). A translation of this resolution appears in William Butler, ed., Collected Legislation of the USSR and the Constituent Union Republics (Dobbs Ferry, N.Y.: Oceana, 1980), part V-2, pp. 1-22.

105. P. Smirnov, "Legal Status of a Foreign Trade Association," Foreign Trade 10 (1978): 38.

106. D.A. Loeber, "USSR: 69 Foreign Trade Organizations Involved on Foreign Markets," Europa Industrie Revue 6 (1978): 38.

107. For example, Loeber, "USSR"; D.A. Loeber, "Foreign Participation in Soviet Enterprises?" Droit et pratique du Commerce Internationale 6, 2 (June 1980): 215-251; Bozek, "The USSR," pp. 506-525; Thomas Shillinglaw and Daniel Stein, "Doing Business in the USSR," Law and Policy in International Relations (Spring 1981).

108. For example, A.I. Bel'chuk, ed., Novyi etap ekonomicheskogo sotrudnichestva SSSR s razvitymi kapitalisticheskimi stranami (Moscow: Nauka, 1978).

109. Smirnov, "Legal Status," 41.

110. Ibid.

111. See, e.g., Louvan Nolting, The Structure and Functions of the USSR State Committee for Science and Technology (Washington, D.C.: U.S. Department of Commerce, 1979).

112. See, e.g., "The Research Center of the USSR State Committee for Foreign Economic Relations," Foreign Trade 7 (1979): 14-15.

113. These charters all follow essentially the same format and have been published in the journal Foreign Trade since 1978.

114. From Promotion of Trade through Industrial Cooperation: Recent Trends in East-West Industrial Cooperation (U.N. Economic and Social Council, August 31, 1978), p. 19: diagrammed

in Eugene Zaleski and Helgard Wienert, Technology Transfer between East and West (Paris: OECD, 1980), p. 125.

115. P. Smirnov, "New Organizations in the Sphere of Foreign Trade - Firms that Are the Components of the Foreign Trade Associations," Foreign Trade 1 (1980): 48.

116. Ibid., 49.

117. Shillinglaw and Stein, "Doing Business," 4.

118. V. S. Pozdniakov, "Legal Status of All-Union Foreign Trade Organizations within the System of the Ministry of Foreign Trade and Other Organizations Authorized to Conclude Foreign Trade Transactions" (paper presented to the Legal Committee of the U.S./USSR Trade and Economic Council, Moscow, September 16, 1980), p. 13.

119. Ibid., p. 14.

120. Shillinglaw and Stein, "Doing Business," 5.

121. Bozek, "The USSR," pp. 507 ff.

122. See, e.g., the chapters by Giuseppe Schiavone and Hans-Jurgen Wagener, in NATO Economics and Information Directorates, eds., Economic Reforms in Eastern Europe and Prospects for the 1980s (Elmsford, N.Y.: Pergamon Press, 1980).

123. Pravda, March 5, 1981, pp. 1-7, translated in The Current Digest of the Soviet Press 33, 16 (May 20, 1981), p. 28 (emphasis added).

124. John Quigley, The Soviet Foreign Trade Monopoly: Institutions and Laws (Columbus, Ohio: Ohio State University Press, 1974), pp. 173-175 ff.

125. Iu. Shiriaev, "The CMEA Countries in World Economic Relations," International Affairs 5 (1979): 8-9.

126. D. Tomashevskii, "How the West is Reacting to Detente," International Affairs 11 (1976): 42.

127. Ibid.

128. Iu. Molchanov, "Peaceful Coexitence and Social Progress," International Affairs 12 (1976): 9.

129. I. Saviolova, "East-West Industrial Cooperation," Foreign Trade 4 (1977): 27.

130. Ibid., 23.

131. Bel'chuk, Novyi etap. This development was brought to our attention by the careful analysis in Loeber, "Foreign Participation."

132. "Brezhnev: Central Committee Report," p. 21 (emphasis added).

133. Maksimova, USSR and International Economic Cooperation, p. 80.

134. 25th Congress of the CPSU, p. 142

135. John Hardt and George Holliday, "Technology Transfer and Change in the Soviet Economic System," in Issues in East-West Commercial Relations (Washington, D.C.: U.S. Government Printing Office, 1979), p. 86.

136. On the importance of distinguishing between sensitivity and vulnerability in conceptualizing interdependence, see Robert Keohane and Joseph Nye, Power and Interdependence: World Politics in Transition (Boston: Little, Brown, 1977), especially part one.

137. For a notable treatment of the American case, see V. F. Petrovskii, "Material'nyi potensial vo vneshne-politicheskoi doktrine SShA," SShA 1 (1980): 10-21.

138. Maksimova, USSR and International Economic Cooperation, p. 81.

139. L. Vidiasova, "Peaceful Coexistence and International Cooperation," International Affairs 3 (1977): 77-78.

140. Iu. Zakharov, "International Cooperation and the Battle of Ideas," International Affairs 1 (1976): 88.

141. Iu. P. Davydov, Mezhdunarodnaia razriadka i ideologicheskaia bor'ba (Kiev: Politizdat Ukraina, 1978), p. 35.

142. D. V. Ermolenko, Sotsiologiia i problemy mezhdunarodnykh otnoshenii (Moscow: Mezhdunarodnye otnosheniia, 1977), pp. 87-109.

143. Zakharov, "International Cooperation," 88.

144. Tomashevskii, "How the West is Reacting," 42.

145. Maksimova, USSR and International Economic Cooperation, pp. 80-81.

146. Iu. P. Davydov, "Razriadka, SShA i zapadnaia evropa," SShA 3 (1979): 20.

147. Ibid., 27.

148. Karenin, Sovetskaia vneshniaia politika, p. 56.

CHAPTER 4

1. For Western views on the impact of nuclear weapons upon Soviet strategy, see, for example, Raymond Garthoff, Soviet Security in the Nuclear Age (New York: Praeger, 1958); Her-

bert Dinerstein, War and the Soviet Union (New York: Praeger, 1958); Thomas Wolfe, Soviet Strategy at the Crossroads
(Cambridge, Mass.: Harvard University Press, 1964).

2. V.D. Sokolovskii, Soviet Military Strategy, 3rd ed. (New
York: Crane, Russak and Co., 1975), p. 190. This is a collective Soviet work that was directed by Marshal Sokolovskii.
For brevity's sake, we refer to this work as if it had been
written by Sokolovskii himself.

3. M. I. Cherednichenko, "On Features in the Development
of Military Art in the Postwar Period," in Selected Soviet
Military Writings, 1970-1975 (Soviet Military Thought, no. 11)
(Washington, D.C.: GPO, 1976), p. 123. These important
Soviet writings are translated under the auspices of the U.S.
Air Force.

4. N.V. Ogarkov, "Na strazhe mirnogo truda," Kommunist 10
(1981): 86.

5. I. A. Grudinin, Dialektika i sovremennoe voennoe delo
(Moscow: Voenizdat, 1971), pp. 61-72.

6. D.D. Gorbatenko, "The Time Factor in Modern Combat,"
in Selected Soviet Military Writings, p. 234.

7. Grudinin, Dialektika, pp. 72-79.

8. V.M. Bondarenko, "Soviet Science and the Strengthening
of the Country's Defense," Kommunist vooruzhennykh sil
(hereafter Kommunist v.s.) 18 (1974), translated in Joint
Publications Research Service (JPRS) 63591, December 5, 1974
(Washington, D.C.), p. 30.

9. V. V. Borisov, Opasnaia stavka: Nauchno-tekhnicheskaia
revoliutsiia i voennye prigotovleniia SShA (Moscow: Voenizdat,
1979), p. 7.

10. Ibid., p. 113.

11. N.V. Ogarkov, "Voennaia nauka i zashchita sotsialisticheskogo otechestva," Kommunist 7 (1978): 116.

12. M.I. Cherednichenko, "Military Strategy and Military
Technology," Voennaia mysl' 4 (1973), translated in Foreign
Press Digest 0043-73, November 12, 1973, p. 53.

13. V.M. Kulish, ed., Voennaia sila i mezhdunarodnye otnosheniia (Moscow: Mezhdunarodnye otnosheniia, 1972), p.
222.

14. Ibid., p. 226.

15. Ibid.

16. Robert Arnett, "Soviet Attitudes toward Nuclear War: Do
They Really Think They Can Win?" Journal of Strategic Studies 2, 2 (1979): 181.

17. Sokolovskii, Soviet Military Strategy, p. 197.

18. V. Karpov and D. Asatiani, in O problemakh razoruzhe-niia, ed. G.M. Kornienko (Moscow: Mezhdunarodnye otnoshe-niia, 1980), p. 75 (emphasis added).

19. Cherednichenko, "Military Strategy," p. 54.

20. M. Simonian, "US and NATO Nuclear Strategy," Zaru-bezhnoe voennoe obozrenia 6 (1980), translated in JPRS 76424, September 12, 1980, p. 35.

21. See, e.g., S. A. Tiushkevich, Filosofiia i voennaia teoriia (Moscow: Nauka, 1975).

22. Marxism-Leninism on War and Army (Moscow: Progress, 1972) (Soviet Military Thought, no. 2) (Washington, D.C.: GPO, n.d.), p. 28.

23. Ibid., p. 260.

24. See, e.g., Christopher Jones, "Just Wars and Limited Wars: Restraints on the Use of the Soviet Armed Forces," World Politics 28, 1 (1975): 44-68.

25. M. P. Skirdo, The People, The Army and the Commander (Soviet Military Thought, no. 14) (Washington, D.C.: GPO, n.d.), p. 37.

26. Tiushkevich, Filosofiia, p. 153.

27. William Husband, "Soviet Perceptions of U.S. 'Positions-of-Strength' Diplomacy in the 1970s," World Politics 31, 4 (1979): 503.

28. See Colin Gray, The Soviet-American Arms Race (Boston: D.C. Heath, 1976).

29. See Colin Gray, The Geopolitics of the Nuclear Era: Heartland, Rimlands, and the Technological Revolution (New York: Crane, Russak and Co., 1977).

30. M.M. Kir'ian, "Revoliutsiia v voennom dele," Sovetskaia voennaia entsiklopediia vol. 7 (Moscow: Voenizdat, 1979), p. 82.

31. Ibid.

32. V. M. Bondarenko, Sovremennaia nauka i razvitie voen-nogo dela (Moscow: Voenizdat, 1976), p. 30.

33. D. F. Ustinov, "Report on the 60th Anniversary of the USSR Armed Forces," translated in Daily Report (Washington, D.C.: Foreign Broadcast Information Service, hereafter FBIS) , February 24, 1978, p. V-9.

34. I. G. Pavlovskii, "The People's Great Exploit," Ekon-omicheskaia gazeta, (May 5, 1980), translated in Daily Report, May 30, 1980, p. R-3.

35. N.V. Ogarkov, "Soviet Military Science," Pravda, February 19, 1978, translated in JPRS 70765, March 10, 1978, p. 91.

36. K. S. Moskalenko, "Speech to Army-Navy Day Ceremony," Krasnaia zvezda, February 22, 1980, translated in Daily Report, March 4, 1980, p. R-2.

37. Ustinov, "Report," p. V-9.

38. G.S. Kravchenko, "Potentsial ekonomicheskii," Sovetskaia voennaia entsiklopediia, vol. 6, (Moscow: Voenizdat, 1978), p. 476.

39. S. Bartenev, "Ekonomika i voennaia moshch," Kommunist vooruzhennykh sil 14 (July 1980): 68.

40. Ibid., p. 70.

41. Pavlovskii, "The People's Great Exploit," p. R-5.

42. D. F. Ustinov, Izbrannye rechi i stati (Moscow: Politizdat, 1979).

43. Ibid., pp. 163-164.

44. "Vo imia mogushchestva i bezopastnosti rodiny," Kommunist vooruzhennykh sil 19 (1979): 12.

45. V.M. Bondarenko, "Potentsial nauchnyi," Sovetskaia voennaia entsiklopediia, vol. 6, p. 475.

46. Ibid.

47. V. G. Afanas'ev, NTR, upravleniia, obrazovanie (Moscow: Politizdat, 1972), p. 277.

48. Ibid., p. 278.

49. V.M. Bondarenko, in Voina i armiia, ed. D.A. Volkogonova et al. (Moscow: Voenizdat, 1977), p. 198.

50. Bondarenko, Sovremennaia nauka, p. 70.

51. A. Kuzin, in Nauchnaia-tekhnicheskaia revoliutsiia (Moscow: Nauka, 1976), p. 77.

52. Razvitoe sotsialisticheskoe obshchestvo, 2nd ed. (Moscow: Mysl', 1975), p. 71.

53. V. G. Kozlov, in The Philosophical Heritage of V. I. Lenin and Problems of Contemporary War (Moscow: Voenizdat, 1972) (Soviet Military Thought, no. 5) (Washington, D.C.: GPO, n.d.), p. 140.

54. "Chelovek-nauka-tekhnika," Voprosy filosofii, 8 (1972): 33 (emphasis added).

55. V.A. Karnoukhov, "Potentsial moral'no-politicheskii," Sovetskaia voennaia entsiklopediia, vol. 6, p. 474.

56. N. A. Lomov, in Problemy revoliutsii v voennom dele (Moscow: Voenizdat, 1965), p. 47.

57. I. E. Shavrov and M. I. Galkin, Metodologiia voenno-nauchnogo poznaniia (Moscow: Voenizdat, 1977), pp. 101-102.

58. Christopher Jones, "Just Wars and Limited Wars," 46.

59. S. K. Il'in, Moral'nyi faktor v sovremennykh voinakh, 3rd ed., (Moscow: Voenizdat, 1979), p. 81.

60. S. K. Il'in, "Ideological Aspects of the Revolution in Military Affairs," Voennaia mysl' 10 (1967): translated in Foreign Press Digest 0146-68, October 25, 1968, p. 42.

61. V.M. Bondarenko, "Scientific-Technical Progress and Strengthening the Country's Defense Capability," Kommunist vooruzhennykh sil 24 (1971): translated in JPRS 55114, February 4, 1972, p. 3.

62. Pravda, April 16, 1979: translated in Daily Report, April 24, 1979, p. R-6.

63. Paul Cocks, "Rethinking the Organizational Weapon: The Soviet System in a Systems Age," World Politics 32, 2 (1980): 247.

64. Kozlov, in Philosophical Heritage of V.I. Lenin, p. 143 (emphasis in original).

65. B. Trushin and M. Gladkov, "The Economic Foundation of the Military-Technical Policy of a Country," Voennaia mysl' 12 (1968): translated in Foreign Press Digest 0102-69, November 1969, p. 38.

66. Dictionary of Basic Military Terms (Moscow: Voenizdat, 1965) (Soviet Military Thought, no. 9) (Washington, D.C.: GPO, 1974), p. 212.

67. "Strategicheskie vooruzheniia," Sovetskaia voennaia entsiklopediia, vol. 7, p. 552.

68. Sovetskie vooruzhennye sily: Istoriia stroitel'stva (Moscow: Voenizdat, 1978), p. 412.

69. A. A. Grechko, The Armed Forces of the Soviet Union (Moscow: Progress, 1977), p. 153.

70. Sokolovskii, Soviet Military Strategy, p. 11.

71. S. Begunov, "The Maneuver of Forces and Materiel in an Offensive," Voennaia mysl' 9 (1968), translated in Foreign Press Digest 0013-69, February 4, 1969, p. 43.

72. V. Mernov and A. Bogomolov, "Characteristics of the Perception of Truth in Military Operations," Voennaia mysl' 7 (1966), translated in Foreign Press Digest 0475-67, May 17, 1967, p. 24.

NOTES   227

73. Joseph Douglass, Jr., Soviet Military Strategy in Europe
(New York: Pergamon, 1980), p. 117.

74. I.G. Pavlovskii, "Guardian of Peaceful Labor," Soviet
Military Review 1 (1978): 25.

75. On the Soviet debates concerning the proper force structure mix, see Edward Warner III, The Military in Contemporary
Soviet Politics: An Institutional Analysis (New York: Praeger,
1977), chapter 4.

76. Skirdo, The People, pp. 20-21.

77. Steve Kime, "The Soviet View of War," Comparative Strategy 2, 3 (1980): 215.

78. K.S. Moskalenko, "Constant Combat Readiness is a Strategic Category," Voennaia mysl' 1 (1969), translated in Foreign
Press Digest 0087-69, September 15, 1969, p. 14.

79. V.V. Larionov, in Problemy revoliutsii, p. 132.

80. N. Krylov, "The Nuclear Missile Shield of the Soviet
State," Voennaia mysl' 11 (1967), translated in Foreign Press
Digest 0157-68, November 18, 1968, p. 18.

81. L. Gareev, "Ever Guarding the Achievements of October,"
Voenno-istoricheskii zhurnal, 11 (1977), translated in JPRS
70538, January 25, 1978, p. 58.

82. N. Vasendin and N. Kuznetsov, "Modern Warfare and
Surprise Attack," Voennaia mysl' 6 (1968), translated in
Foreign Press Digest 0005-69, January 16, 1969, p. 46.

83. Sokolovskii, Soviet Military Strategy, p. 202.

84. M. Shirokov, "Military Geography at the Present Stage,"
Voennaia mysl' 11 (1966), translated in Foreign Press Digest
0730-67, July 27, 1967, p. 63.

85. See, e.g., P. T. Egorov et al., Civil Defense (Moscow:
Vysshaia shkola, 1970) (Soviet Military Thought, no. 10)
(Washington, D.C.: GPO, 1971).

86. S.S. Gorshkov, The Sea Power of the State (Moscow:
Voenizdat, 1976), translation (Annapolis, Maryland: Naval
Institute Press, 1979), p. 279.

87. Ibid.

88. Sokolovskii, Soviet Military Strategy, p. 205.

89. N.V. Ogarkov, "Strategiia voennaia," Sovetskaia voennaia
entsiklopediia, vol. 7, p. 565.

90. See the excellent study by David Holloway, Technology,
Management and the Soviet Military Establishment (London:
International Institute for Strategic Studies, Adelphi Paper 76,
April 1971).

91. See, e.g., B. I. Strel'chenko, "Kibernetika voennaia," Sovetskaia voennaia entsiklopediia, vol. 4, (Moscow: Voenizdat, 1977), pp. 151-153; Iu. N. Sushkov, Kibernetika v voinu (Moscow: Voenizdat, 1972).

92. See, e.g., V.M. Bondarenko and A. F. Volkovia, eds., Avtomatizatsiia upravleniia voiskami (Moscow: Voenizdat, 1977); V. V. Druzhinin and D. S. Kontorov, Concept, Algorithim, Decision (Moscow: Voenizdat, 1972) (Soviet Military Thought, no. 6) (Washington, D.C.: GPO, n.d.).

93. A. Parkhomenko, "Analiz sistem vooruzheniia," Voennaia mysl' 1 (1968): 13.

94. P. K. Altukhov, "Upravlenie voiskami," Sovetskaia voennaia entsiklopediia, vol. 8, (Moscow: Voenizdat, 1980), p. 204.

95. V.D. Sokolovskii and M.I. Cherednichenko, "Military Strategy and its Problems," Voennaia mysl' 10 (1968), translated in Foreign Press Digest 0084-69, August 29, 1969, p. 37.

96. P. F. Batitskii, "Combat Readiness--The Law of Life," Krasnaia zvezda, January 13, 1978, translated in Daily Report January 17, 1978, p. V-3.

97. Bondarenko, in Voina i armiia, p. 207.

98. Bondarenko, Sovremennaia nauka, p. 62.

99. See, e.g., David Holloway, in John Thomas and Ursula Kruse-Vaucienne, eds., Soviet Science and Technology: Domestic and Foreign Perspectives (Washington, D.C.: George Washington University Press, 1976), pp. 189-229.

100. See, e.g., A. B. Pupko, Sistema: Chelovek i voennaia tekhnika (Moscow: Voenizdat, 1976), pp. 62-107.

101. I. G. Pavlovskii, "Ekonomika--osnova oboronosposobnosti SSSR," Planovoe khoziastvo 2 (1978): 36.

102. See, e.g., Grechko, The Armed Forces, p. 154; Iu. I. Mashkov, "Nauchno-issledovatel'skie uchrezhdenie," Sovetskaia voennaia entsiklopediia, vol. 5, (Moscow: Voenizdat, 1978), p. 531.

103. See especially Bondarenko's arguments in Sovremennaia nauka, chapter 2.

104. See, e.g., David Holloway, in Ronald Amann et al., eds., The Technological Level of Soviet Industry (New Haven: Yale University Press, 1977), pp. 407-489; David Holloway, "War, Militarism and the Soviet State," Alternatives 6, 1 (1980): 71-77.

105. G. Semenov and V. Prokhorov, "Scientific-Technical Progress and Some Questions of Strategy," Voennaia mysl' 2 (1969), translated in Foreign Press Digest 0060-69, June 18, 1969, p. 31.

106. A. Kornienko and V. Korolev, "Economic Aspects of Soviet Military Doctrine," Voennaia mysl' 7 (1967), translated in Foreign Press Digest 0120-68, July 30, 1968, p. 33.

107. Holloway, Technology, Management, p. 6.

108. I. Gorshechnikov, "On the Effectiveness of Defense Expenditures," Voennaia mysl' 8 (1973), translated in Foreign Press Digest 0038, July 10, 1974, p. 71.

109. M. I. Cherednichenko, "Military-Political Forecasting as a Type of Scientific Prediction," Kommunist vooruzhennykh sil 20 (1970): translated in JPRS 51887, December 1, 1970, p. 49.

110. See, e.g., S. P. Ivanov, O nauchnykh osnovakh upravleniia voiskami (Moscow: Voenizdat, 1975), chapter 3; D. A. Ivanov et al., Osnovy upravleniia voiskami v boiu (Moscow: Voenizdat, 1977), especially chapter 2.

111. Kozlov, in Philosophical Heritage of V. I. Lenin, p. 141.

112. V. A. Bokarev, Kibernetika i voennoe delo (Moscow: Voenizdat, 1969), pp. 226-227.

113. Holloway, Technology, Management, p. 34.

114. V. Kulikov, "Economic Factors and Armament," Voennaia mysl' 12 (1973), translated in Foreign Press Digest 0048, August 20, 1974, p. 119.

115. Moskalenko, "Constant Combat Readiness," pp. 16, 18.

116. M. I. Azkhmatov, ed., SShA: Vneshneekonomicheskaia strategiia (Moscow: Nauka, 1976); E. S. Shershnev, ed., Problemy i protivorechiia amerikanskoi ekonomiki (Moscow: Nauka, 1978).

117. See, e.g., V. V. Borisov, Opasnaia stavka: NTR i voennye prigotovleniia (Moscow: Voenizdat, 1979).

118. See, e.g., G. A. Arbatov et al., eds., SShA: NTR i tendentsii vneshnei politiki (Moscow: Mezhdunarodnye otnosheniia, 1974); G. A. Arbatov et al., eds., Global'naia strategiia SShA v usloviiakh NTR (Moscow: Mysl', 1979); V. F. Petrovskii, Doktrina natsional'noi bezopasnosti v global'noi strategiia SShA (Moscow: Mezhdunarodnye otnosheniia, 1980).

119. See, e.g., B. D. Piadyshev, Voenno-promyshlennyi kompleks SShA (Moscow: Voenizdat, 1974).

120. V. Rut'kov, "The Military-Economic Might of the Socialist Countries is a Factor in the Security of Peoples," Kommunist vooruzhennykh sil 23 (1974), translated in JPRS 63902, January 17, 1975, p. 11.

121. Zakhmatov, SShA: Vneshneekonomicheskaia strategiia, pp. 24-25.

122. See, e.g., V.I. Gromeka, NTR i sovremennyi kapitalizm (Moscow: Politizdat, 1976); V. I. Gromeka, SShA: Nauchno-tekhnicheskii potentsial (Moscow: Mysl, 1977).

123. Gromeka, NTR, p. 29.

124. See, e.g., the discussion of engineering psychology in the managerial process in V.G. Marakhov, NTR i ee sotsial'nye posledstviia (Moscow: Vysshaia shkola, 1975).

125. See, e.g., M. M. Kreisberg, SShA: Sistemnyi podkhod v upravlenii (Moscow: Nauka, 1974).

126. See, e.g., I. G. Minervin, SShA: Problemy upravlen-cheskikh kadrov v promyshlennosti (Moscow: Nauka, 1974).

127. See, e.g., I. D. Ivanov, ed., SShA: Promyshlennye korporatsii i nauchnye issledovaniia (Moscow: Nauka, 1975).

128. Gromeka, NTR, p. 90.

129. On the problems that Western economic theory confronts as the economic environment within which state intervention changes, see I. Osadchaia, From Keynes to Neo-Classical Syntheses (Moscow: Progress, 1974).

130. G. Evgenev, "The Military-Industrial Potential of the USA," Voennaia mysl' 12 (1967), translated in Foreign Press Digest 0103-68, June 18, 1968, p. 71.

131. See, e.g., B. G. Boldyrev, Finansy i razoruzhenia (Moscow: Finansy, 1980).

132. See, e.g., V. M. Mil'shtein, Voenno-promyshlennyi kompleks i vneshniaia politika SShA (Moscow: Mezhdunarodnye otnosheniia, 1975).

133. R. A. Faramazian, Razoruzhenia i ekonomika (Moscow: Mysl', 1978), p. 108.

134. See, e.g., G. S. Khozin, in Budushchee nauki (Moscow: Znanie, 1972), pp. 157-168.

135. Petrovskii, Doktrina, p. 256.

136. See, e.g., ibid., chapter 5; R. G. Bogdanov and A. A. Kokoshin, SShA: Informatsiia i vneshniaia politika (Moscow: Nauka, 1979).

137. Piadyshev, Voenno-promyshlennyi kompleks, p. 109.

138. Ibid., p. 108.

139. Ibid., p. 97.

140. V. A Fedorovich, Amerikanskii kapitalizm i gosudarst-vennoe khoziaistvovanie (Moscow: Nauka, 1979), p. 151.

141. Gromeka, SShA, p. 57.

142. Gromeka, NTR, p. 98.

143. Ibid.

144. Gromeka, SShA, p. 58.

145. Borisov, Opasnaia stavka, pp. 115-116.

146. R. G. Bogdanov et al., SShA: Voenno-strategicheskie kontseptsii (Moscow: Nauka, 1980), p. 35.

147. Piadyshev, Voenno-promyshlennyi kompleks, p. 112.

148. R. Faramazian and V. Borisov, "Bremia militarizma i zhiznennye interesy narodov," Mirovaia ekonomika 5 (1981): 28.

149. Iu. Vlas'evich, "Dynamics of Military Economy Expenditures," Kommunist vooruzhennykh sil 16 (1970), translated in JPRS 51698, November, 2, 1970, p. 5.

150. A. Kornienko, "Concerning the Economic Aspects of US Military Doctrine," Voennaia mysl' 11 (1972), translated in Foreign Press Digest, 0049 December 3, 1973, pp. 102, 107.

151. I. Sidel'nikov, in Selected Soviet Military Writings, p. 41.

152. "Soviet Statements on the Consequences of Nuclear War," Trends in Communist Media (Washington, D.C.: FBIS, August 17, 1977), p. S-4.

153. V. F. Khalipov, in Philosophical Heritage of V. I. Lenin, p. 17.

154. N. A. Ponomarev, in ibid., p. 61.

155. Marxism-Leninism on War and Army, p. 37.

156. Sidel'nikov, in Selected Soviet Military Writings, p. 43.

157. Skirdo, The People, the Army, the Commander, p. 17.

158. Izvestiia, September 8, 1968, as quoted by Warner, The Military, p. 155.

159. Skirdo, The People, the Army, the Commander, p. 101.

160. Ibid.

161. See, e.g., Egorov et al., Civil Defense.

162. Moskalenko, "Constant Combat Readiness," 14.

163. E. Nikitin and S. Baranov, "The Revolution in Military Affairs and Measures of the CPSU for Raising the Combat Might of the Armed Forces," Voennaia mysl' 6 (1968), translated in Foreign Press Digest 0005-69, January 16, 1969, p. 7.

164. Kime, "The Soviet View of War," 217.

165. Samuel Payne, Jr., The Soviet Union and SALT (Cambridge, Mass.: MIT Press, 1980), p. 56.

232   "THE SCIENTIFIC-TECHNOLOGICAL REVOLUTION"

166. A. Fedorov, "US: 'New Nuclear Strategy'," Zarubezhnoe voennoe obozrenia 11 (1980), translated in JPRS 77879, April 20, 1981, p. 95.

167. N. A. Talenskii, "The Last War: Some Reflections," International Affairs 5 (1965): 23.

168. See, e.g., O.N. Bykov et al., Aktual'nye problemy razoruzheniia (Moscow: Nauka, 1978), chapter 1.

169. G. A. Trofimenko, SShA: Politika, voina, ideologiia (Moscow: Mysl', 1976), pp. 318-319.

170. T. Kondratkov, "What is Concealed Behind the Bourgeois Concepts of the Essence of War?" Kommunist vooruzhennykh sil 20 (1980), translated in JPRS 77268, January 28, 1981, p. 67.

171. Mil'shtein, Voenno-promyshlennyi kompleks.

172. N. M. Nikol'skii and A. V. Grishin, Nauchno-tekhnicheskii progress i mezhdunarodnye otnosheniia (Moscow: Mezhdunarodnye otnosheniia, 1978), p. 263.

173. V. F. Petrovskii, "On the Need to Continue Detente," Novaia i noveshaia istoriia 1 (1981), translated in JPRS 77676, March 26, 1981, p. 6.

174. Ogarkov, "Strategiia voennaia," 564.

175. Raymond Garthoff, "Mutual Deterrence and Strategic Arms Limitation in Soviet Policy," International Security 3, 1 (1978): 133.

176. A. G. Arbatov, Bezopasnost' v iadernyi vek i politika vashingtona (Moscow: Politizdat, 1980), p. 270.

177. Petrovskii, "On the Need to Continue Detente," 9.

178. R. G. Bogdanov et al., eds., SShA: Voenno-strategicheskie kontseptssi (Moscow: Nauka, 1980), p. 11.

179. Fritz Ermarth, "Contrasts in American and Soviet Strategic Thought," International Security 3, 2 (1978): 146.

180. See footnote 13 above.

181. Karpov and Asatiani, in O problemakh razoruzheniia, p. 75.

182. G.A. Arbatov et al., Global'naia strategiia SShA, p. 109.

183. Ibid.

184. See, e.g., A. G. Arbatov, Bezopasnost'.

185. Dennis Ross, "Rethinking Soviet Strategic Policy: Inputs and Implications," Journal of Strategic Studies 1, 1 (1978): 11.

186. A. G. Arbatov, "Strategicheskii paritet i politika administratsii Kartera," SShA 11 (1980): 40.

187. O. Bykov, "V avangarde bor'by za uprochenie mira," Mirovaia ekonomika 10 (1980): 11.

188. Roman Kolkowicz, "Strategic Parity and Beyond: Soviet Perspectives," World Politics 23, 3 (1971): 449.

189. Dimitri Simes, "Deterrence and Coercion in Soviet Policy," International Security 5, 3 (1980): 95.

CONCLUSION

1. N. A. Lomov, ed., Scientific-Technical Progress and the Revolution in Military Affairs, translated and published under the auspices of the U.S. Air Force (Washington, D.C.: GPO, 1974), p. 31.

2. R. A. Novikov, "Obshchaia kharakteristika osnovnykh mezhdunarodnykh aspektov problemy okruzhaiushchei sredy i priodnykh resursov na sovremennom etape," in Problema okruzhaiushchei sredy v mirovoi ekonomike i mezhdunarodnykh otnosheniiakh (Moscow: Mysl', 1976) p. 31.

3. N. I. Lebedev, A New Stage in International Relations (Elmsford, N. Y.: Pergamon Press, 1978), p. 131.

4. M. M. Maksimova, "The Soviet Union and the World Economy," 130.

5. V. L. Mal'kevich, East-West Economic Cooperation and Technological Exchange (Moscow: Social Sciences Today, 1981), p. 25.

6. See, for example, Y. Sheinin, Science Policy: Problems and Trends (Moscow: Progress, 1978), pp. 122 ff.

7. Lebedev, A New Stage, p. 129; and Mal'kevich, East-West Economic Cooperation, p. 23.

8. Vneshniaia torgovlia SSSR: Itogi deviatoi piatiletki i perspektivy (Moscow: Mezhdunarodnye otnosheniia, 1977), p. 30.

9. Georgii Skorov, in Foreword to Mal'kevich, East-West Economic Cooperation, p. 15.

10. A. P. Aleksandrov, interview in Literaturnaia gazeta, February 18, 1976, translated in Daily Report, February 27, 1976, pp. A5-A6 (emphasis added).

11. Oleg Bykov, "The Key Problem of Our Time," Social Sciences 4 (1980): 159.

12. See, for example, L. Maier et al., "Zapadnoevropeiskii tsentr imperialisticheskogo sopernichestva," Mirovaia ekonomika 12 (1978): 22-32.

13. V. N. Shenaiev et al., eds., Western Europe Today: Economics, Politics, the Class Struggle, and International Relations (Moscow: Progress, 1980), p. 290.

14. G. A. Arbatov, "Nauchno-tekhnicheskaia revoliutsiia i vneshniaia politika SShA," in SShA: Nauchno-tekhnicheskaia revoliutsiia i tendentsii vneshnei politika (Moscow: Mezhdunarodnye otnosheniia, 1974), p. 26.

15. See, for example, R. A. Avakov, Ravivaiushchiesia strany: Nauchno-tekhnicheskaia revoliutsiia i problema nezavisimosti (Moscow: Mysl', 1976).

16. Y. Kashlev, "International Relations and Information," International Affairs 8 (1978): 82.

17. Kashlev, "International Relations"; Y. Zakharov, "International Cooperation and the Battle of Ideas," International Affairs 1 (1976): 86.

18. Zakharov, "International Cooperation," 86.

19. See, for example, N. M. Nikol'skii, Nauchno-tekhnicheskaia revoliutsiia: Mirovaia ekonomika, politika, naselenie (Moscow: Mezhdunarodnye otnosheniia, 1970). Nikol'skii analyzes the effects of the STR upon the institutions and processes of diplomacy on pp. 163-188.

20. Lebedev, A New Stage, p. 58.

21. For elaboration of the discussion about Soviet conservatives and modernizers in this and the following section, see Hoffmann and Laird, The Politics of Economic Modernization in the Soviet Union.

22. Mal'kevich, East-West Economic Cooperation, p. 23 (emphasis added).

23. Shenaiev et al., Western Europe Today, p. 310.

24. V. Sobeslavsky and P. Beazley, The Transfer of Technology to Socialist Countries (Cambridge, Mass.: Oelgeschlager, Gunn & Hann, 1980), p. 110.

25. Thane Gustafson, Selling the Russians the Rope? Soviet Technology Policy and U. S. Export Controls (Santa Monica, Calif.: Rand, 1981), p. 69.

26. "Brezhnev's Report to the Congress," in Current Digest of the Soviet Press 33, 8 (March 25, 1981): 18.

27. Lebedev, A New Stage, p. 94.

28. "Brezhnev: Central Committee Report," in Current Soviet Policies VII, p. 18.

29. See Hoffmann and Laird, In Quest of Progress: Soviet Perspectives on Advanced Society.

30. Jerry Hough, "The Evolution in the Soviet World View," World Politics 32, 4 (July 1980): 521 (emphasis added).

31. See, for example, A. A. Grechko, "Rukovodiashchaia rol' KPSS v stroitel'stve armii razvitogo sotsialisticheskogo obshchestva," in Voprosy istorii KPSS (May 1974), translated in Strategic Review (Winter 1975).

32. See Zhores Medvedev's perceptive comments on the Soviet approach to detente in Soviet Science (New York: Norton, 1978), pp. 137-203.

33. Gustafson, Selling the Russians the Rope, p. 70.

34. Sobeslavsky and Beazley, The Transfer of Technology, p. 112.

35. Hanson, Trade and Technology, p. 5.

36. See, for example, Rennselaer Lee, Soviet Perceptions of Western Technology (Bethesda, Md.: Mathtech, Inc., 1978); and Bruce Parrott, Soviet Technological Progress and Western Technology Transfer to the USSR: An Analysis of Soviet Attitudes (Washington, D. C.: U.S. Department of State, 1978).

37. D. Ustinov, Izbrannye rechi i stat'i, 1942-1979 (Moscow: Voenizdat, 1979), p. 193 (emphasis added).

Index

About the Authors

ERIK P. HOFFMANN is Associate Professor of Political Science, Graduate School of Public Affairs, State University of New York at Albany. He is an Associate of the Research Institute on International Change, Columbia University, and Managing Editor of Soviet Union. He coauthored, with Robbin F. Laird, The Politics of Economic Modernization in the Soviet Union (Cornell University Press) and In Quest of Progress: Soviet Perspectives on Advanced Society (forthcoming). He also coedited, with Frederic J. Fleron, Jr., The Conduct of Soviet Foreign Policy (Aldine Publishing Co.) and with Robbin F. Laird, The Soviet Polity in the Modern Era (Aldine Publishing Co.). Hoffmann is the author of numerous studies on contemporary Soviet politics, economics, administration, and law; East-West diplomatic and economic relations; and science, technology, and political change in industrialized societies.

ROBBIN F. LAIRD is an Associate of the Research Institute on International Change, Columbia University. He is a consultant to various U. S. governmental and nongovernmental institutions and lectures periodically in Western Europe. He coauthored, with Erik P. Hoffmann, The Politics of Economic Modernization in the Soviet Union (Cornell University Press) and In Quest of Progress: Soviet Perspectives on Advanced Society (forthcoming). He coedited, with Erik P. Hoffmann, The Soviet Polity in the Modern Era (Aldine Publishing Co.). Laird is the author of a number of studies on contemporary Soviet politics, economics, and administration; East-West military, economic, and diplomatic relations; and science, technology, and political change in industrialized societies.